PENGUIN  CLASSICS

PENGUIN POETS IN TRANSLATION
GENERAL EDITOR: CHRISTOPHER RICKS

PETRARCH IN ENGLISH

FRANCESCO PETRARCA (PETRARCH), the son of an exiled Florentine notary, was born in 1304 in Arezzo. In 1312 he went with his father to Avignon, then the seat of the papal court, and in nearby Carpentras began a traditional training in rhetoric. After further education in law at Montpellier and Bologna, he was recalled by his father's death to Avignon. There, on 6 April 1327, he first saw Laura who inspired the passion commemorated in the *Canzoniere*, the poetic sequence that future generations throughout Europe were to revere as the great model for love poetry. After some years in the service of Cardinal Colonna, a powerful and enlightened patron, and after travel in France, Germany and Flanders, Petrarch withdrew to Vaucluse (Provence) where he began the Latin epic *Africa* and the *Triumphs*. The fame of his learning and poetry grew rapidly and in 1341, on Easter Sunday, he was crowned poet laureate at the Capitol in Rome. In 1353, after the deaths of Laura and Cardinal Colonna, Petrarch left Avignon in disgust at the corruption of the papal court. Welcomed by the Visconti in Milan, he performed a number of diplomatic missions in Europe before moving on to Venice and finally to Padua. In his last years he completed the *Triumphs* and reordered and revised the poems of the *Canzoniere*. He died in July 1374.

THOMAS P. ROCHE, JR., Professor of English at Princeton University, was born in New Haven, Connecticut, in 1931. He was educated at Yale, Cambridge and Princeton where he became Murray Professor of English Literature, Emeritus in 2002. He is the author of *The Kindly Flame: A Study of the Third and Fourth Books of the Faerie Queene* (1964) and *Petrarch and the English Sonnet Sequences* (1989). He has edited the essays of Rosemond Tuve and D. W. Robertson and is co-editor with William Oram and Anne Lake Prescott of *Spenser Studies: A Renaissance Poetry Annual*. He has also published on Sidney, Shakespeare, Petrarch, Ariosto and Tasso. He is currently at work on the iconography of the muses from Hesiod to Milton.

PETRARCH IN ENGLISH

Edited by THOMAS P. ROCHE, JR.

PENGUIN BOOKS

To Cleopatra, Julie and Valentina – and Bo, without whose
help this volume might have taken even longer.

PENGUIN CLASSICS

Published by the Penguin Group
Penguin Books Ltd, 80 Strand, London WC2R ORL, England
Penguin Group (USA) Inc., 375 Hudson Street, New York, New York 10014, USA
Penguin Group (Canada), 90 Eglinton Avenue East, Suite 700, Toronto, Ontario, Canada M4P 2Y3
(a division of Pearson Penguin Canada Inc.)
Penguin Ireland, 25 St Stephen's Green, Dublin 2, Ireland
(a division of Penguin Books Ltd)
Penguin Group (Australia), 250 Camberwell Road, Camberwell, Victoria 3124, Australia
(a division of Pearson Australia Group Pty Ltd)
Penguin Books India Pvt Ltd, 11 Community Centre, Panchsheel Park, New Delhi – 110 017, India
Penguin Group (NZ), cnr Airborne and Rosedale Roads, Albany, Auckland 1310, New Zealand
(a division of Pearson New Zealand Ltd)
Penguin Books (South Africa) (Pty) Ltd, 24 Sturdee Avenue, Rosebank, Johannesburg 2196, South Africa

Penguin Books Ltd, Registered Offices: 80 Strand, London WC2R ORL, England

www.penguin.com

First published 2005
2

Editorial material and selection copyright © Thomas P. Roche, Jr., 2005
All rights reserved

The moral right of the editor has been asserted

The Acknowledgements on pp. 311–12 constitute an extension of this copyright page

Set in 10/12.5 pt PostScript Monotype Bembo
Typeset by Rowland Phototypesetting Ltd, Bury St Edmunds, Suffolk
Printed in England by Clays Ltd, St Ives plc

ISBN 978-0-14-043448-4

www.greenpenguin.co.uk

MIX
Paper | Supporting
responsible forestry
FSC® C018179
www.fsc.org

Penguin Books is committed to a sustainable future
for our business, our readers and our planet.
The book in your hands is made from paper
certified by the Forest Stewardship Council.

CONTENTS

INTRODUCTION

In a century where Dante seems to reign supreme, it is time to recognize the simple fact that Francesco Petrarca (1304–74) was the most important Italian poet for three centuries following his death. No lyric poet in Europe escaped his influence. On the other hand, it must be admitted that more than fifty complete translations of *The Divine Comedy* have appeared since the first translation by the Reverend Henry Boyd in 1802, and this cannot be said of Petrarch's *Rerum vulgarium fragmenta*, the Latin title for his *Canzoniere*, or *Rime sparse*, which have been translated only six times in their entirety, the first being the leisure avocation of Captain Robert Guthrie Macgregor while on military service in India (*Odes of Petrarch*, 1851, and *Indian Leisure*, 1854).[1]

The paucity of complete translations of Petrarch argues not so much a lack of interest in the poetry as the extraordinary difficulty of translating lyrics of such opacity; they seem almost impervious to translation, just like Dante's lyrics. *The Divine Comedy* has a narrative that eases the translator over the really tough linguistic problems, but a lyric has no narrative, no set of stable characters, no immediately apprehensible narrator. In reading or translating lyrics we are intruders on an overheard conversation or monologue, of which we try to make sense, in order to become part of the conversation, and for this reason translators are fond of appending descriptive titles such as 'On receiving a pair of his lady's gloves' or 'On seeing his lady bathing', which more often than not impose a more fleshly/physical *mise-en-scène* than was intended by the author or delivered by the poem.

Because of these anomalies of the lyric mode, translators are much more apt to seize on a single poem or a group of poems and to feel no compulsion to complete the entire lyric sequence. Such is the case with Petrarch, who has attracted more gifted amateurs since the Renaissance than any other poet (with the possible exception of Horace) to try their skill at getting a Petrarch sonnet or *canzone* into English. In the sixteenth and seventeenth centuries such translation was made not only to show the translator's skill but also to show that English was as powerful a linguistic medium as Italian. Once English had established its own literary tradition, the translation was to show the poetic superiority of the poet or poetaster. Needless to say, the latter group was dominant.

The aim of this volume, *Petrarch in English*, is accurately summarized by its immediate predecessor, *Bohn's Illustrated Library*, which produced its complete Petrarch by various hands, in London, 1859. The Preface to that volume contains a paragraph that is no less true today:

It is rather a singular fact that, while the other three Poets of this world-famed series — Dante, Ariosto, and Tasso — have each found several translators, no complete version of the fourth [Petrarch], and in Italy the most popular, has hitherto been presented to the English reader. This lacune becomes the more remarkable when we consider the great influence which Petrarch has undoubtedly exercised on our poetry from the time of Chaucer downwards.

Bohn's collection of Petrarch in translation — and mine — deal only with his poems in the vernacular, although he wrote in Latin an unfinished epic poem, *Africa*, as well as treatises that were to influence the intellectual history of Europe, and thousands of pages of prose letters to friends, to classical authors, which were also to become important documents in European intellectual history. Petrarch saw his audience as the past, the present, and the future. He was certainly the most important intellectual in fourteenth-century Italy, and the least important of his works for his own century, the *Canzoniere*, and the *Trionfi*, his vernacular poems, have become for the most part the only fragment of his almost universal fame to endure in the twentieth-first century. His curse is that his story is known, but his poems are not.

His relationship to Dante is substantial, although Petrarch in a letter to Boccaccio is loath to answer Boccaccio's question of why he never mentions Dante. The letter is a work of superb skill, in which Petrarch manages to praise Dante and his works better than any contemporary writer – without even mentioning Dante's name. That his older contemporary Dante (1265–1321) influenced Petrarch's writing in the vernacular is without question. Dante's *La divina commedia*, from its first appearance, became the Italian rival to Virgil's *Aeneid*, and Petrarch acceded to this just fame by writing his *Africa* in Latin, an attempt to rival Virgil in his own language. His rivalry with Dante took the form of writing his *Trionfi* in the same *terza rima* verse form (*aba bcb cdc*) as the *Commedia*. These six poems use Dante's meter to contract the exquisite vision of Dante to a paradigm based solely on Petrarch's putative love of Laura, itself an imitation of Dante's love for Beatrice. The six poems carry Petrarch's love of Laura through the Triumph of Love (6 April 1327, Petrarch's first sight of Laura), to the Triumph of Chastity (Laura's refusal of his love), to the Triumph of Death (6 April 1348, the death of Laura), to the Triumph of Fame (his celebration of her), to the Triumph of Time (the obliteration of earthly memory), to the Triumph of Eternity (the turn from earthly things to God). The poems are a sonnet sequence of love and value within the framework of fourteenth-century Christianity and were meant to do what Dante had done in epic form, which Petrarch knew he could not, or would not, rival. The *Trionfi*, in fact, had more printed editions than Dante's *Commedia* in the following two centuries.

His second work in the vernacular shows Petrarch again rivalling Dante, whose first poetic work was *La vita nuova*, the story of the inception and growth of his love for Beatrice, written in the form of sonnets and canzoni held together in a prose framework that ultimately was an imitation of the *De consolatione philosophiae* of Boethius. Here Petrarch felt he had a chance to surpass Dante. He wrote 366 poems, mostly sonnets, interspersed with *ballate*, *sestine*, *madrigali* and *canzoni*, that were to become the model of love poetry ever afterward.

The *Canzoniere* is a sad story of a young poet smitten with love for a married woman who does not return his love, and who dies, but the poet continues in his torment for the rest of his life. It is the paradigm for human love that continues until Edgar Allen Poe's classic statement that there is nothing more poetical than the death of a beautiful woman. The story is an unjustifiable ethic, almost Thurberian in its tenacity, and depends on the death of the woman, and it is the beginning of the sonnet sequence tradition, that virus of European poetry that has hounded love poetry to the present day.

The story is simply recorded on the flyleaf of Petrarch's copy of Virgil, now in the Ambrosiana Library, Milan. This should be read in its entirety for its poignancy and intellectual rigor.

Laurea, illustrious for her own virtues and long celebrated in my poems, first appeared to my eyes about the time of my early manhood in the year of the Lord 1327 on the sixth day of the month of April, in the church of St. Clare in Avignon in the morning; and in the same city, in the same month of April, on the same sixth day, at the same first hour, in the year 1348, her light was withdrawn from this light when I by chance was then at Verona, unaware of my fate. Moreover, the unhappy news reached me through a letter of Ludovico in the same year, in the month of May, the nineteenth day early. That most chaste and most beautiful body was placed in the church of the Franciscans on the very day of her death at vespers. But her soul has, I am persuaded, returned to the heaven whence it came, as Seneca says of Scipio Africanus. As a memorial, afflicting yet mixed with a certain bitter sweetness, I have decided to make this record in this place of all places, which often falls under my eyes, that I may reflect that there can be no more pleasure for me in this life, and that, now that the chief bond is broken, I may be warned by frequently looking at these words and by the thought of the flying years that it is time to flee from Babylon. This, by God's Grace will be easy for me, when I think courageously and manfully of the past's vain concerns and empty hopes and unexpected outcomes.

Even after her death he struggled with his passion until he himself died on 19 July 1374, the day before his seventieth birthday.

The *Canzoniere* is the record of this extraordinary infatuation, and it is even more extraordinary in that we do not know if Laura existed. We know from an Abbé de Sade, an eighteenth-century ancestor of the Marquis de Sade, that a Laure de Noves was married to a Hugues de Sade on 16 January 1325 and that this same Laura made a will on 3 April 1348, when the Black Plague was ravaging Europe. The speed with which she was buried on that sixth of April does suggest that she was a victim of the Plague. We know also that she bore Hugues de

Sade eleven children (although Thomas Campbell claims there were merely ten). Unfortunately the documents cited by the Abbé were destroyed during the French Revolution, and we cannot be certain that the Abbé was not creating a French muse for the famous Italian poet. The Abbé was not the first to make a connection between this woman and Petrarch's Laura. Vellutello's commentary (1525 and thereafter) suggests a slightly different time and place for their first meeting in 1327. Also the French poet Maurice Scève, while studying law in Avignon, discovered the tomb almost two hundred years later and found there a metal box, inside which was a medal depicting a woman ripping out her heart and a sonnet 'Qui reposan quei caste & felice ossa', apparently by Petrarch (see Giovanni di Tournes, 'The Tomb Sonnet').

The *Canzoniere*, beginning with sonnet 4's acronym of Lau–Re–Ta (see Basil Kennet), are modelled on another Laura, as described in Ovid's myth of Apollo's pursuit of Daphne in Book I of the *Metamorphoses*. It is an Apollo, fresh from his victory over the serpent Python, celebrated ever after by the Pythian games, in which the victor was crowned with oak leaves because the Laurel was not yet [*laurus nondum est*], and then Ovid swings into his story of Apollo and Daphne, whose metamorphosis into the laurel defeated Apollo's desires and provided him with the leaves to crown himself as god of poetry. In short, love thwarted crowns itself with the spoils of its poetic talents. Ovid concludes his story of Apollo and Daphne by linking the myth to the custom of crowning both Caesars and poets with laurel on the Capitoline Hill in Rome.

That Petrarch knew this myth intimately cannot be doubted because he weaves it into the fabric of his life. He tells us in a letter that on the first day of September 1340, in the morning he received an invitation from the Roman Senate to be crowned laureate, and on the afternoon of that very same day a similar invitation from the University of Paris. Although we may be surprised that Italian mail service in the fourteenth century seems infinitely superior to that of the twenty-first century, we should be even more surprised that either the Roman Senate or the University of Paris should have issued such an invitation since neither body had a custom of laureation before Petrarch tells us of their invitation to him. On advice from friends (and no doubt from his own preference) he chose the invitation of the Roman Senate and asked for the sponsorship of King Robert of Naples, for which purpose he travelled to Naples, reaching there sometime in February 1341. Petrarch was duly examined by King Robert as to his eligibility for the honour of laureation and satisfied the requirement. King Robert, because of his age, wanted the ceremony to be performed in Naples, but Petrarch requested that his coronation take place in the Senatorial Palace on the Capitoline in Rome. The request was granted, and armed with a 'robe of honour' from the king, Petrarch set out for Rome, arriving there most probably on Good Friday, 6 April 1341. On Easter Sunday Petrarch gave his Coronation Oration on the virtues of the Laurel, received the triple crown of *poeta laureatus* from the hands of his friend, Roman Senator, Orso dell'Anguillara, and after the ceremony proceeded to old St Peter's where he placed his crown on the high altar. Petrarch would no doubt have seen that his coronation was quite literally the fulfilment of Apollo's prophecy about the laurel, for not since antiquity had a poet been crowned in Rome, if indeed any such ceremonies ever took place, and only three other laureations had occurred anywhere. We can only suppose that Petrarch invented the occasion and orchestrated its execution.[2]

We may also wonder about the continual recurrence of the date 6 April in Petrarch's narratives. On that date he first saw Laura (1327), on that date she died (1348). On that date he was first inspired to begin his epic *Africa* (1338). On that date he arrived in Rome to begin the occasion of his laureation (1341). The recurrence of this date beggars coincidence. In sonnet 3 he states that he first saw Laura on the day that Christ died. This statement has caused much consternation among Petrarch scholars because 6 April 1327 was the Monday, not the Friday, of Holy Week; but they need not have feared Petrarch's accuracy because according to the best chronologies of the fourteenth century, Adam was created on 6 April and Christ was crucified on that same date. Hence the Old Adam and the New Adam were linked to a date in the calendar. In using this date Petrarch is reinforcing the opposition he continually repeats throughout the *Canzoniere* of his love for Laura and his love of God.

In fact, the two-part structure of the poems of the *Canzoniere* repeats this crucial opposition. The *Canzoniere* consists of 366 poems, divided into a first part of 263 poems, *In vita di Laura*, and a second part of 103 poems, *In morte di Laura*. If we take Petrarch seriously (and we always must) and imagine his *Canzoniere* as a leap-year of 366 days, and take the further step of faith in imagining that sonnet 1 is a 6 April date, we come to the beginning of *In morte* on the 25th of December, the date on which we celebrate the birth of Christ. Thus, Petrarch celebrates the initiation of his love for Laura on the same day that Christ died and the death of Laura on the day that Christ was born. It is a genuine opposition that only the poems themselves can fully engage and disentangle, but it should already be clear that this story, or concatenation of myths, is not the simple story of a young man who could write poetry, falling in love with a married woman.

What makes Petrarch's love for Laura different from almost all other love stories is that within the sequence he tries to use his errant love as a symbol of the malaise affecting his age. He introduces poems that are clearly political, and from the time of Alessandro Vellutello's printed edition of the *Canzoniere* (1525; 26 editions thereafter) these political poems were printed in a separate section, a dreadful violation of Petrarch's intention. Ovid's prophecy about the laurel intended that garland both for poets and Caesars, and Petrarch projected not only his personal but his political desires into his poetic aspirations. It must be remembered that Petrarch was born in exile, his parents along with Dante banished from their native Florence in 1302. He lived in exile all his life, the exile of his fallen condition, the exile of a totally disunited Italy, in which he was given preferment by many of the dukes and princes of Italy's city states, the exile of a Christian whose pope had abandoned Rome in favour of a Babylonian Captivity in Avignon, where he laboured for those popes and where he first saw Laura. He fought all his life to bring the papacy back to Rome, which he saw as the proper site both of Ovid's prophecy and Peter's chair. His life-long association with the noble Colonna family, whom he celebrates in Petrarch (P) 10, P28, P266, P269, etc., his early espousal of Cola di Rienzo (P53), all point towards a return to a revivified Rome as the proper political solution. Petrarch's love is directed both towards a woman and a city. His laurels come from his intercession to both, and the signature emblem of this double quest is the image of the old man (*il veccheriel*, P16) – not a Dickensian whimsy, but an allegory of St Paul's Old Man, stumbling toward Rome to see the Veronica, that venerated image of the face of Christ in St Peter's.

What caught the fancy of the fifteenth and sixteenth centuries was not only this extremely convoluted story but the supple elegance of Petrarch's verse. It has the limpidity of Tennyson matched with the strength of Milton, which goes far to explain the lack of praise for Petrarch by T. S. Eliot and the New Critics, for whom the limpidity seemed mere simplicity and the strength mere rhetorical stance. Hence Petrarch achieved adjectival status – of a bad sort.

It is a fortuitous coincidence that Petrarch should make his first appear-ance in English poetry by the hand of Geoffrey Chaucer (*c.* 1343–1400), the father of English poetry. That Chaucer knew of Petrarch is beyond doubt; in the *Canterbury Tales* he makes his Clerk refer to 'Fraunceys Petrak, the lauriat poete . . . whos rethorike sweete / Enlumyned all Ytaille of poetrie' in the Prologue to 'The Clerk's Tale'. That Chaucer knew Petrarch personally is possible but doubtful. Chaucer's journey to Italy in 1368 as part of the entourage accom-panying Prince Lionel to his marriage with Violante Visconti, daughter of the Duke of Milan, provides a provocative possibility because Petrarch also attended this wedding. We will have to leave the fictive encounter to Tom Stoppard. Chaucer's second trip to Italy presents another possibility, but Petrarch's erratic presence in the northern city of Arguà during the last years of his life because of the war between Venice and Padua and Chaucer's own diplomatic concerns in 1372 make that later meeting doubtful unless new records are found. That Chaucer knew at least one of Petrarch's sonnets is undeniable be-cause he translates sonnet 132, 'S'amor non è', into three rhyme royal stanzas in *Troilus and Criseyde*, Book I.400–420 as 'Canticus Troili', Troilus's first declaration of his love for Criseyde. It is a typical medieval statement of the submission of the lover's will to the power of the God of Love, the substance of which could be documented in count-less examples from the period. What makes this example important is that Chaucer clearly has his eye on the progress of Petrarch's diction and imagery in 132. Chaucer must have seen or owned a manuscript of Petrarch to have such a controlled knowledge of 132. At any rate, the 'Canticus Troili' is the introduction of Petrarch to English literature.

The next important appearance of Petrarch in English is more than a century and a half later just before the beginning of the reign of Elizabeth I. In 1557 a small volume of poems, *Songes and Sonnettes, written by the ryght honorable Lorde Henry H[o]ward, late Earle of Surrey, and other,* was printed by Richard Tottel; this first anthology of English poetry is now more generally known as *Tottel's Miscellany.* It ran through ten editions by 1587 and is important because it was the first time that the poems of Henry Howard, Earl of Surrey (1517?–47), and Sir Thomas Wyatt the Elder (*c.* 1503–42) were printed. It is the most important collection of poetry written during the reign of Henry VIII, but for the purposes of this volume its importance rests in the fact that it introduces the sonnet form to English and that this form appears mainly in translations of Petrarch: five by Surrey, twenty-three by Wyatt and two by anonymous authors. It cannot be said that Tottel is mainly responsible for popularizing Petrarch in England because he was already known and read in the Italian, but the enormous influence of Tottel on later collections such as *The Paradise of Dainty Devises* (1576), *A Handful of Pleasant Delights* (1584), *The Phoenix Nest* (1593), *England's Helicon* (1600) and *A Poetical Rhapsody* (1602), in addition to his having made Wyatt and Surrey available in printed form, gives Tottel a significant role in the promotion of Petrarch in English. At the same time, nonetheless, manuscript collections of English poetry such as the Hill MS (Add. MS 36529) and the Arundel Harington MS (Egerton MS 2711), the second of which contains autograph copies of Wyatt's poems, continued the earlier tradition of collecting manuscript poetry.

Such printed and manuscript evidence from the Elizabethan period makes it very clear that Petrarchan influence was everywhere, whether that influence ended up in translation or not. What is difficult to determine is whether the influence on the English poets is from Petrarch, from Petrarch's already abundant Italian and French imitators, or from the general psychology of love that dominated the medieval and Renaissance periods. In attempting to answer these questions it is better to avoid imputing Bloomian anxiety of influence to the translators but rather to recall Pope's 'True wit is nature to advantage dress'd / What oft was thought but ne'er so well express'd'. Poetry expresses thoughts already in the public realm; the trick of the poet is simply to express them better.

Another complicating factor is the form that the translation takes. Since Italian is an inflected language, it is almost impossible not to rhyme; English, even with its much greater lexicon, is relatively poor in rhymes – something that Spenser might well have considered with more care before inventing his rhymed stanza, a point that Milton saw only too well in choosing blank verse for his epic.

It is conventional in English studies to distinguish three basic forms for the sonnet: the Italian, or Petrarchan, the Spenserian and the English, or Shakespearean. The Italian form divides the fourteen lines into an octave (*ab ba ab ba*) and a sestet, using some combination of *cde* rhymes that will avoid a final couplet. The form of both the Spenserian (*abab bcbc cdcd ee*) and the Shakespearean (*abab cdcd efef gg*) insist on a final rhyming couplet. Beyond this basic discrimination it is pointless to make generalizations about the form of the sonnet – unless one has a specific sonnet in mind. This is particularly true of the earlier sixteenth century in England. Writers were trying to make their language sit in a form something like an Italian sonnet. Beyond that there were no rules, just attempts. Surrey translated five of Petrarch's poems: four sonnets and one *ballata*.[3]

In the first three of the sonnets, he chooses what has come to be called the 'Shakespearean sonnet': three quatrains rhymed *abab* and a concluding couplet. Surrey carries this form to extravagant limits in Tottel 2, with only two rhymes, which tends to destroy any sense of progressive argument in the poem. It seems a brilliant exercise in testing the rhyming power of the English language. This interest may also account for the fact that Tottel 276 and 277 by an anonymous author, or authors, included in this selection, translate Petrarch 1 and 3 into rhyming septenary couplets. Wyatt, on the other hand, tends to retain the Petrarchan division into an octave and a sestet, but even this observation pales as a significant statement about poetic form when one considers the problems that Tottel faced in rendering to the public of the mid sixteenth century Wyatt's and Surrey's renderings of the Petrarchan Italian of the fourteenth century.

It is clear from all the poetry in *Tottel*, for which we have manuscripts (most notably those of Wyatt – his personal copy is Egerton MS 2711), that Tottel knew that he had a literary winner (the poetry of an earl and a knight!), and also that he wanted to make them pass as *au courant* contemporaries; therefore he edited whatever manuscript material he had to achieve his purpose. One example must suffice.

The first poem in Wyatt's copy is a translation of P121, a *madrigale* of 9 lines, which Wyatt translated into a *rondeau* of 15 lines, which Tottel then tried to shape into a regular sonnet. The course of this successful fiasco must be traced by quoting the originals

P121, 'Or vedi, Amor, che giovenetta donna', was a late imposition on the structure of the *Canzoniere*, the *madrigale* replacing an earlier *ballata*, 'Donna mi vene spesso nella mente', which had been in place from the time of Petrarch's earliest plans for his collection.

> Or vedi, Amor, che giovenetta donna
> tuo regno sprezza, et del mio mal non cura,
> et tra duo ta' nemici è sí secura.
>
> Tu se' armato, et ella in treccie e 'n gonna
> si siede, et scalza, in mezzo i fiori et l'erba
> ver' me spietata, e 'ncontra te superba.
>
> I' son pregion; ma se pietà anchor serba
> l'arco tuo saldo, et qualchuna saetta,
> fa' di te et di me, signor, vendetta.

The jaunty and tricky rhythms and rhymes of the Italian were not known to Wyatt as a form, and so he turned to models he knew from the French. The rhythms suggested the French rondeau and its connection to the dance, and Wyatt made this spirited English rondeau:

> Behold, love, thy power how she dispiseth!
> My great payne how litle she regardeth!
> The holy oth, wherof she taketh no cure
> Broken she hath: and yet she bideth sure,
> Right at her ease: and litle she dredeth
> Wepened thou art and she vnarmed sitteth:
>   To the disdaynfull, her liff she ledeth:
> To me spitefull, withoute cause, or mesure,
>   Behold, love!
> I ame in hold: if pitie the meveth
> Goo bend thy bowe: that stony hertes breketh
> And, with some stroke, revenge the displeasure
> Of thee and him, that sorrowe doeth endure,
> And, as his lorde, the lowly entreateth
>   Behold, love!

The *abb acc cdd* rhyme scheme of the Petrarchan poem gets translated into the francophile English: *aabbaaab x aabba x*. This form was apparently not to the taste of Tottel, and so he converted it into a 14-line sonnet, by filling out the first refrain line *Behold, love!* and deleting the second refrain line.

> Behold, Loue, thy power how she despiseth:
> My greuous payn how litle she regardeth,
> The solemne othe, wherof she takes no cure,
> Broken she hath: and yet, she bydeth sure,
> Right at her ease, and litle thee she dredeth.
> Weaponed thou art, and she vnarmed sitteth:
> To the disdainful, all her life she leadeth:
> To me spiteful, without iust cause, or measure.
> Behold Loue, how proudly she triumpheth,
> I am in hold, but if thee pitie meueth
> Go, bend thy bow that stony hartes breaketh:
> And with some stroke reuenge the great displeasure
> Of thee, and him that sorow doth endure,
> And as his Lord thee lowly here entreateth.

But the metamorphosis from *madrigale* to *rondeau* to sonnet is a most parlous transformation, especially into the sonnet form, with its rhyme scheme: *aabb aaab aaab ba*, a form not seen before nor after. The rough meter and rhyme of Wyatt gets lost in an attempt to be 'regular.' And so the achievement of Tottel.

The next step in getting Petrarch into English introduces another problem of translation. Edmund Spenser in 1569, when he was in his late teens, was probably asked by his headmaster Richard Mulcaster of the Merchants' Taylor School to translate Petrarch 323, 'Standomi un giorno', a visionary *canzone*, previously translated by Clément Marot, for an English version of a Dutch Protestant polemic by Jan van der Noot, *A Theatre for Worldlings*. It is Spenser's first published work and is important not only for that reason but also because it shows Petrarch's poems to Laura taking on a political significance, not often accorded them by readers of the original Italian.

The other selections from the sixteenth and seventeenth centuries are examples of the vast sonneteering vogue of the period, many of which will appear very familiar but which may not have been fully associated with the petrarchizing passion of those centuries. One can detect a tendency to domesticate the love affair, which Spenser had already achieved in his *Amoretti and Epithalamium* (1595) by writing the only sonnet sequence that ends in marriage; but Spenser, after his early encounter with P323, did not include Petrarchan translations in his own sequence. Other sonneteers did, and their contributions will be more fully described in the headnotes to the selections.

The Renaissance seems to have expended the English enthusiasm about Petrarch. He is still there, through his well-known tropes and rhetorical ploys, but there is little activity in making him over into English verse. The eighteenth century gave as much attention to Petrarch as they did to the sonnet form: very little. Just as in the later sixteenth and seventeenth centuries, no first-rate poets turned their hand to the translation of Petrarch, neither 'great Anna' nor any of the Georges attempted to vie with their Tudor predecessor. Those poetasters who did include translations of Petrarch in their poetic outputs fall into three distinct social groups: peers, gentry, academic clerics.

Peers
James Caulfeild, Earl of Charlemont (1728–99)
Alexander Fraser Tytler, Lord Woodhouselee (1747–1813)
Sir Samuel Egerton Brydges (1762–1837)
Barbarina Brand, Lady Dacre (1768–1854)

Gentry
John Langhorne (1735–79)
George Hardynge (1743–1816)
Charlotte Turner Smith (1749–1806)
Dr John Nott (1751–1825)
Thomas Le Mesurier of Guernsey (1757–1822)
John Penn (1760–1834)

Clerics
Basil Kennet (1674–1715)
Reverend William Collier (1743–1803)
Archdeacon Francis Wrangham (1767–1843)

(Biographical details may be found in the headnotes to their selections; Hardynge and Le Mesurier are not included in this volume.)

Even through the middle of the nineteenth century there are merely sporadic attempts to do Petrarch anew. Interest in Petrarch was undoubtedly stirred by the revelations of the Abbé de Sade that Laura was a married woman and mother of numerous children, *Memoires pour la vie François de Petrarque* (1764–7). Reactions to this most shocking 'fact' were frequent because it all but deconstructed the myth of the unfulfilled and suffering poet. The 'real' Laura had been found: the Italians did not like it because she was French; other Europeans did not like it because it brought the poet they wanted to admire too close to the man he was, a brilliant intellectual in minor orders with two illegitimate children. It domesticated the whole sonnet sequence tradition and brought it much closer to the emerging world of the novel.

In fact, the major tendency of Petrarchan criticism was to reify the love of Petrarch for Laura. It begins with the commentary of Vellutello (twenty-six editions), whose main aim is to historify the poems by identifying as many of them with the actual places and events he thought they represented, and thus the poems become merely a disguised biography, complete with a chronology and a map. Time and space invade the sonnet world to render it more accessible but merely reduce the impact of the fiction that Petrarch wrought. What happens when that desire, that love, that torment, that betrayal – loses the icy edge of the damnation threatened by late-medieval, Christian moral theology, vividly described by Petrarch in his other writings? Very soon we arrive at an aesthetic and sentimental rationale for the poetic fiction. We are but one step from the fantasies of Walter Mitty.

The tradition of writing sonnet sequences foundered in England long before the mid seventeenth century. What had been sonnet sequences became miscellanies of the works of individual poets, such as William Habington's *Castara* (1634) or Abraham Cowley's *The Mistresse* (1647), in which topical and occasional poems still ride under the rubric of that presiding female figure who has lost all substance. Interest in the sonnet as a form waned, although there are important exceptions in the *Elegiac Sonnets* (1784) of Charlotte Turner Smith, which went through eleven editions, and the *Fourteen Sonnets and Other Poems* (1789) of William Lisle Bowles, which so excited the imagination of the young Coleridge, who remarks in the *Biographia Literaria*: 'Bowles and Cowper were, to the best of my knowledge, the first who combined natural thought with natural diction; the first who reconciled the heart with the head.' The Petrarchan sonnet would never be the same again. Its nature would become the nature of Wordsworth; its diction distorted by the Romantic ego, which has cast its shadow over the reading of Petrarch to the present day.

Late eighteenth-century and early nineteenth-century sonnet writing owes much to the fact that the Romantics resuscitated the sonnet almost as the standard of their 'newness': every river, brook and nook could have its sonnet as an expression of the poet's individuality. But this is a problem for the scholar of poetic diction, since most rivers, brooks and nooks do not contribute much to the individuality of any poet. If you have seen one, you have seen them all, unless you live there. Wordsworth's River Duddon series and his more than five hundred other sonnets merely added to the stream.

The appearance of George Henderson's *Petrarca: a Selection of Sonnets from Various Authors, with an Introductory Dissertation on the Origin and Structure of the Sonnet* (1803) prepares us for the renewed interest in the historical Petrarch and the history of the englishing of Petrarch, shown in Henderson's selection of translators from Surrey to Thomas Moore, but Petrarch's continuing influence is known mainly through two large publishing ventures, the first, a five-volume anthology of sonnets from Italian, French, English, German, Greek and Hebrew, chosen by Capel Lofft in 1813–14, and the second, the first complete translation of Petrarch by English hands published by Henry Bohn in 1859 in his famous Illustrated Libraries (833 volumes *in toto*). At last the *Canzoniere* had made it in English.

But let us start with Capel Lofft (1751–1824), the son of Christopher Lofft, secretary to Sarah, Duchess of Marlborough, and Anne Capell, sister of the Edward Capell who edited Shakespeare. He was educated at Eton, Peterhouse, Cambridge, and Lincoln's Inn, an incendiary Whig, reformer par excellence, whom Boswell called 'this little David of popular spirit' and whom Napoleon accounted 'parmi [mes] amis les plus affectionés', classical scholar, lover of literature, music, botany and astronomy. In 1813–14 he produced his five-volume *Laura, or an Anthology of Sonnets (on the Petrarchan model) and Quatorzains, English, Italian, Spanish, Portuguese, French and German*. It is an astonishing feat, and certainly his almost two-hundred page introduction on the nature and history of the sonnet is the most learned discourse we have today. His insights into the variations on the sonnet form should be mandatory reading for any creative writing course still interested in poetic form. It is the kind of book that could not be produced today. He ranges from the earliest examples of the sonnet in Italian to examples from his contemporaries: Bowles, Coleridge, Charlotte Turner Smith, his wife Sarah Watson Finch, and his own. Permission fees alone would militate against publication. He obviously read everything, knew everyone and was passionately concerned about the sonnet as a poetic form. His collection shows beyond any doubt that the sonnet as a form was very much alive in the early years of the nineteenth century. The four volumes of text contain 1000 sonnets, 250 to each volume, 300 of which are Italian sonnets, only 40 of which are by Petrarch, but the entire collection is called *Laura*, in tribute to the primary influence of Petrarch. From the small number of Petrarchan sonnets translated by a number of hands it might almost seem that there was a competition to show who would make the best English translation, but emulation of the Italian was not the main point since there are over 600 original English sonnets in the collection. Surprisingly, the most often reproduced early English sonneteer is Milton, whose Italian sonnets invited many translations. Shakespeare, Spenser, Sidney, Daniel, Drayton come lagging far behind. No one dealing with the subject of the sonnet in the Romantic period should ignore this massive compendium, which puts Henderson's *Petrarca* totally out of court.

It was only a logical progression to go beyond Capel Lofft's achievement of surveying the whole field of sonneteering for Bohn to produce the first complete translation of Petrarch in English by various hands. The presence in London in the early 1820s of Ugo Foscolo, the vagabond prince of Italian Romantic poets, and the publication of his *Essays on Petrarch* (1821, 1823), dedicated to Lady Dacre, could only have spurred interest. Thomas Campbell's two-volume *Life of Petrarch* (1841) was reprinted several times and also appeared in a condensed form as the introduction to Bohn. The world was ready for Bohn's popular venture, and it still should be read carefully by all interested in Petrarchan influence in England.

In the late nineteenth and early twentieth century, Yeats played through his Petrarchan romance with Maude Gonne and her daughter Isolde with no more success than Petrarch with Laura, but it is less well known that Synge turned to his prose versions of Petrarch after a similar failure of romantic success, the defeated playboy of the world of Italy. How much of Tennyson's Lady of Shallott was playing through their endeavours? How much of Lancelot and Elaine? When does the adjective 'tender' become an operative word in translations of Petrarch? These early twentieth-century Petrarchans are filled with a spirituality about their love that would have horrified Petrarch.

Translations in the latter part of the twentieth century are, with a few notable exceptions, the work of professional Italianist academics. Gone are the dilettante nobility and the literate clergy. The Italian text is presented with the translation on facing pages. In this century the earliest translation of the entire *Canzoniere* was the work of Anna Maria Armi, whose attempt to maintain the rhyme scheme of the original introduces many inaccuracies, but for whom I still have a personal attachment since it was my introduction to the *Canzoniere*, at a time when the Italian by itself would have proved too inaccessible. In 1976 the appearance of Robert Durling's prose versions provided a learned and necessary step in helping those of us in English literary studies with a more accurate aid to the mastery of Petrarch's poetry. Most recently, the editions of James Wyatt Cook and Germaine Warkentin (1995) and Mark Musa (1996) have appeared with all the apparatus of scholarly editions. None of the four saw fit to include the *Trionfi* as part of their mighty labours, an observation that I hope will seem less churlish than it might appear at first; I mean only to point to a desideratum to make English Petrarch more complete.

Notes

1. The others are Charles Bagot Cayley, *The Sonnets and Stanzas of Petrarch*, translated by C. B. Cayley (1879), Anna Maria Armi, *Petrarch: Sonnets and Songs* (1946), Robert Durling, *Petrarch's Lyric Poems: The Rime Sparse and Other Lyrics* (1976), James Wyatt Cook, *Petrarch's Songbook* (1995) and Mark Musa, *Petrarch: The Canzoniere, or, Rerum vulgarium fragmenta* (1996). In addition to which we now have Anthony Mortimer's lavish selection in the Penguin Classics series, *Petrarch's Canzoniere: Selected Poems* (2002).

2. There were only two poetic coronations before Petrarch. Albertino Mussato was crowned in his native city of Padua on 3 December 1315. Dante was crowned posthumously in September 1321 at his funeral, as was Convenevole da Prato, Petrarch's teacher, at his funeral. See Ernest Hatch Wilkins, *The Making of the 'Canzoniere' and Other Petrarchan Studies* (1951), pp. 21–4, and J. B. Trapp, *Journal of the Warburg and Courtauld Institutes* 21 (1958), pp. 227–55.

3. The sonnets are P140 (Tottel 2), P145 (Tottel 12), P164 (Tottel 10) and P310 (Tottel 2); the *ballata* is P11 (Tottel 13).

EDITOR'S NOTE

It is the purpose of this anthology of English translations of Petrarch to make available a wide range of his vernacular output and to show how deeply embedded Petrarch is in the English tradition of poetry from Chaucer to the present day. If to no other purpose it will add body to that emaciated and much misunderstood adjective 'Petrarchan'.

I begin with the *Trionfi*, which all but sank from poetic sight in the twentieth century, and offer translations by three amateur poets of the sixteenth century, Henry Parker, Lord Morley, Queen Elizabeth, one by the Countess of Pembroke, and one Scot of the mid-seventeenth century, Anna Hume. I also include the fragment of Lady Dacre's *Triumph of Death* and the entire *Triumph of Eternity* by the Reverend Henry Boyd to complete the fragment by Queen Elizabeth. I then present the most popular Petrarchan poems, as witnessed by the number of times they have been translated over the centuries, beginning with Chaucer who was the first Englishman to translate Petrarch. Thereafter the chronology is that of the English translation rather than the position of the poem in the *Canzoniere* for the simple reason that (as I hope will be apparent) certain themes and poetic topoi appeal to each succeeding generation of English poets.

I have tried to give a broad spectrum of translators of Petrarch into English to show his enormous influence on the language of English poetry and I conclude with a *Coda: Parodies and Replays* that attempts to show how Petrarchan we still are.

I have tried for every selection to use the earliest printed text and to maintain the typography, spelling and punctuation of that edition. Hence for the earlier writers, especially, I retain the *i* for *j*, and *u* for *v* of the original orthography but substitute modern *s* for the long *s* (*f*) and modernize the old form *vv* to our *w*. Punctuation is retained even when modern punctuation demands a comma or a full stop; dashes have been made consistent and single quotation marks are used throughout.

Information about the source of each selection is given in the headnote to each author or in the Acknowledgements. George Watson's *The English Petrarchans: A Critical Bibliography of the Canzoniere* (1966) is used as a frequent reference in the headnotes (abbreviated as 'Watson, *English Petrarchans*'). Above most of the poems is a letter P followed by a number – the number of the Petrarchan original – and the first line of that poem. If there is no P-notation, the poem is an original poem of that author, so remarkably Petrarchan that I could not exclude it. At the end of the volume is an appendix of all the selected translations in the order of Petrarch's original.

TRIONFI

PREFACE

The *Trionfi* are the intellectual grammar of Petrarch's *Canzoniere*; they present the framework within which we should read the passionate declaration of his love for Laura in those sonnets, *canzoni, ballate, sestine* and *madrigali* in which the unremitting voice of the poet-lover hovers between hope of finding his love and fear of losing her. They teach us how to read the torrent of his outpourings, as violent as the torrent of Vaucluse, in Provence, at whose base he wrote many of the poems. They teach us that the secret of grasping and understanding the contradictions and non sequiturs of the lyrics lies in the intellectual world most apparent to Petrarch, the double world of classical literature and Christian moral thought, that skillfully intermeddled, inter-texted world which was the intellectual gift to Petrarch from the preceding two thousand years.

The ground of his *Trionfi* is his covert contest with Dante, for the *Trionfi* are written in the *terza rima* of Dante's *Commedia*. The substantive subject of these poems is the Roman *triumphus*, that paean to victory in battle which the Romans perfected as they conquered the world, the welcome home to the conquering hero. But Petrarch's *Trionfi* as we read them bear less resemblance to Roman *triumphi* than they do to the literary adaptations beginning with Ovid's *Amores* I.2, in which Amor makes his triumph over the poet-lover. Petrarch also had in mind Dante's *Purgatorio* 29 and Boccaccio's *L'amorosa visione*, by which the Roman *triumphus* and Ovid himself are translated into the Christian moral vision of the Middle Ages, in which Love does triumph but only as the Christian God Who is Love. Petrarch's triumphs take on an unmistakable Christian determination in that we move from triumphs possible for Romans – Love, Death, Fame and Time – to a victory that no Roman could have foreseen – Eternity, which resoundingly cancels the Roman triumph against the triumph of eternal life, promised only to the believing Christian. Petrarch's particular innovation in this tradition is the *Triumph of Chastity*, a triumph not significant in Roman literature but inescapable in sonnet literature, for if the lady should succumb to the blandishments of the poet-lover, the whole poetic enterprise would collapse, as Byron saw with perfect clarity:

> Think you if Laura had been Petrarch's wife,
> He would have written sonnets all his life?
> > *Don Juan*, III.8

The *Trionfi* are deceptive poems if one does not understand their grammar, because there is, in fact, only one triumphal procession described by Petrarch – the triumph of Love, which has a cart and a *triumphator* and the attendant-conquered victims. All the rest are singularly lacking in depicting the pictorial qualities of a procession, in spite of the fourteenth- and fifteenth-century illustrators, who drew triumphal chariots and victors that Petrarch does not describe. The narrator is constantly in control of the images he presents to the reader, and the narrative is essentially the same as that of the *Canzoniere*: Petrarch's love for Laura, her indifference to his love, her death, his laureation because of his continued poetic devotion, and the rest is history.

The appeal of the *Trionfi* during the sixteenth century is attested to by the fact that the Queen of England and the leading literary lady of the realm both tried their hands at turning Petrarch into English, Elizabeth by translating the first 88 lines of the *Triumph of Eternity* and Mary Sidney Herbert, Countess of Pembroke, by translating all of the *Triumph of Death*. One may understand why neither continued on in this pursuit because they tried to retain the *terza rima* of the original, a linguistic chore that can be appreciated only by those Anglophone writers who have attempted to translate all of Dante in his meter.

There were two complete translations in the sixteenth century. The first by Henry Parker, Lord Morley, appeared in 1554; there is an excellent edition edited by D. D. Carnicelli (1971). The second translation is that of William Fowler (fl. 1603), tutor to the young James VI, and uncle to William Drummond of Hawthornden, among whose papers two versions of the manuscript exist in Edinburgh; published versions are printed in the sixth volume, new series, of the Scottish Text Society, edited by Henry W. Meikle (1914). Both men resorted to the couplet as their form, and the first line of Fowler's *Triumph of Love* will give the reader some indication why none of Fowler is reproduced here: 'That tyme that did my sobbing sobbs and sorye sighes renewe . . .', although much of the translation reads better than Morley.

The last of the Renaissance translators is Anna Hume, the daughter of David Hume of Godscroft, who may or may not have seen her father's *History of the Houses of Douglas and Angus* through the press, but who most certainly translated the first three of the triumphs, which appeared in 1644. She too chose the couplet as her form, and her English is more comfortable to modern ears. To round out Elizabeth I's translation I print that of the Reverend Henry Boyd, who was the first English speaker to translate the *Divina commedia* (1802). In 1807 he brought out his *Triumphs of Petrarch*.

With the exception of the Countess of Pembroke none of these translators is a poet, but I felt that it was more important to have a text of the *Trionfi* included in this volume to give a context for the outpouring of sonnets that follow. I am encouraged in this decision by the fact that almost all Renaissance editions of Petrarch contain both *Trionfi* and *Canzoniere*. They must, or should, be read together.

The Triumph of Love

ANNA HUME (fl. 1644)

Little is known of Anna Hume except as the translator of the first three of Petrarch's *Trionfi* (1644) and also as the daughter of David Hume of Godscroft (b. 1573), whose *History of the Houses of Douglas and Angus* she edited in one of its troubled versions. She was known by William Drummond of Hawthornden, who mentions her troubles in publishing the *History* in one of his letters. She dedicated her translation to Elizabeth of Bohemia (1618–80), who was the daughter of Frederick V, the Elector Palatine (elected King of Bohemia by the Protestant Union in 1619), and Elizabeth Stuart, the eldest daughter of James I and Anne of Denmark. This learned lady had a voluminous correspondence with Descartes, and in later life became the abbess of the Protestant nunnery at Hertford in Westphalia. Copy-text for both Hume's Triumphs: Harvard University Library Ital 7122.9★

The Triumph of Love, translated out of Petrarch

Chap. I
The Argument
A vision shews the captived
By mighty Love in triumph led.

It was the time, when I doe sadly pay
My sighs, in tribute to that sweet-sowre-day,
Which first gave being to my tedious woes:
The Sunne, now o're the Bulls horns proudly goes,
And *Phaëton* had renew'd his wonted race:
When Love, the Season, and my owne ill case,
Drew me that solitary place to finde,
In which I oft unload my charged minde:

There tir'd with raving thoughts and helplesse moans,
Sleep seal'd my eyes up, and, my senses gone,
My waking fancie spied a shining light,
In which appear'd long pain, and short delight.
A mighty Generall, I then did see,
Like one, who (for some glorious victory)
Should to the Capitol in triumph go:
I (who had not been us'd to such a show
In this soft age, where we no valour have
But pride) admir'd his habit, strange and brave,
And having rais'd mine eyes, which wearied were,
To understand this sight was all my care.
Foure snowie steeds a fiery Chariot drew;
There sat the cruel boy; a threatning ewe
His right hand bore, his Quiver arrowes held,
Against whose force, no helme or shield prevail'd.
Two party-coloured wings his shoulders ware;
All naked else; and round about his chaire
Were thousand mortals: some in battell tain,
Many were hurt with darts, and many slain.
Glad to learn newes I rose, and forward prest
So farre, that I was one amongst the rest;
As if I had been kill'd with loving pain
Before my time; and looking through the train
Of this teare-thirsty King, I would have spi'd
Some of my old acquaintance, but descri'd
No face I knew: If any such there were,
They were transform'd with prison, death and care.
At last one Ghost, lesse sad than th'others, came,
Who neare approaching, call'd me by my name.
And said: This comes of Love: What may you be,
(I answer'd, wondring much) that thus know me?
For I remember not t'have seen your face.
He thus reply'd: It is the duskie place
That dull's thy sight, and this hard yoake I beare:
Else I a Thuscan am; thy friend, and deare

To thy remembrance: his wonted phrase
And voyce did then discover what he was.
So we retir'd aside, and left the throng,
When thus he spake; I have expected long
To see you here with us; your face did seem
50   To threaten you no lesse. I doe esteem
Your prophesies; but I have seen what care
Attends a Lovers life; and must beware.
Yet have I oft been beaten in the field,
And sometimes hurt, said I, but scorn'd to yeeld.
He smil'd and said: Alas! thou dost not see,
(My sonne) how great a flame's prepar'd for thee.
I knew not then what by his words he meant;
But since I finde it by the dire event:
And in my memory 'tis fixt so fast,
60   That marble gravings cannot firmer last.
Mean while my forward youth did thus enquire:
What may these people be? I much desire
To know their names, pray, give me leave to aske.
I thinke ere long, 'twill be a needlesse taske
(Replied my friend) thou shalt be of the train,
And know them all; this captivating chain
Thy neck must beare, (though thou dost little feare)
And sooner change thy comely forme and haire,
Then be unfettered from the cruell tie,
70   How ere thou struggle for thy liberty;
Yet to fulfill thy wish, I wil relate
What I have learn'd. The first that keeps such state,
By whom, our lives and freedomes we foregoe,
The world hath call'd him Love; and he (you know
But shal know better when he comes to be
A Lord to you, as now he is to me)
Is in his child-hood milde, fierce in his age;
'Tis best beleev'd of those that feel his rage.
The truth of this thou in thy selfe shalt finde,
80   I warn thee now, pray keep it in thy mind.

Of idle loosenesse, he is oft the childe;
With pleasant fancies nourisht, and is stil'd
Or made a God by vain and foolish men:
And for a recompense, some meet their bane:
Others, a harder slavery must endure,
Than many thousand chains and bolts procure.
That other gallant Lord, is conquerour
Of conquering Rome, led captive by the faire
Egyptian Queen, with her perswasive Art
90   Who in his honours claimes the greatest part:
For binding the worlds victor with her charmes,
His Trophees are all hers by right of armes.
The next is his adoptive sonne, whose love
May seem more just, but doth no better prove;
For though he did his loved *Livia* wed,
She was seduced from her husbands bed.
Nero is third, disdainfull, wicked, fierce;
And yet a woman found a way to pierce
His angry soul. Behold *Marcus* the grave
100 Wise Emperour is fair *Faustina's* slave:
These two are tyrants: *Dionysius*,
And *Alexander*, both suspicious,
And yet both loved: the last a just reward
Found of his causeless feare. I know y' have heard
Of him, who for *Creusa* on the rock
Antandrus mourn'd so long; whose-warlike stroke
At once, reveng'd his friend, and wonne his love:
And of the youth whom *Phedra* could not move
T' abuse his fathers bed; he left the place,
110 And by his vertue lost his life (for base
Unworthy loves to rage doe quickly change)
It kill'd her too; perhaps in just revenge
Of wrong'd *Theseus*, slain *Hyppolito*,
And poore forsaken *Ariadne*: so
It often proves that they who falsely blame
Another, in one breath themselves condemme:

And who have guilty been of treachery,
Need not complain, if they deceived be.
Behold the brave *Heros* a captive made
120   With all his fame, and twixt these sisters led:
Who, as he joy'd the death of th' one to see,
His death did ease the others misery.
The next that followeth, though the world admire
His strength, Love bound him. Th' other full of ire
Is great *Achilles*, he whose pittied fate
Was caus'd by love. *Demophoon* did not hate
Impatient *Phyllis*, yet procur'd her death.
This *Jason* is, he whom *Medea* hath
Oblig'd by mischief; she to her father prov'd
130   False, to her brother cruel; t'him she lov'd
Grew furious, by her merit over-priz'd.
Hypsiphile comes next, mournfull, despis'd,
Wounded to see a strangers love prevail
More then her owne a Greek. Here is the frail
Fair *Helena*, with her the Shepherd boy,
Whose gazing looks hurt Greece, and ruin'd Troy.
'Mongst other weeping souls, you heare the moan
Enone makes, her *Paris* being gone,
And *Menelaus*, for the woe he had
140   To lose his wife. *Hermione* is sad,
And cals her deare *Orestes* to her aid.
And *Laodamia*, that haplesse maide
Bewails *Protesilaus*. *Argia* prov'd
To *Polinice* more faithfull then the lov'd
(But false and covetous) *Amphiaraos* wife.
The groanes, and sighes of those who lose their life
By this kind Lord, in unrelenting flames
You heare: I cannot tell you halfe their names,
For they appeare not onely men that love,
150   The gods themselves doe fill this mirtle grove:
You see faire *Venus* catch't by *Vulcan's* Art
With angry *Mars*: *Proserpina* apart

From *Pluto*, jealous *Juno*, yellow-hair'd
Apollo, who the young god's courage dar'd;
And of his trophees proud, laught at the bow,
Which in Thessalia gave him such a blow.
What shal I say? here, in a word, are all
The gods that *Varro* mentions, great and small;
Each with innumerable bonds detain'd,
160   And *Jupiter* before the chariot chain'd.

Chap. II
The Argument
Brave Massinissa *doth relate*
His Love: Seleucus *his hard fate.*

Weari'd, not satisfi'd, with much delight,
Now here, now there I turn'd my greedy sight,
And many things I view'd: to write were long,
The time is short, great store of passions throng
Within my brest: when loe, a lovely paire,
Joyn'd hand in hand, who kindly talking were,
Drew my attention that way: their attire
And forrain language quickned my desire
Of further knowledge, which I soon might gain;
10   My kinde Interpreter did all explain.
When both I knew, I boldly then drew neare;
He lov'd our countrey, though she made it feare.
O! *Massinissa*; I adjure thee by
Great *Scipio*, and her who from thine eye
Drew manly tears (said I) let it not be
A trouble, what I must demand of thee.
He lookt, and said: I first desire to know
Your name and qualitie, for well you show
Y'have heard the combate in my wounded soul,
20   When Love did Friendship, Friendship Love controul.
I am not worth your knowledge, my poore flame
Gives little light (said I:) your royall fame,

Sets hearts on fire, that never see your face:
But (pray you) say: are you two led in peace
By him? (I shew'd their guide) your History
Deserves record: it seemeth strange to me,
That faith and cruelty should come so neare.
He said; Thine owne expressions witnesse beare.
Thou knowst enough, yet I will all relate
30 To thee, 't will somewhat ease my heavie state.
On that brave man my heart was fixt so much,
That *Lelius* love to him could be but such;
Where ere his colours marched, I was nigh,
And Fortune did attend with victory:
Yet still his merit call' d for more then she
Could give; or any else deserve but he.
When to the West the Romane Eagles came
My self was also there, and catcht a flame,
A purer never burnt in Lovers brest:
40 But such a joy could not long be possesst!
Our nuptiall knot (alas!) he soone untide,
Who had more power then all the world beside!
He car'd not for our sighes; and though 't be true
That he divided us, his worth I knew:
He must be blinde that cannot see the Sunne,
But by strict justice Love is quite undone:
Counsel from such a friend gave such a stroke
To Love, it almost split, as on a rock:
For as my father I his wrath did feare,
50 And as a sonne he in my love was deare;
Brothers in age we were, him I obey'd,
But with a troubled soul and look dismaid:
Thus my dear halfe had an untimely death,
She priz'd her freedome far above her breath;
And I th'unhappy instrument was made;
Such force th' intreaty and intreater had!
I rather chose myself than him t'offend,
And sent the poyson brought her to her end:

With what sad thoughts I know, and she'l confesse,
60   And you, if you have sense of Love, may guess;
No heire she left me, but my tedious moan;
And though in her my hopes, and joyes were gone,
She was of lower value than my faith!
But now farewell, and trie if this troup hath
Another wonder; for the time is lesse
Then is the taske: I pittied their distresse,
Whose short joy ended in so sharp a woe:
My soft heart melted: As they onward goe,
This youth for his part, I perhaps could love
70   (She said) but nothing can my minde remove
From hatred of the Nation; He replide,
Good *Sophonisba* you may leave this pride,
Your City hath by us been three times beat,
The last of which (you know) we laid it flat.
Pray use these words t' another, not to me
(Said she) if Africk mourned, Italy
Needs not rejoyce; search your records, and there
See what you gained by the Punick warre.
He that was friend to both, without reply
80   A little smiling, vanisht from mine eye
Amongst the croud: As one in doubtfull way
At every step looks round, and fears to stray
(Care stops his journey) so the varied store
Of Lovers staid me, to examine more,
And trie what kinde of fire burnt every brest:
When on my left hand strayed from the rest
Was one, whose looke exprest a ready minde
In seeking what he joy'd, (yet sham'd to finde;)
He freely gave away his dearest wife,
90   (A new found way to save a Lovers life)
She, though she joy'd, yet blushed at the change.
As they recounted their affections strange,
And for their Syria mourn'd; I tooke the way
Of these three Ghosts, who seem'd their course to stay,

And take another path: the first I held
And bid him turne; he started, and beheld
Me with a troubled look, hearing my tongue
Was Romane, such a pause he made, as sprung
From some deep thought; then spake as if inspir'd,
100   For to my wish, he told what I desir'd
To know: *Seleucus* is (said he) my name,
This is *Antiochus* my sonne, whose fame
Hath reacht your eare; he warred much with Rome,
But Reason oft by Power is overcome.
This woman, once my Wife, doth now belong
To him; I gave her, and it was no wrong
In our Religion; it staid his death,
Threatned by Love; *Stratonica* she hath
To name: so now we may enjoy one state,
110   And our fast friendship shal out-last all date.
She from her height was willing to descend;
I quit my joy; he rather chose his end
Then our offence; and in his prime had dide,
Had not the wise Physician been our guide;
Silence in Love oercame his vitall part;
His love was force, his silence vertuous Art.
A fathers tender care made me agree
To this strange change. This said, he turn'd from me,
As changing his designe, with such a pace,
120   Ere I could take my leave, h' had quit the place.
After the Ghost was carried from mine eye
Amazedly I walkt; nor could untie
My minde from his sad story; till my friend
Admonisht me, and said: You must not lend
Attention thus to every thing you meet;
You know the number's great, and time is fleet.
More naked prisoners this triumph had
Than *Xerxes* souldiers in his army led:
And stretched further than my sight could reach;
130   Of severall Countreyes, and of differing speech.

One of a thousand were not knowne to me,
Yet might those few make a large History.
Perseus was one; and well you know the way
How he was catched by *Andromida*:
She was a lovely brownet, black her haire
And eyes. *Narcissus*, too, the foolish faire,
Who for his own love did himselfe destroy;
He had so much, he nothing could enjoy.
And she, who for his losse, deep sorrow's slave,
140   Chang'd to a voyce, dwells in a hollow cave.
Iphis was there, who hasted his own fate,
He lov'd another, but himselfe did hate;
And many moe condemn'd like woes to prove,
Whose life was made a curse by haplesse love.
Some modern Lovers in my minde remain,
But those to reckon here were needlesse pain.
The two, whose constant loves for ever last,
On whom the winds wait while they build their nest;
For *Halcion* dayes poore labouring saylers please,
150   And in rough winter calme the boystrous seas.
Far off the thoughtfull *Æsacus*, in quest
Of his *Epiria*, findes a rocky rest,
Then diveth in the floods, then mounts i'th' aire.
And she who stole old *Nisus* purple haire
His cruel daughter, I observ'd to fly.
Swift *Atalanta* ran for victory,
But three gold apples, and a lovely face,
Slackt her quick paces, till she lost the race:
She brought *Hippomanes* along, and joy'd
160   That he, as others, had not been destroy'd,
But of the victory could singly boast.
I saw amidst the vain, and fabulous hoast,
Fair *Galatea* lean'd on *A[c]is'* brest;
Rude *Polyphemus* noise disturbs their rest.
Glaucus alone swims through the dangerous seas,
And missing her who should his phansie please,

Curseth the cruels Love transform'd her shape.
Canens laments that *Picus* could not scape
The dire enchantresse; he in Italy
170　Was once a King, now a pie'd Bird; for she
Who made him such, chang'd not his clothes nor name,
His Princely habit still appears the same.
Egeria, while she wept, became a Well:
Scylla (a horrid rock by *Circes* spell)
Hath made infamous the Sicilian strand.
Next, she who holdeth in her trembling hand
A guilty knife, her right hand writ her name.
Pygmalion next, with his live mistresse came.
Sweet *Aganippe*, and *Castalia* have
180　A thousand more; all there sung by the brave
And deathlesse Poets, on their faire banks plac'd;
Cydippe by an apple fool'd at last.

Chap. III
The Argument
Love woundeth Petrarchs *wary heart,*
Who well describes that dying smart.

My heart was fill'd with wonder and amaze,
As one struck dumb, in silence stands at gaze
Expecting Counsel, when my friend drew neare,
And said: What doe you looke? why stay you here?
What mean you? know you not that I am one
Of these? and must attend ? pray, let's be gone
Deare friend (said I) consider what desire
To learn the rest hath set my heart on fire;
My owne haste stops me. I beleeve't (said he)
10　And I will help; 'tis not forbidden me.
This Noble man, on whom the others wait,
(You see) is *Pompey*, justly call'd, The great:
Cornelia followeth, weeping his hard fate,
And *Ptolemies* unworthy causelesse hate.

You see farre off the Grecian general;
His base wife, with *Ægisthus* wrought his fal:
Behold them there, and judge if Love be blinde.
But here are Lovers of another kinde,
And other faith they kept. *Lyncus* was sav'd
20   By *Hypermnestra*: *Pyramus* bereav'd
Himselfe of life, thinking his mistresse slain:
Thisbes like end, shortned her mourning pain.
Leander swimming often, drown'd at last;
Hero her faire selfe from her window cast.
Courteous *Ulisses* his long stay doth mourn;
His chaste wife prayeth for his safe return,
While *Circes* amarous charmes her prayers controule,
And rather vexe then please his vertuous soule.
Amilcars sonne, who made great Rome afraid,
30   By a mean wench of Spain is captive led.
This *Hipsicrates* is, the vertuous faire,
Who for her husbands deare Love cut her haire,
And serv'd in all his warres: This is the wife
Of *Brutus*; *Portia*, constant in her life
And death: this *Julia* is, who seems to mone,
That *Pompey* loved best, when she was gone.
Looke here and see the Patriarch much abus'd
Who twice seven years for his fair *Rachel* choos'd
To serve: O! powerfull love increast by woe!
40   His father this: Now see his Grandsire goe
With *Sarah* from his home. This cruel Love
O'recame good *David*; so it had power to move
His righteous heart to that abhorrid crime,
For which he sorrowed all his following time.
Just such like errour soil'd his wise sonnes fame,
For whose idolatry Gods anger came;
Here's he who in one houre could love and hate:
Here *Tamar* full of anguish wailes her state;
Her brother *Absolon* attempts t' appease
50   Her grieved soul. *Sampson* takes care to please

His fancy; and appeares more strong then wise,
Who in a traitresse bosome sleeping lies.
Amongst those pikes and speares which guard the place,
Love, wine, and sleep, a beauteous widdowes face
And pleasing Art hath *Holophernes* taine;
She backe again retires, who hath him slain,
With her one maide, bearing the horrid head
In haste, and thanks God that so wel she sped.
The next is *Sichem*, he who found his death
60   In circumcision, his father hath
Like mischiefe felt; the City all did prove
The same effect of his rash violent Love.
You see *Ahasuerus* how well he bears
His losse; a new love soon expels his cares:
This cure in this disease doth seldom fail,
One naile best driveth out another nail.
If you would see Love mingled oft with hate,
Bitter with sweet; behold fierce *Herods* state,
Beset with Love and crueltie at once:
70   Enraged first, then late his fault bemoans,
And *Mariamne* cals; those three faire Dames
(Who in the list of Captives write their names)
P[r]ocris, Deidamia, Artimesia were
All good, the other three as wicked are;
Semiramis, Biblis, and *Myrrha* nam'd,
Who of their crooked wayes are now asham'd:
Here be the erring Knights in ancient scroules,
Lancelot, Tristram, and the vulgar soules
That wait on these; *Jiniver*, and the faire
80   *Isond*, with other Lovers; and the pair
Who, as they walke together, seeme to plain
Their just, but cruel fate, by one hand slaine;
Thus he discours'd: and as a man that feares
Approching harme, when he a trumpet heares,
Starts at the blow ere touch't, my frighted blood
Retir'd: as one rais'd from his Tombe I stood;

When by my side I spi'd a lovely maide,
(No Turtle ever purer whitenesse had)
And straight was caught (who lately swore I would
90   Defend me from a man at Armes) nor could
Resist the wounds of words with motion grac't;
The image yet is in my phansie plac't.
My friend was willing to increase my woe,
And smiling whisperd; You alone may goe
Conferre with whom you please, for now we are
All stained with one crime: My sullen care
Was like to theirs, who are more griev'd to know
Anothers happinesse then their owne woe:
For seeing her, who had enthral'd my minde,
100   Live free in peace, and no disturbance finde:
And seeing that I knew my hurt too late,
And that her beauty was my dying fate:
Love, jealousie, and envie held my sight
So fixt on that faire face, no other light
I could behold; like one who in the rage
Of sicknesse greedily his thirst would swage
With hurtfull drinke, which doth his palat please,
Thus (blinde and deaf t' all other joyes are ease)
So many doubtful wayes I followed her
110   The memory still shakes my soul with feare.
Since when mine eyes are moist, and view the ground;
My heart is heavie, and my steps have found
A solitary dwelling 'mongst the woods,
I stray ore rocks, and fountains, hils and floods:
Since when such store my scattered papers hold
Of thoughts, of tears, of inke; which oft I fold,
Unfold, and teare: since when I know the scope
Of Love, and what they feare, and what they hope;
And how they live that in his Cloyster dwell,
120   The skilfull in their face may reade it well.
Mean while I see, how fierce and gallant she
Cares not for me, nor for my misery,

Proud of her vertue, and my overthrow:
And on the other side (if ought I know)
This Lord, who hath the world in triumph led,
She keeps in feare; thus all my hopes are dead,
No strength nor courage left, nor can I be
Reveng'd, as I expected once; for he,
Who tortures me and others, is abused
130   By her; she'le not be caught, and long hath used
(Rebellious as she is!) to shun his warres,
And is a Sunne amidst the lesser starres.
Her grace, smiles, slights, her words in order set;
Her haire disperst, or in a golden net;
Her eyes enflaming with a light divine
So burn my heart, I dare no more repine.
Ah, who is able fully to expresse
Her pleasing wayes, her merit? no excesse,
No bold Hyperboles I need to feare
140   My humble stile cannot enough come neare
The truth; my words are like a little stream
Compar'd with th' Ocean, so large a theame
Is that high prayse; new worth, not seen before,
Is seen in her, and can be seen no more
Therefore all tongues are silenced; and I,
Her prisoner now, see her at liberty:
And night and day implore (O unjust fate!)
She neither heares, nor pitties my estate:
Hard lawes of Love! But though a partiall lot
150   I plainly see in this, yet must I not
Refuse to serve: the gods, as well as men,
With like reward of old have felt like pain.
Now know I how the mind itselfe doth part,
(Now making peace, now warre, now truce) what art
Poore Lovers use to hide their stinging woe:
And how their bloud now comes, and now doth goe
Betwixt their heart and cheeks, by shame or feare:
How they be eloquent, yet speechlesse are:

And how they both wayes leane, they watch and sleep,
160 Languish to death, yet life and vigor keep:
I trode the pathes made happy by her feet,
And search the foe; I am afraid to meet.
I know how lovers metamorphos'd are
To that they love: I know what tedious care
I feele; how vain my joy, how oft I change
Designe, and countenance; and (which is strange)
I live without a soul: I know the way
To cheat my selfe a thousand times a day:
I know to follow whiles I flee my fire:
170 I freeze when present; absent, my desire
Is hot: I know what cruel rigour Love
Practiseth on the minde, and doth remove
All reason thence, and how he racks the heart;
And how a soul, hath neither strength nor Art
Without a helper to resist his blowes;
And how he flees, and how his darts he throwes:
And how his threats the fearful Lover feels;
And how he robs by force, and how he steales:
How oft his wheels turne round (now high, now low)
180 With how uncertain hope, how certain wo:
How all his promises be voyd of faith,
And how a fire hid in our bones he hath;
How in our vains he makes a secret wound,
Whence open flames and death doe soone abound.
In summe, I know how giddy and how vain
Be Lovers lives; what feare and boldnesse raigne
In all their wayes; how every sweet is paide,
And with a double weight of sowre allaide:
I also know their customes, sighs, and songs;
190 Their sudden mutenesse, and their stammering tongues,
How short their joy, how long their pain doth last,
How Wormwood spoyleth all their hunni's taste.

Chap. IV
The Argument
Himselfe with other slaves of Love
Are all shut up in Venus grove.

When once my will was captive by my fate,
And I had lost the liberty, which late
Made my life happy; I, who us'd before
To flee from Love (as fearefull Deere abhorre
The following huntsman) suddenly became
(Like all my fellow-servants) calme and tame;
And viewd the travels, wrestlings, and the smart,
The crooked by-pathes, and the cosening Art
That guides the amarous flock: then whil'st mine eye
10   I cast in every corner, to espie
Some Ancient or Modern who had prov'd
Famous: I saw him, who had onely lov'd
Euridice, and found out Hel, to call
Her deare Ghost back; he nam'd her in his fall
For whom he died. *Alceus* there was knowne
Skilfull in Love and verse: *Anacreon*
Whose Muse sung nought but Love: *Pindarus*, he
Was also there: there I might *Virgil* see:
Many brave wits I found, some looser rimes,
20   By others Writ hath pleas'd the ancient times,
Ovid was one: After *Catullus* came;
Propertius next, his Elegies the name
Of *Cynthia* beare: *Tibullus*, and the young
Greeke Poetesse, who is receiv'd among
The noble Troup for her rare Saphick Muse.
Thus looking here and there (as oft I use)
I spi'd much people on a flowry plaine,
Amongst themselves disputes of Love maintaine.
Behold *Beatrix* with *Dant*; *Selvagia*, she
30   Brought her *Pistoyon Cin*; *Guiton* may be
Offended that he is the later nam'd:
Behold both *Guidoes* for their learning fam'd:

Th'honest *Bullonian*: the *Scicilians* first
Wrote Love in rimes, but wrote their rimes the worst.
Francischin and *Senuchio*, (who all know)
Were worthy and humane; after did go
A squadron of another garbe and phrase,
Of whom *Arnaldo Daniel* hath most praise,
Great master in Loves Art, his stile as new
40   As sweet, honoures his Countrey: next, a few
Whom Love did lightly wound; both *Peters* made
Two; one, the lesse *Arnaldo*: some have had
A harder warre; both the *Rimbaldoes*, th' one
Sung *Beatrix*, though her quality was known
Too much above his reach in Mont-ferrat.
Alvernia's, old *Piero*, and *Girault*:
Flocchetto, who from *Genua* was estrang'd
And call'd *Marsilian*, he wisely chang'd
His name, his state, his countrey, and did gain
50   In all: *Jeffray* made haste to catch his bane
With sails and oares: *Guilliam* too sweetly sung
That pleasing Art, was cause he di'd so young.
Amareg, *Bernard*, *Hugo*, and *Anselme*
Were there, with thousands more, whose tongues were helme,
Shield, sword, and speare, all their offensive armes,
And their defensive to prevent their harmes.
From those I turn'd, comparing my own woe,
To view my countrey-folks; and there might know
The good *Thomasso*, who did once adorne
60   *Boloigna*, now *Messina* holds his urne.
Ah vanisht joyes! Ah life too full of bane!
How wert thou from mine eyes so quickly tane?
Since without thee nothing is in my power
To doe; Where art thou from me at this houre?
What is our life? If ought it bring of ease,
A sick mans dreame, a fable, told to please.
Some few there from the common road did stray;
Lelius and *Socrates*, with whom I may

A longer progresse take: O! what a paire
70   Of deare esteemed friends to me they were!
'Tis not my verse, nor prose, may reach their praise;
Neither of these can naked Vertue raise
Above her owne true place: with them I have
Reach't many heights; one yoke of learning gave
Lawes to our steps, to them my festered wound
I oft have shew'd; no time or place I found
To part from them; and hope, and wish we may
Be undivided till my breath decay:
With them I us'd (too early) to adorne
80   My head with th'honoured branches, onely worne
For her deare sake I did so deeply love,
Who fill'd my thoughts (but ah!) I dayly prove,
No fruit nor leaves from thence can gathered be;
The root hath sharp and bitter been to me.
For this I was accustom'd much to vexe,
But I have seen that which my anger checks:
(A Theame for buskins, not a Comick stage)
She tooke the God, adored by the rage
Of such dul fooles, as he hath captive led:
90   But first, Ile tel you what of us he made;
Then from her hand what was his owne sad fate,
Which *Orpheus* or *Homer* might relate.
His winged coursers ore the ditches leapt,
And we their way as desperately kept,
Till he had reached where his mother raignes,
Nor would he ever pul or turne the reignes;
But scour'd ore woods and mountains, none did care
Nor could discerne in what strange world they were.
Beyond the place, where old *Ægeus* mournes,
100   An Iland lies, *Phoebus* none sweeter burnes,
Nor *Neptune* ever bath'd a better shore:
About the midst a beauteous hill, with store
Of shades and pleasing smels, so fresh a spring
As drownes all manly thoughts: this place doth bring

Venus much joy; 't was given her Deity,
Ere blinde man knew a truer god than she:
Of which original it yet retaines
Too much, so little goodnesse there remains
That it the vicious doth onely please,
Is by the vertuous shun'd as a disease.
Here this fine Lord insulteth o're us all
Tied in a chaine, from Thule to Ganges fall.
Griefes in our breasts, vanity in our armes;
Fleeting delights are there, and weighty harmes:
Repentance swiftly following to annoy:
(Such *Tarquine* found it, and the bane of Troy)
All that whole valley with the Ecchoes rung
Of running brookes, and birds that gently sung:
The banks were cloath'd in yellow, purple, green,
Scarlet and white, their pleasing springs were seen;
And gliding streames amongst the tender grasse,
Thickets and soft winds to refresh the place.
After when Winter maketh sharp the Aire,
Warme leaves, and leasure, sports, and gallant cheare
Enthrall low minds. Now th' equinox hath made
The day t' equal the night; and *Progne* had
With her sweet sister, each their old taske taine:
(Ah! how the faith in Fortune plac't is vain!)
Just in the time, and place, and in the houre
When humble tears should earthly joys devoure,
It pleased him, whom th' vulgar honour so,
To triumph over me; and now I know
What miserable servitude they prove,
What ruine, and what death, that fall in Love.
Errours, dreams, palenesse waiteth on his chair,
False fancies o're the doore, and on the stair
Are slipry hopes, unprofitable gain,
And gainfull losse; such steps it doth contain,
As who descend, may boast their fortune best:
Who most ascend, most fall: a wearied rest,

And resting trouble, glorious disgrace;
A duskish and obscure illustriousnesse;
Unfaithful loyalty, and cozening faith,
That nimble fury, lazy reason hath:
A prison, whose wide wayes doe all receive,
Whose narrow paths a hard retiring leave:
A steep descent, by which we slide with ease,
But finde no hold our crawling steps to raise:
Within confusion, turbulence, annoy
150   Are mixt; undoubted woe, and doubtful joy:
Vulcano, where the sooty Cyclops dwel;
Lyparis, *Strombolli*, nor *Mongibel*,
Nor *Ischia*, have more horrid noise and smoke:
He hates himselfe that stoops to such a yoke.
Thus were we all throng'd in so strait a cage,
I chang'd my looks and hair, before my age,
Dreaming on liberty (by strong desire
My soul made apt to hope) and did admire
Those gallant mindes, enslav'd to such a woe,
160   (My heart within my brest dissolv'd like snow
Before the Sunne) as one would side-wayes cast
His eye on pictures, which his feet hath past.

The Triumph of Chastity

ANNA HUME (fl. 1644)

The Triumph of Chastitie

Chap. I
The Argument
Chastitie binds the winged god,
And makes him subject to her rod.

WHEN to one yoke at once I saw the height
Of gods and men subdu'd by *Cupids* might;
I tooke example from their cruel fate,
And by their sufferings eas'd my owne hard state:
Since *Phoebus* and *Leander* felt like paine,
The one a God, the other but humane.
One snare catcht *Juno*, and the Carthage Dame,
(Her Husbands death prepar'd her funerall flame,
'Twas not a cause that *Virgil* maketh one)
10   I need not grieve, that unprepar'd, alone,
Unarm'd, and young, I did receive a wound,
Or that my enemy no hurt hath found
By Love; or that she cloath'd him in my sight,
And tooke his wings, and marr'd his winding flight:
No angry Lions send more hideous noyse
From their beat breasts, nor clashing thunders voyce
Rends Heav'n, frights Earth, and roareth through the aire
With greater force, then Love had rais'd, to dare
Encounter her, of whom I write; and she
20   As quicke and ready to assaile, as he:

Enceladus when *Ætna* most he shakes,
Nor angry Scylla, nor Charybdis makes
So great and frightfull noyse, as did the shock
Of this (first doubtfull) battel, none could mock
Such earnest warre; all drew them to the height
To see what maz'd their hearts, and dimm'd their sight.
Victorious Love a threatening dart did show
His right hand held; the other bore a bow,
The string of which he drew just by his eare;
No Leopard could chase a frighted Deere
(Free, or broke loose) with quicker speed, then he
Made haste to wound; fire sparkled from his eye:
I burn'd, and had a combat in my brest,
Glad t' have her company, yet 'twas not best
(Me thought) to see her lost, but 'tis in vain
T'abandon goodnesse, and of fate complaine:
Vertue her servants never will forsake,
As now 'twas seen, she could resistance make:
No Fencer ever better warded blow,
Nor Pilot did to shore more wisely row
To shun a shelfe, then with undaunted power
She wav'd the stroke of this sharp Conquerour.
Mine eyes and heart were watchfull to attend,
In hope the victory would that way bend
It ever did; and that I might no more
Be barr'd from her; as one, whose thoughts, before
His tongue hath utter'd them, you well may see
Writ in his looks; O! if you victour be
Great Sir, (said I) let her and me be bound
Both with one yoke; I may be worthy found,
And will not set her free, doubt not my faith:
When I beheld her with disdain and wrath
So fill'd, that to relate it, would demand
A better Muse then mine: her vertuous hand
Had quickly quench't those guilded fiery darts,
Which dipt in beauties pleasure, poyson hearts.

30

40

50

Neither *Camilla*, nor the warre-like hoast,
That cut their brests, could so much valour boast;
Nor *Caesar* in Pharsalia fought so well,
As she 'gainst him, who pierceth coats of mail;
All her brave vertues arm'd, attended there,
(A glorious troup!) and marched paire by paire:
Honour and blushes first in ranke; the two
Religious vertues make the second row;
(By those she other women doth excell)
Prudence, and Modesty, the twins that dwell
Together, both were lodged in her brest;
Glory and Perseverance ever blest:
Fair Entertainment, Providence without,
Sweet courtesie and purenesse round about;
Respect of credit, fear of infamy;
Grave thoughts in youth, and what not oft agree,
True Chastitie, and rarest beauty; these
All came 'gainst Love, and this the heav'ns did please,
And every generous soule in that full height,
He had no power left to beare the weight!
A thousand famous prizes hardly gain'd
She tooke; and thousand glorious palms obtain'd,
Shooke from his hands; the fall was not more strange
Of *Hannibal*, when Fortune pleas'd to change
Her minde, and on the Romane youth bestow
The favours he enjoy'd; nor was he so
Amaz'd, who frighted th' Isralitish hoast
Struck by the Hebrew boy, that quit his boast;
Nor *Cirus* more astonisht at the fall
The Jewish widow gave his Generall:
As one that sickens suddenly, and feares
His life, or as a man tane unawares
In some base act, and doth the finder hate;
Just so was he, or in a worse estate:
Feare, griefe and shame, and anger in his face
Were seen, no troubled Seas more rage, the place

Where huge *Typheus* grones, nor Etna when
Her Giant sighs, were mov'd as he was then.
I passe by many noble things I see;
(To write them, were too hard a taske for me)
To her and those that did attend, I go;
Her armour was a robe more white than snow;
And in her hand a shield like his she bare
100 Who slew *Medusa*, a faire pillar there
Of Jasp was fixt, and with a chain (first wet
In *Lethe* floud) of Jewels fitly set,
Diamonds mixt with Topasses (of old
'Twas worne by Ladies, now 'tis not) first hold
She catch't, then bound him fast, then such revenge
She tooke, as might suffice: my thoughts did change;
And I who wisht him victory before,
Was satisfi'd, he now could hurt no more.
I cannot in my rimes the names contain
110 Of blessed Maids that did make up her train;
Calliope nor *Clio* could suffice,
Nor all the other seven, for th' enterprise:
Yet some I will insert may justly claime
Precedency of others. *Lucrece* came
On her right hand; *Penelope* was by,
Those broke his bow, and made his arrowes ly
Split on the ground, and pull'd his plumes away
From off his wings: after *Virginia*
Nere her vext father, arm'd with wrath and hate,
120 Fury, and iron and Love, he freed the state
And her from slavery, with a manly blow:
Next were those barbarous women, who could show
They judg'd it better die then suffer wrong
To their rude Chastitie: the wise and strong
The chaste Hebræan *Judith* followeth these;
The Greeke that sav'd her honour in the Seas.
With these and other famous soules I see
Her Triumph over him, who us'd to be

Master of all the world: Amongst the rest
130   The vestal Nunne I spide, who was so blest
As by a wonder to preserve her fame.
Next came *Hersilia* the Romane Dame
(Or *Sabine* rather) with her valarous train,
Who prove all slanders on that sexe are vain.
Then 'mongst the forraign Ladies, she whose faith
T' her husband (not *Æneas*) caus'd her death;
The vulgar ignorant may hold their peace,
Her safety to her Chastitie gave place;
Dido I mean, whom no vain passion led,
140   (As fame belies her) last, the vertuous Maide
Retir'd to Aruns, who no rest could finde,
Her friends constraining power forc't her mind:
The Triumph thither went, where salt waves wet
The Bayan shore, eastward; her foot she set
There on firme land, and did *Avernus* leave
On the one hand, on th' other Sybils Cave,
So to Lencernus marcht, the Village where
The noble Africane lies buried; there
The great newes of her Triumph did appeare
150   As glorious to the eye, as to the eare,
The fame had been; and the most chaste did show
Most beautifull; it griev'd Love much to go
Anothers prisoner, expos'd to scorne,
Who to command whole Empires seemed borne.
Thus to the chiefest City all were led,
Entering the Temple which *Sulpitia* made
Sacred; it drives all madnesse from the minde;
And chastities pure Temple next we finde,
Which in brave soules doth modest thoughts beget,
160   Not by *Plebeians* entred, but the great
Patrician Dames; there were the spoyles displaid
Of the faire victresse; there her palmes she laid,
And did commit them to the Thuscan youth,
Whose marring scarres beare witnesse of his truth:

With others more, whose names I fully knew,
(My guide instructed me) that overthrew
The power of Love 'mongst whom of all the rest,
Hyppolito and *Joseph* were the best.

The Triumph of Death

MARY SIDNEY, COUNTESS OF PEMBROKE (1561–1621)

'Sidney's sister, Pembroke's mother', as William Browne called her, Mary Sidney was the younger sister of Sir Philip Sidney. Together they collaborated on translating the Psalms, and after his death she brought out a version of his *Arcadia* (1598). She also published her translation of Robert Garnier's *Antonius*, as well as Philippe de Mornay's *A Discourse of Life and Death*. She is the first lady of English literary history. Text from MS Petyt 538 (Inner Temple Library) as presented by Frances Berkeley Young in *PMLA* (1912).

The Triumphe of death translated out of Italian by the Countesse of Pembrooke: the first chapter

That gallant Ladie, gloriouslie bright,
    The statelie pillar once of worthinesse,
    And now a little dust, a naked spright:
Turn'd from hir warres a ioyefull conqueresse:
    Hir warres, where she had foyled the mightie foe,
    Whose wylie stratagems the world distresse,
And foyl'd him, not with sword, with speare or bowe,
    But with chaste heart, faire visage, upright thought,
    wise speache, which did with honor linked goe:

10 And love's new plight to see strange wonders wrought
      With shiuered bowe, chaste arrowes, quenched flame
      While here som slaine, and there laye others caught.
She, and the rest, who in the glorious fame
      Of the exploit, hir chosen mates, did share,
      All in one squadronet close ranged came.
A few, for nature makes true glorie rare,
      But eache alone (so eache alone did shine)
      Claym'd whole Historian's, whole Poete's care.
Borne in greene field, a snowy Ermiline
20   Colored with [topaces], sett in fine golde
      Was this faire companies unfoyled signe.
No earthlie marche, but heauenly, did they hould;
      Their speaches holie ware, and happie those,
      Whoso are borne, to be with them enroll'd.
Cleare starrs they send, which did a Sunne unclose,
      Who hyding none, yett all did beawtifie
      With coronets deckt with violet and rose;
And as gain'd honor, filled with iollitie
      Each gentle heart, so made they merrie cheere,
30   When loe, an ensigne sad I might descrie,
Black, and in black a woman did appeere,
      Furie with hir, such as I scarcelie knowe
      If lyke at Phlegra with the Giants were.
Thow Dame, quoth she, that doeth so proudlie goe,
      Standing upon thy youth, and beauties state,
      And of thy life the limits doest not knowe,
Loe, I am shee, so fierce, importunate,
      And deafe, and blinde, entytled oft by yow,
      Yow, whom with night ere euening I awate.
40 I to their end, the Greekish nation drewe,
      The Troian first, the Romane afterward,
      With edge and point of this my blade I slewe.
And no Barbarian my blowe could warde,
      Who stealing on with unexpected wound
      Of idle thoughts have manie thousand marr'd.

And now no lesse to yow-ward am I bound
   While life is dearest, ere to cause [you] moane.
   Fortune som bitter with [your] sweetes compound.
To this, thow right or interest hast none,
50   Little to me, but onelie to this spoile.
   Replide then she, who in the world was one.
This charge of woe on others will recoyle,
   I know, whose safetie on my life depends:
   For me I thank who shall me hence assoile.
As one whose eyes som noveltie attend,
   And what it mark't not first, it spyde at last,
   New wonders with it-self, now comprehends.
So far'd the cruell, deepelie over-cast
   With doubt awhile, then spake, I know them now.
60   I now remember when my teeth they past.
Then with lesse frowning, and lesse darkned browe,
   But thow that lead'st this goodlie companie,
   Didst neuer yett unto my scepter bowe.
But on my counsell if thow wilt relye,
   Who maie inforce thee; better is by farre
   From age and ages lothsomnesse to flye.
More honored by me, then others are
   Thow shalt thee finde; and neither feare nor paine
   The passage shall of thy departure barre.
70   As lykes that Lord, who in the heau'n doeth raigne,
   And thence this all doeth moderatelie guide:
   As others doe, I shall thee entretaine:
So answered she, and I with-all descryde
   Of dead appeare a neuer-numbred summe,
   Pestring the plaine, from one to th'other side.
From India, Spaine, Cattay, Marocco, [come],
   So manie Ages did together falle,
   That worlds were fill'd, and yett they wanted roome.
There saw I, whom their times did happie calle,
80   Popes, Emperors, and kings, but strangelie growen,
   All naked now, all needie, beggars all.

Where is that wealth? where are those honors gonne?
   Scepters, and crownes, and roabes and purple dye?
   And costlie myters, sett with pearle and stone?
O wretch who doest in mortall things affye:
   (Yett who but doeth) and if in end they dye
   Them-selues beguil'd, they find but right, saie I.
What meanes this toyle? Oh blinde, oh more then blinde:
   Yow all returne, to your greate Mother, olde,
90   And hardlie leave your verie names behinde.
Bring me, who doeth your studies well behoulde.
   And of your cares not manifestlie vaine
   One lett him tell me, when he all hath tolde.
So manie lands to winne, what bootes the paine?
   And on strange lands, tributes to impose,
   With hearts still griedie, their owne losse to gaine,
After all theise, wherin yow winning loose
   Treasures and territories deere bought with blood;
   Water, and bread hath a farre sweeter close.
100 And golde and gem gives place to glasse and wood:
   But leaste I should too-long degression make
   To turne to my first taske I think it good.
Now that short-glorious life hir leave to take
   Did neere unto the uttmost instant goe,
   And doubtfull stepp, at which the world doeth quake.
An other number then themselves did shewe
   Of Ladies, such as bodies yett did lade,
   If death could pitious be, they faine would knowe.
And deepe they did in contemplacion wade
110 Of that colde end, presented there to view,
   Which must be once, and must but once be made.
All friends and neighbors were this carefull crue
   But death with ruthlesse hand on golden haire
   Chosen from out those amber-tresses drewe.
So cropt the flower, of all this world most faire,
   To shewe upon the excellentest thing
   Hir supreame force, And for no hate she bare.

How manie dropps did flowe from brynie spring
   In who there sawe those sightfull fountaines drye,
120   For whom this heart so long did burne and [sing].
For hir in midst of moane and miserie,
   Now reaping once what vertues life did sowe,
   With ioye she sate retired silentlie.
In peace cryde they, right mortall Goddesse goe,
   And soe she was but that in noe degree
   Could death entreate, hir comming to forslowe.
What confidence for others? if that she
   Could frye and freese in few nights changing cheere:
   Oh humane hopes, how fond and false yow bee.
130 And for this gentle Soule, if manie a teare
   By pittie shed, did bathe the ground and grasse,
   Who sawe doeth knowe; think thow, that doest but heare.
The sixt of Aprill, one a clock it was
   That tyde me once, and did me nowe untye,
   Changing hir copie: Thus doeth fortune passe.
None so his thralle, as I my libertie;
   None so his death, as I my life doe rue,
   Staying with me, who faine from it would flye.
Due to the world, and to my yeares was due,
140 That I, as first I came, should first be gonne,
   Not hir leafe quail'd, as yett but freshlie newe.
Now for my woe, guesse not by't, what is showne.
   For I dare scarce once cast a thought there too,
   So farre I am of, in words to make it knowne.
Vertue is dead; and dead is beawtie too.
   And dead is curtesie, in mournefull plight.
   The ladies saide: And now, what shall we doe?
Neuer again such grace shall blesse our sight
   Neuer like witt shall we from woman heare.
150 And voice repleate with Angell-lyke delight.
The Soule now prest to leave that bosome deare
   Hir vertues all uniting now in one,
   There where it past did make the heauens cleare.

And of the enemies so hardlie none,
    That once before hir shew'd his face obscure
    With hir assault, till death had thorough gonne.
Past plaint and feare when first they could endure
    To hould their eyes on that faire visage bent,
    And that dispaire had made them now secure.
160   Not as great fyers violently spent,
    But in them-selues consuming, so hir flight
    Tooke that sweete spright, and past in peace content,
Right lyke unto som lamp of cleerest light,
    Little and little wanting nutriture.
    Houlding to end a neuer-changing plight
Pale? No: but whitelie: and more whitelie pure,
    Then snow on wyndless hill, that flaking falles:
    As one, whom labor did to rest allure.
And when that heauenlie guest those mortall walles
170   Had leaft; it nought but sweetelie sleeping was
    In hir faire eyes: what follie dying calles
Death faire did seeme to be in hir faire face.

The second chapter of the Triumph of death

That night which did the dreadfull happ ensue
    That quite eclips't; naie rather did replace
    The sunne in skies, and me bereave of view.
Did sweetelie sprinkle through the ayrie space
    The Summers frost, which with Tithon's bryde
    Cleareth of dreame the darke-confused face
When loe, a Ladie, lyke unto the tyde
    With Orient iewells crown'd from thousands moe
    Crowned as she: to me I coming spyde;
10   And first hir hand somtime desyred so
    Reaching to me, at once she sygh't and spake:
    Whence endlesse ioyes yett in my heart doe growe.

And know'st thow hir, who made thee first forsake
    The vulgar path, and ordinarie trade?
    While hir, their marke, thy youthfull thoughts did make?
Then doune she sate, and me sitt-doune she made,
    Thought, wisedom, Meekenesse in one grace did striue
    [On pleasing] bank in bay, and beeches shade
My Goddesse, who me did and doeth reuiue,
20   Can I but knowe? (I sobbing answered)
    But art thow dead? Ah speake or yett aliue?
Aliue am I: And thow as yett are dead,
    And as thow art shalt soe continue still
    Till by thy ending hower, thow hence be led.
Short is our time to liue, and long our will:
    Then lett with heede, thy deedes, and speaches goe.
    Ere that approaching terme his course fullfill.
Quoth I, when this our light to end doth growe,
    Which we calle life (for thow by proofe hast tryde)
30   Is it such payne to dye? That, make me knowe.
While thow (quoth she) the vulgar make thy guide,
    And on their iudgements (all obscurelie blynde)
    Doest yett relye: no bliss can thee betyde.
Of lothesom prison to eache gentle mynde
    Death is the end: And onelie who employe
    Their cares on mudd, therin displeasure finde.
Even this my death, which yealds thee such annoye
    Would make in thee farre greater gladnesse ryse
    Couldst thou but taste least portion of my ioye.
40 So spake she with devoutlie-fixed eyes
    Upon the Heauens; then did in silence foulde
    Those rosie lips, attending there replyes:
Torments, invented by the Tyrranes olde:
    Diseases, which each parte torment and tosse
    Causes that death we most bitter houlde,
I not denye (quoth she) but that the crosse
    Preceeding death, extreemelie martireth,
    And more the feare of that eternall losse.

But when the panting soule in God takes breath;
50   And wearie heart affecteth heauenlie rest,
        An unrepented syghe, not els, is death.
With bodie, but with spirit readie prest,
        Now at the furthest of my liuing wayes.
        There sadlie uttered sounds my eare possest.
Oh happless he; who counting times and dayes
        Thinks each a thousand yeares, and liues in vayne
        No more to meete hir while on earth he stayes.
And on the water now, now on the Maine
        Onelie on hir doeth think, doeth speake, doeth write.
60   And in all times one manner still retaine.
Heere-with, I thither cast my failing-sight,
        And soone espyde, presented to my view,
        Who oft did thee restraining, me encyte.
Well, I hir face, and well hir voice I knewe,
        Which often did my heart reconsolate;
        Now wiselie graue, then beawtifulie true.
And sure, when I, was in my fairest state,
        My yeares most greene, myself to thee most deare,
        Whence manie much did think, and much debate.
70 That life's best ioye was all most bitter cheere,
        Compared to that death, most myldelie sweete,
        Which coms to men, but coms not euerie-where.
For I, that iournie past with gladder feete,
        Then he from hard exile, that homeward goes.
        (But onelie ruth of thee) without regreete.
For that faith's sake, time once enough did shewe,
        Yett now to thee more manifestlie plaine,
        In face of him, who all doeth see and knowe,
Saie Ladie, did you euer entretaine
80   Motion or thought more louinglie to me
        (Not louing honor's-height) my tedious paine?
For those sweete wraths, those sweete disdaines in yow
        In those sweete peaces written in your eye
        Diverslie manie yeares my fanzies drewe.

Scarce had I spoken but in lightning wise
   Beaming I saw that gentle smile appeare,
   Sometimes the sunne of my woe-darkned skyes.
Then sighing thus she answered: Neuer were
   Our hearts but one, nor neuer two shall be:
90   Onelie thy flame I tempred with my cheere:
This onlie way could saue both thee and me:
   Our tender fame did this supporte require,
   The mother hath a rodd, yett kinde is she.
How oft saide this my thoughts: In loue, naie fire
   Is he: Now to prouide must I beginne,
   And ill prouiders are feare and desire.
Thow sawe'st what was without, not what within,
   And as the brake the wanton steede doeth tame,
   So this did thee from thy disorders winne.
100 A thousand times wrath in my face did flame.
   My heart meane-while with loue did inlie burne,
   But neuer will; my reason overcame.
For, if woe-vanquisht once, I sawe thee mourne;
   Thy life, or honor, ioyntlie to preserve
   Myne eyes to thee sweetelie did I turne.
But if thy passions did from reason [swarue],
   Feare in my words, and sorrowe in my face
   Did then to thee for salutation serve.
Their artes I us'd with thee: thow ran'st this race
110   With kinde acceptance; now sharp disdaine
   Thow know'st, and hast it sung in manie a place.
Sometimes thine eyes pregnant with tearie rayne
   I sawe, and at the sight: Behould he dyes:
   But if I help, saide I, the signes are plaine.
Vertue for ayde, did then with loue aduise:
   If spurr'd by [loue], thow took'st som running toye,
   So soft a bitt (quoth I) will not suffice.
Thus glad, and sad, in pleasure, and annoye:
   What red, cold, pale: thus farre I have thee brought
120   Wearie but safe to my no little ioye.

Then I with teares, and trembling; what it sought
　　My faith hath found, whose more then equall neede
　　Were this; if this, for truth could passe my thought.
Of little faith (quoth she) should this proceede;
　　If false it were, or if unknowne from me:
　　The flames withall seem'd in hir face to breede.
If lyking in myne eyes the world did see
　　I saie not, now, of this, right faine I am,
　　Those cheines that tyde my heart well lyked me,
130　And well me lykes (if true it be) my flame,
　　Which farre and neere by thee related goes,
　　Nor in thy loue could ought but measure blame.
That onelie fail'd; and while in acted woes
　　Thow needes wouldst shewe, what I could not but see
　　Thow didst thy heart to all the world disclose.
Hence sprang my zeale, which yett distempreth thee,
　　Our concorde such in euerie thing beside,
　　As when united loue and vertue be.
In equale flames our louing hearts were tryde,
140　At leaste when once thy loue had notice gott,
　　But one to shewe, the other sought to hyde.
Thow didst for mercie calle with wearie throte
　　In feare and shame, I did in silence goe,
　　So much desire became of little note.
But not the lesse becoms concealed woe,
　　Nor greater growes it uttèred, then before,
　　Through fiction, Truth will neither ebbe nor flowe.
But clear'd I not the darkest mists of yore?
　　When I thy words alone did entretaine
150　Singing for thee? my loue dares speake no more.
With thee my heart, to me I did restraine
　　Myne eyes: and thow thy share canst hardlie brooke
　　Leesing by me the lesse, the more to gayne.
Not thinking if a thousand times I tooke
　　Myne eyes from thee; I manie thousands cast
　　Myne eyes on thee; and still with pittying looke.

Whose shine no cloud had euer ouer-cast:
   Had I not fear'd in thee those coles to fyres
   I thought would burne too-dangerouslie fast.
160 But to content thee more, ere I retyre
   For end of this, I somthing wilt thee tell,
   Perchance agreable to thy desire:
In all things fullie blest, and pleased well,
   Onelie in this I did myself displease:
   Borne in too-base a toune for me to dwell:
And much I grieved, that for thy greater ease,
   At leaste, it stood not neere thy flowrie nest.
   Els farre-enough, from whence I did thee please.
So might the heart on which I onelie rest
170   Not knowing me, haue fitt it-self elswhere,
   And I lesse name, lesse notice haue possest.
Oh no (quoth I) for me, the heauens third spheare
   To so high loue advanc't by speciall grace,
   Changelesse to me though chang'd thy dwelling were.
Be as it will, yett my great Honor was,
   And is as yett (she saide) but thy delight
   Makes thee not mark how fast the howers doe passe.
She from hir golden bed aurora bright
   To mortall eyes returning Sunne and daye
180   Breast-high aboue the Ocean bare to sight.
Shee to my sorrowe, calles me hence awaie,
   Therfore thy words in times short limits binde,
   And saie in-brief, if more thow haue to saie.
Ladie, (quoth I) your words most sweetlie kinde
   Have easie made what euer erst I bare,
   But what is left of yow to liue behinde.
Therfore to knowe this, my onelie care,
   If sloe or swift shall com our meeting-daye.
   She parting saide, As my coniectures are
190 Thow without me long time on earth shalt staie.

                 Marie Sydney Countesse of Pembrooke

BARBARINA OGLE BRAND, LADY DACRE (1768–1854)

Lady Dacre was a poet and dramatist as well as ardent Petrarchist. Her *Dramas, Translations and Occasional Poems* appeared in two volumes in 1821, but some of them also appeared in an appendix to Ugo Foscolo's *Essays on Petrarch* (1821, 1823), which Foscolo dedicated to her (Watson, *English Petrarchans*, pp. 8–9). This fragment is taken from *Bohn's Illustrated Library* (1859).

The Triumph of Death (line 103 to the end)

And now closed in the last hour's narrow span
Of that so glorious and so brief career,
Ere the dark pass so terrible to man!
And a fair troop of ladies gather'd there,
Still of this earth, with grace and honour crown'd
To mark if ever Death remorsefull were.
This gentle company thus throng'd around,
In her contemplating the awful end
All once must make, by law of nature bound:
Each was a neighbour, each a sorrowing friend.
Then Death stretch'd forth his hand, in that dread hour,
From her bright head a golden hair to rend,
Thus culling of this earth the fairest flower:
Nor hate impell'd the deed, but pride, to dare
Assert o'er highest excellence his power.
What tearful lamentations fill the air
The while those beauteous eyes alone are dry,
Whose sway my burning thoughts and lays declare!
And while in grief dissolved all weep and sigh,
She, in meek silence, joyous sits secure,
Gathering already virtue's guerdon high.

110

120

'Depart in peace, O mortal goddess pure!'
They said; and such she was: although it nought
'Gainst mightier Death avail'd, so stern – so sure!
Alas for others! if a few nights wrought
In her each change of suffering dust below!
Oh! Hope, how false! How blind all human thought!
130   Whether in earth sank deep the dews of woe
For the bright spirit that had pass'd away,
Think, ye who listen! They who witness'd know.
'Twas the first hour, of April the sixth day,
That bound me, and, alas! now sets me free:
How Fortune doth her fickleness display!
None ever grieved for loss of liberty
Or doom of death as I for freedom grieve,
And life prolong'd, who only ask to die.
Due to the world it had been her to leave,
140   And me, of earlier birth, to have laid low,
Nor of its pride and bost the age bereave.
How great the grief it is not mine to show
Scarce dare I think, still less by numbers try,
Or by vain speech to ease my weight of woe.
Virtue is dead, beauty and courtesy!
The sorrowing dames her honour'd couch around
'For what are we reserved?' in anguish cry;
'Where now in women will all grace be found?
Who with her wise and gentle words be blest,
150   And drink of her sweet song th' angelic sound?'
The spirit parting from that beauteous breast,
In its meek virtues wrapt, and best prepared,
Had with serenity the heavens imprest:
No power of darkness, with ill influence, dared
Within a space so holy to intrude,
Till Death his terrible triumph had declared.
Then hush'd was all lament, all fear subdued;
Each on those beauteous features gazed intent,
And from despair was arm'd with fortitude.

160   As a pure flame that not by force is spent,
      But faint and fainter softly dies away,
      Pass'd gently forth in peace the soul content:
      And as a light of clear and steady ray.
      When fails the souirce from which its brightness flows,
      She to the last held on her wonted way.
      Pale, was she? No, but white as shrouding snows,
      That, when the winds are lull'd, fall silently,
      She seem'd as one o'erewearied to repose.
      E'en as in balmy slumbers lapt to lie
170   (The spirit parted from the form below),
      In her appear'd what th' unwise term to die:
      And Death sate beauteous on her beauteous brow.

The Triumph of Fame

HENRY PARKER, LORD MORLEY (1476–1556)

Lord Morley was an inveterate translator, who gave his efforts as New Year's gifts. In addition to the *Trionfi*, he translated Boccaccio's *De claris mulieribus*. Text from *The Triumphes of Petrarch Translated by Henry Parker Lord Morley* (1554); reprinted by Stafford Henry Earl of Iddesleigh (1877) [Roxburghe Club].

The Excellent Tryumphe of Fame

After that deathe had triumphed in that face
Which often of me had tryumphed in lyke case
And that the sonne of our world was dead and past
This ougly and dispytefull beaste at the last
Pale and horrible and proud for to se
With hyr blacke baner awaye goeth she
When that she had extincte out quyte
Of perfyt beutye the very clere lyght
Then as I dyd loke about on euery part
Commyng towardes me there I dyd aduert
Hyr that mans lyfe for euer doth saue
And pulleth hym out alyue from his graue
This gloryous fayre Lady muche lyke was she
Vnto that bryght starre that goeth trust me
In the orient of the cleare day appeare
Euen in lyke maner was this Ladyes chere
So that there is no mayster in no Scole
Can take vpon them to descrybe that Sole

That I go aboute with symple wordes to tell
20   So muche great in glory this Lady dyd excell
That all the element about her dyd shyne
Not as a mortall but lyke a thyng deuyne
Grauen in theyr foreheades were the names
Of the honorable people whose hyghe fames
By valure and vertue can neuer dye
Folowynge this noble fame there sawe I
Many of those of whiche I tofore haue rehersed
That by loue (as sayd is) were sore oppressed
On her ryght hand there fyrst in my syght
30   Was Cesar and Scipion that honorable knyghte
But which of them twayne next [to] fame was
I do not remember but there they both dyd pas
The tone in vertue the tother in loue
Was taken though he semed somewhat aboue
And then forthwith was shewed vnto me
After these twayne captaynes that so excellent be
Men of hyghe valure armed full bright
As vnto the Capitall they went full ryghte
By that selfe waye that sacra called was
40   Or by via lata wherevnto they dyd passe
They came in suche an honest ordre as I saye
And had wrytten and graued this is no nay
Theyr excellent names in theyr foreheads on hie
And euen as I behelde them thus attentyfely
Their maner, their port, their chere & euerithing
To these twayne most hyest in ordre folowyng
Ensued the tone his neuew to hym dere
The tother his sonne that neuer yet had pere
And those that thou seest with the swerde in [the hand]
50   The twayn fathers and the sonnes that by him [stand]
Agaynst these enemies that Italy dyd inuade
Armed in bryght stele they no dreade hadde
Two there folowed fyrst, and twayne after past
But he that in ordre was semyng to be laste

In dede of the thre was worthyest of fame
And after these of excellent and renoumed name
Euen as the Ruby most oriently doth shyne
Went he with his hand and with his councel fyne
It was Claudius that with his wyse foresyght
60   As a swyfte byrde that taketh hys flyght
So dyd he go to the fielde at Metaurus
And pulled vp the wede, this knyght gloryouse
He had eyes and tymes convenient for to spy
And wynges as a byrde to execute it by and by
There folowed then after in that worthy race
The great old captayne that let not byd bace
Vnto the fierce captayne Hannibal and thervnto
Adioyned vnto hym was annother Fabio
Twayne named Catones with these also went
70   And two noble Paulus wyse to all intent
Two Brutus and also twayne Marcellus
And one renowmed worthy captayne Regulus
That more truly layed Rome then I saye that he
Loued his owne selfe excedyng in degree
There was there also Curio and Fabricius
That with theyr wyse pouertie maruelouse
Were more prayse worthy then [M]yde was
Or Crassus with all the great golde that he has
For golde made them vertue to expell
80   And pouertye these twayne in glory to excell
There folowed these twayne euen syde by syde
Cincinato to whom the Romaynes cryed
For helpe in theyr extreme daunger and nede
He was equall to the tother twayne in dede
Camillus ensued the noble valyaunt knyght
That had liuer dye for the maintenaunce of ryght
Then otherwise to do but as a vertuouse man
The fauour of heauen brought him to Rome [than]
Where enuy had banyshed hym from the towne
90   Home to his countrye this knyght of high renoun

There was also the vallyaunt & fresh Torquatus
That slewe his owne welbeloued son Cheualerus
Rather then he would knyghtly ordre breake
He would be childles thus the olde stories speake
Both the twayne Decius were also in the place
That theyr cruell enemies cleane for to deface
Vowed them selfes alas and that willingly
O cruell vowe them selfes forthwith to dye
No lesse dyd he the vallyaunt hardy Curio
100   That entred vnto the great large hole so
That horrybly was opened in Rome [that] riall tow[n]e
Wyllyngly hymselfe therein he entred downe
Mummio Leuio went also in ordre there
And the good noble [Attilio] with a manly chere
Titus Flami[ni]us that the grekes dyd subdue
Most with gentle pytie there dyd he ensue
There was also there in the presse he that made
A large great circle in Syria with hys rode
And with his hardy and ferse loke & cou[n]tenaunce
110   To his wylle & intent so was this romaines chau[n]ce
He the great & pussaunt kyng so constrayned
That all his hole request thereby he obteyned
And by hym in good ordre there was also he
That kept as he was armed most valliauntly
The hyll from his cruell enymies all
And after in that same place hym selfe had a fall
And with this company was [that] most valiaunt man
That kept the brydge from all Toscan
And next in ordre vnto this hardy knyght
120   Stode that ferse warrear that in great dispyte
Burnte hys ryght hand because he fayled
To sley the king his enemie which he the[n] assayled
Euen in the mides of all his noble men.
Thys was a merueylouse hardy dede there & the[n]
And I sawe also there in the hugh prese
He that fyrst vanquished on the great Seese

The Carthagines and scatred all abroade
By Cycell and Sardinia by euyll chanse al [the] rode
I sawe among the others him with [the] graue sight
130   Called Appius that wyth his forse and myght
Kept the men vulgar people in great dread & awe
So strayt & hard he bound pore men to a lawe
And after as all about I dyd cast myne eye
I dyd that person among other rest espye
That with his swete facyons vsyd hym soo
That next the fyrst in fame he myght goo
But that the ende turnyd vnto blame
Wherefore I may ryght well affirme the same
That often it is sene a long prolonged lyfe
140   Turneth good renowne into payne and stryfe
And certenly he was no lesse in fame and myght
But as Bacus and great Alcides by ryght
Or as to Thebus the good Impaminunda was
Among the other nobly he dyd there pas
And after this great and worthy myghty man
I sawe folowing among the other than
Hym that in his yonge flowryng age
Had great lawde and prayse for his vassalage
And euen asmuch as thys ferse champion
150   Was terrible and cruell in his naturall regyon
He that folowed hym was as merciable
I know noo Duke to be more commendable
There went in ordre after by and by
He that wyth hys wysdome sapiently
The noble [V]olumines he was there in the prese
Hys lawde is praysed and shall neuer sease
Cosso was there Philon and Rutilio
And the hardy captayne Lucio Dentato
With Marco, Sergio and Sceua the bolde
160   In armys as lyghtnyng one myght them behold
Their harnes broke[n] their shelde in twenty places
Persyde thorowe with swordes dartes & mases

The last of them that there was in dede
With no lytle fame the rest dyd succede
And after these noble men afore rehearsed
Dyd folowe ferse Marius which reuersyd
Iugurta of Numedy the myghty kyng
And the Cymbers that with them dyd brynge
The Almaynes in fury and in rage
170   Thys Marius dyd their great myght asswage
There went by the Marius by and by
Fuluius [Flaccus], that with witty polecy
Destroyed those that at Rome dyd rebell
But he that folowed dyd farre passyng exell
It was Fuluio so was his very name
Well worthy among other to folowe fame
There was also one Romayne named Graccus
[That] had among [that] people much matter contrariouse
To his ruyne at the last in Rome towne
180   There was he thys knyght of high renowne
And he also that much fortunate semyde
Though by me he cannot so be demyde
Was there and after hym there came
The two worthy Marcelles in ordre than
That kept all close in theyr hartes I say
Theyr secretes they went aboute alway
These two had great prayse in Numyddia
In Macedon also and in the Yle of Creta
And in lyke maner in the Realme of Spayne
190   Three vallyaunt famouse Knyghtes for certayne
And I sawe also euen at that tyde
The good Vespacian and by his famouse syde
His eldest sonne but not his cruell brother
He was not worthy to be amonge the other
And so folowed after in good ordre than
Narva the auncient and gentle Traian
Helio and Adrian and the mercifull Antonius
With fayre succession vnto Macronius

That were no more couetouse of croune imperial
200   Then desirous for to lyue in vertuous naturall
And whiles that I thus loked all aboute
I sawe fyue Kynges amonges that rowte
The syxte an euyll happe dyd hym take
As one that foloweth vice & vertue doth forsake.

The Seconde Chapiter of Fame

Full of greate and infynyte maruayle
I stode beholding these noble Romaynes well
Whiche of al other hadde neuer no peere
And as I reuolued their famous actes cleere
Which I haue sene in bookes wrytten and tolde
More was there of them dyuers and manyfolde
Then I haue here in this place set in by name.
Therfore I now for this tyme passe the same
To loke vpon straungers vertuous and excelle[n]t
10   The fyrst was Hannybal that in ordre went
The next was he that syngyng made his men
To haue the vyctory, and there folowed then
Achylles the Greke, that in his hauynge dayes
Gate by his prowes a great laude and prayse
Twayne noble worthy Troyans were there also
And twayne hardy Persiens in ordre ther did go
Philip of Macedon, and his sonne Alexander
That dyd bryng downe [the] Persiens great power
Vnto subiection, as in olde bookes we fynde
20   And conquered thervnto al the regyon of Inde
After noble fame they passed in that place
And another named Alexander folowed apace
Not farre from the tother that went before
But O fortune howe doest thou euermore
Dyuyde those that in the put theyr truste
From true honoure thou arte so vniuste

There ensued in ordre there by and by
The gloryouse captayne valyaunt and worthy
Of Thebes that ryall Citie of hygh renowne
30   There was also he that had the famous crowne
And twayne Achilles, and the wyse Vlixes
And the hardy valiaunt greke Dyomedes
Nestor the sage that lyued so many yeares
There was the olde kynge amonge his peeres
Agamenon the great and the kynge Menelaus
That both their two wyues to v[n]gracious
Muche hurt vnto the hole worlde dyd they
Folowed hardy Leonydes that purposed I saye
To his men a harde Dyner, but hardyest of all
40   Was the supper whereto he dyd them call
With a fewe men he dyd a meruelouse dede
Amonge the other there this captayne yede
There was also the fayre knyght Alcibiades
That dyd straunge & great wonders in Athenes
With his fayre eloquent speche and fayre face
Amonge the rest he was there in that place
Melciedes was next that made all Grece free
His sonne folowed the example of pytye
That alyue and dead his father dyd ensue
50   That among the other in preace there I knewe
The[mistocles] and the valyaunt Theseus
Arystides and the good faythfull Fabricius
Whiche theyr vnkynde countrey I do saye
Woulde not suffre theyr bodyes to lye in claye
Alas this was a foule and an vnkynde dede
So to reward them for theyr well doynge mede
The good Phocion folowed whom I did regard
For his good dedes they gaue hym lyke rewarde
And as I turned here and there my syght
60   I sawe Pyrrus that noble warlyke knyght
And the good gentle kynge Masinises
That semed angry because that doubtles

Amonge the Romaynes that he was not set
With hym I knewe Iero of Syracuse the greate
And cruell Amylcar deuyded from these twayne
It was he that yssued from the fyre and rayne
A manyfest token that nether helme nor shielde
Agaynst false fortune can neuer wynne the fyelde
There was Sciphas much after that rate and sorte
70   and Brennius for all his great pryde and porte
That was cast downe by Apollos temple syde
after the other in ordre there he hyde
In dyuers straunge garmentes and araye
Went this tryumphe onwarde on theyr waye
And I that chaunced to cast my loke asyde
I sawe a great huge number go and ryde
amonge them one that would Gods temple make
and he fyrst began it for his loue and sake
This was the fyrst I saye in all that rowte
80   But he that fynyshed that worke out of doubte
That holy buyldyng of whiche that I do meane
Was not inwarde so vertuouse nor so cleane
as the fyrst good kynge wheron I do saye
Nowe he that folowed him in that greate arraye
Was he that spake to God face to face
There was few or none that euer had such grace
And after hym in lyke order by and by
Came he that stayde the Sonne so wonderly
Tyll he his enemies had taken and slayne
90   O gentle trust most sure and certayne
In servynge God as dyd this noble knyght
With symple worde to stay the heauenly lyght,
I sawe after hym where that there went
Our olde father whiche for good entent
God badde he shoulde his lande forsake
And he for that shoulde possesse and take
The place that was helthfull to all mankynde
Electe of God there dyd he that countre fynde

Folowed after this father his sonne moost dere
And his welbeloued neuew also he was there
Whiche had the yoke in hauynge wyues two
There was with hym the chast Joseph also
That from his father went full many a daye
Thus here and there castynge myne eyes alwaye
I sawe the iuste and good kynge Ezechias
And Sampson that so stronge and myghtye was
And not farre distaunt from hym there went he
That made the great wonderfull shyppe of Noe
And he also that the great hygh towre began
Charged with synne and with errour than
The good valyaunt Iudas that noble knyght
He there folowed after in ordre ryght
That would not his holy godly lawe forsake
Alas he for Justice the death dyd take
My desyre with seyng all these noble men
Was well nere fully satisfyed there and then
When that sodenly I dyd there espye
Of worthy ladyes a more gorgeous company
That pleased my syght as much or more
As all the syght that I had sene before
There sawe I goyng together in a bande
Antiope and Arithia well armyd stand
And fayre swete Ipolita sory and sadde
Because that no comforth of her son she had
And Manylipe that vanquished Hercules
And her Suster also was there in prese
The tone Hercules toke vnto hys wyfe
The tother with Theseus led her lyfe
There folowed the hardy wydowe that dyd se
Hyr dere sone slayne most constantly
And reuenged hys death vpon kyng Cyrus
It was a noble hardy acte and valerouse
She abatyd therby so his gloriouse fame
That wel nere it blotted his dedes & eke his name

100
110
120
130

There was also she her selfe that lost her ioye
By great mysfortune comming vnto Troye
And among other that bolde Lady of Italye
That domaged bi armes the Troia[n]s maruelously
And euen by her went that hardy Lady
140   That halfe her fayre here bounde vp curiously
And let the tother for to hange besyde
Tyll she abatyd the babilonicall pryde
Cleopatra that was burnte with loues fyre
There she was with all her hote desire
And among the thickest of the prese
Was Xenobia which was doutelesse
Wondre fayre and swete for to beholde
Soo much of hardines her high harte dyd holde
That with her helme of stele on her hedde
150   She put in daunger in feare and eke in dreade
The high mightye Emperoure of Rome towne
Tyll fortune vnkynde dyd thrawe her downe
That at the last she was made I saye
Vnto the Romaynes a great huge pray
And albeit that I do here forgete
Both men and women that wer highe and great
Yet the chast Iudeth wyll I call to mynde
That slewe dronken Holyferne in loue blynde
And dronken as he lay routing in his bedde
160   Wyth hys owne sworde she smote of his hedd
But alas why do I present her forget
That noble gentelman among the rest to sett
Which pride brought from his trone dou[n]e opprest
To lyue seuen yeares as a brutyshe beste
Or why do I not remember in this place
Zorastro that the fyrst Inuentor was
Of arte magyke of Errour the ground
Or why art not thys twayne here founde
That passyd Euphrates and put Italye to sorow
170   Or Metridates that both euen and morowe
To the Romaynes was ennemie perpetuall

And wynter and somer fled ouer all
Great thynges in fewe wordes I do tell
Where is kyng Arthur that dyd excell
And the thre Cesares surnamed Augustus
One was of Aufryke a Prynce gloriouse
The tother he was of the Regyone of Spayne
And the thyrde of the country of Lorrayne
But setting this nobles for a whyle a syde
180 The good Godfrey after fame faste hyde
Surnamed Bulleyne that toke with his hand
Iherusalem the Cytie and eke the holy lande
Nowe alas I say a place neclecte of vs
Wherfore ryght well I may saye thus
Go ye proude and wreched christen men
And consume the tone the tother then
And care not for shame among you at all
Though dogges possesse the sepulcre royall
Alas why do you suffer it for pitie
190 But after these as farre as I coulde se
Fewe or none was that deserued fame
Sauing that behynde there went by name
One Sarracene that dyd much payne and wo
To christen men it is euen playnely soo
and Saladyne after dyd folowe a great pase
and one Duke of Lancaster after there was
That with sheilde, and swerde, and bowe & launce
Was a sharpe scourge vnto the realme of fraunce
and thus marueylyng as I lokte all aboute
200 as one that was desyrouse amongest the route
To se more of these valliaunt men
At the last I dyd behold there and then
Twayne worthy men that lately alas dyd dye
There they went in that honorable companye
The good kyng Robert of Cecyll he was there
That with his wyse syght sawe fare and nere
And my good Columnes went in that arraye
Vallyaunt and free and constant alway.

The Thirde Chapiter of Fame

I coulde not in noo wyse away put my syght
From these greate honorable men of myght
When as me thoughte one to me dyd saye
Loke on the lefte hande there see thou may
The dyuyne Plato that goeth I say full nye
Vnto the marke of fame euen by and by
Next vnto Plato Aristotle there he is
Pytagoras foloweth that mekely calde Iwys
Phylosophy he dyd geue it that name
10   Socrates and Xenophontes folowed the same
And that fyery olde auncient man
To whome the musys were so fra[n]dely than
That dyscryued Argo Micena and Troye
Howe that for Helene they lost all their ioye
And he dyd wryte of Laertes sonne also
And of Achilles that was the Troyanes woo
He was the fyrst paynter it is so tolde
Of the auncient and venerable actes olde
There went with hym in that place hand in hand
20   The Mantuan poete I do well vnderstand
Stryuyng which of them should goo before
And there folowed after in hast more and more
He that as he passyde in that noble passe
It semed the flowres dyd spryng on the grasse
It is he the most eloquent Marcus Tullius
The selfe same eyes and the tunge gloriouse
Vnto all the Latynes there was he
And after hym there there came Demostyne
That semyd to be not very well content
30   Because he was not accompted most excellent
To goo hymselfe next vnto worthy fame
He toke it to be to hym great wrong and shame

He semyd to be a lyghtnyng all one fyre
But next vnto hym all full of grete desyre
Went Eschy[n]es which myght perceaue and se
Howe vnmete he was vnto Demostyne
I cannot saye in ordre nether wryte nor tell
Of one and other that dyd there exell
Nor howe I dyd them se nor when
40 Nor who went foremost nor hynmost then
For it were so to do to great a wondre
They went not fare these clarkes a sondre
But so thycke that both eye and mynd
In lokyng on them theyr names I could not find
But well I knowe that Solon he was there
That planted soo good holsome frute to bere
And yet to lytle effect at length it was
With hym the syx wyse sage grekes dyd pas
Which Grece doth boste of for theyr wyt
50 In one bande together they were knyt
and I dyd with these also well beholde
Varro which all our nacione had enrolde
As theyr Duke the thyrde in place was he
Of all the Romaynes in that high degree
The more that I lokte vpon hym there
The more his face semed fayre and clere
Crispo Salustius went with him hande in hande
And Tytus Liuius by hym dyd there stande
Scant contented but lokyng very sadde
60 Because the fyrst honoure there he ne had
And as I loked fast on this Tytus Liuius
Came by me the excellent naturall Pl[in]ius
Quick in wrytyng but quycker to the death
To muche boldenes dyd stoppe alas, his breath
I sawe after hym the great clarcke Plotinus
That wenyng by hys lyfe solytariouse
To haue preuented his harde chaunce & destenye
yet fell he therin for truth this is no lye

His sage foresyght dyd profyt hym nothyng
70 When necessitie therto dyd hym brynge
There was in lykewyse among the rest also
Crasso, Antonio, and sage Hortensio
Sergius, Galba, and the disdayning Licinius
Whiche were to muche proude and to to curiouse
For with theyr tunges vntrue and vniuste
They sclau[n]dered Cicero they were [the] lesse to trust
There folowed after [Th]ucides in that pres
That ordeyned [with] wisedome the howres doutles
And wrote of the battels & wher they were done
80 And Herodotus with his style holesome
And he beganne the crafty sciense of Geometre
The triangle and the rounde Arball in degree
And of the quadrant fyrme and fast also
The Sophisticall Porphirus next hym dyd go
And falsely dysputed agaynst our religion
And he of Coo that with his disputacion
Made muche matter in his Amphorisomis
Apollo and Esculapius with hym is
Howbeit they were so auncyent and olde
90 That scant I could decerne what they would
There was one in that prease of Pargamo
His science is now past it is verye so
But in his tyme it was muche set by
Anaxarco without dread most hardye
And [X]enocrates more fyrme then a stone
So that there coulde no euyll temptation
Moue hym in any thinge that was vyle
Or by vnclennes his chast body defyle
There folowed hym self there Archemenides
100 With sadde regarde he stode in that pres
And the pensyfe Democryte next in ordre there
Blynde of both his eyes he had no pere
There was Hyppia also of great auncient age
That durst affyrme that he was so wyse and sage

That he knewe and vnderstode all thynge
Archisilao ensued not much vnlyke such rekenyng
That he accompted by hys scyence playne
All thynge to be doubtfull and certayne
I saw Heraclito with wordes couert and close
110   And Diogenes folowyng his sensual purpose
That lytle shamed his desyre to ensue
Amonge the other this straunge clerke I knewe
And he that shewed a gladde mery chere
When al his landes were lost and other gere
There was also Dicearco the curyouse
Quintilian, Sceneke, and Plutarke the famouse
And after these excellent and connynge men
I sawe a great number together then
Disputinge of dyuers sundry cases
120   Not to knowe but to fynde secret places
One contrarye vnto the tother alwayes
That it semed there clateryng was lyke iayes
With a romblynge as the shyppes that be
In a [ragynge] tempest vpon the large see
Euen as Lyons and serpentes hurle together
Withoute profyte nowe hyther nowe thyther
Was there disputation and after these than
Wyttye Carneades that well lerned man
That coulde with speach a case so fyle
130   That were it true or false hys subtyll style
It was harde his craft to knowe and discerne
He lyued longe without all syknes and harme
Tyll false enuy agaynst hym dyd soo aryse
That he coulde not although he were wyse
Resyst the fury of them that hym hatyd
Nor the veneme that agaynst hym was debatyd
There was also the bablynge Epicurus
That agaynst Cirus was greatlye contrariouse
That affirmed oure soules neuer to dye
140   This Epycure cleene contrary dyd denye

And sayd that our soules were very mortall
And perysshe as best soules do with the body all
Wherby he deserued to have reproue and blame
And scant worthy for to folowe fame
I sawe dyuers other folowinge thys secte
Lyppo and Metrodorus and Aristippus [the] electe
For theyr excellent conninge that they then hade
Praysed greatly though theyr saynges were bad
There was also that Phylozopher [that] in very dede
150   Spune the subtle and wonderouse crafty threde
Hys wyt was so excellent and his learning so fine
That he semed to haue a knowledge deuyne
[Z]e[n]one the Father of the Stoykes secte
Aboue the rest he was best electe
Well declared he as he dyd there stande
By the palme and closyng of his hande
Howe the truth was in eche season and case
For he so declared it with his wyse face
The vayne argumentes from the true euen so
160   That many after hym dyd ensue and go
Here I do leue to speake more of the rest
And nowe wyll tell of that thyng which is best.

The Triumph of Time

HENRY PARKER, LORD
MORLEY (1476–1556)

The Excellente and Moste Dyuyne Tryumphe of Time

Frome hys golden harboroughe & restyng place
The fayre Aurora going afore his face
Yssewed out the sonne so clear & fyrmely set
With radient and bryght beames burnished & bet
That thou woldest haue said euen with a thought
Thys faire swete planet was gotten vp a loft
Thus vp rysen in lyke maner and guyse
As do these sage men sober sadde and wyse
He loked all about and to hymselfe he sayde
What doest thou nowe I se well at this brayde
Yf to thyne one selfe thou take no better hede
All thy great glory wylbe gone in dede
Take thou then I aduyse the good and wise cure
For yf that it be very certeyne and sure
That worthy men by fame dyeng do not dye
Thys vniuersall and fyrme course eternally
Of the large heuen most sure and certayne
Shalbe accompted at the last but vayne
And yf fame mortall for euer do encrease
That a litle short houre shuld cause to sease
I se my great excellence shall soone declyne
And howe can I haue a worse ende and fyne
Than to haue no more in the heuenly skye
Than man in earth that dying cannot dye
That thynkes myselfe equall by speciall grace
Aboue all other to haue the highest place

10

20

In the great wyde and large see Occeane
Foure horses of myne are there and than
That with great studye I nourishe and dresse
30   In theyr rennyng course of infinite switenesse
And yet for all theyr great wonderfull hoste
Cannot a mortall man that is dead and past
Put in forgetting neyther his laude nor fame
It muste neades greue and anger me that same
Not onely I my selfe the chefe in my degree
But the thyrde or seconde wold therat greued be
I must than hast my selfe with a great zele
Agaynst these men for the wrong that I fele
In doublyng my course to there double harme
40   For I do enuy there fame that is so farme
That after a thousand and a thousand yeares
Theyr hyghe renowme and theyr glory cleres
Muche more after theyr death then in theyr lyfe
Which playne is vnto me a perpetuall stryfe
That am nowe no higher nor in no better rate
Than I was or the earth was in his firste state
Goyng in compasse with my beames bryght
By thys great round bole which is infinite
When this fayre beautifull sonne had thus sayde
50   Dysdaynyng furthwith and euen at a brayde
She toke her course far more swyfter I say
Then Faukon that from a high flyeth to [the] praye
Her wonders swiftnes I can nether tel nor write
For it is not possible for me it to endyte
Noo I say with my thought to expresse it in dede
So that to remember it I am in feare and dreade
Then I saye when that wyttely I mynded this
I compted oure lyfe to be a vyle thinge as it is
And none other nor no better but a terrible vanite
60   To put oure hartes on that which sone doth fle
So fast away that euen with a thought
Wenyng to holde hym we holde hym nought

He whosoeuer doth loke vnto his state
Let hym sone prouyde for hym selfe algate
Whyles he hath his fre wyl in his propre myghte
In thynges that be stable to set his delyght
For when I sawe the tyme goo so fast
After his guyde that maketh post hast
I wyll not saye it, for tell it I ne can
For I sawe euen at one verye poynte than
The yse and the rose one after the other
Nowe colde nowe hote euen with the tother
That for to tell it is a maruelous case
Howe after the tone the tother hyeth a pase
He that with a wyse iudgement this markes
Shall se by true experience all these warkes
Whiche lytle I noted in my yonge lusty age
And that maketh me nowe with my selfe to rage
For then I confesse all my hoole delyght
Was in folowyng my folysh appetyte
But now afore my feble eyes is a glasse
Wherin I spye my greate faulte that was
Styll goynge downeward to my last ende & fyne
Remembryng therto how fast it doth declyne
I was a chylde euen this same present daye
And nowe an olde man prest to passe away
So that for a very truth to tell it I shall
Lesse then a sely daye is oure lyfe mortall
Cloudy and colde, and ful of woo and payne
That semeth to be fayre, and yet is but vayne
This is the vnstable hope of all our kynde
Why are we then so proude why are we so blynd?
When no man knoweth hys lyfe nor his death
And this note onely as the sage man sayeth
Doth not touche me but all that be alyue
The fast course of the Sonne doth away dryue
That plainly and manifestly the truth note I shal
The ruyne of the worlde is knowen to vs all

Then ye yonge men that be in your fresh lust
100   Measure [the] tyme longe and put therto your trust
Folyshly I say playnly why cal ye not to mynd
Afore consydered hurte lesse hurteth by kynde
Onles I blowe these wordes to you in vayne
But I do tel you note it for truth and certayne
ye that do not mynde, nor well remember this
With a slepy lytargy your braynes combred is
For the howres flyes a pace, so doth the dayes
The monethes and the yeares, folowe alwayes
Together in a breif shorte distaunce and tyme
110   So that yf ye well and wysely note this ryme
We must all mortall men to another countre pas
And all our great glory shalbe turned to was
Goo ye not then agayne the truth I do saye
But amende your euyl lyues whyles that ye may
Do not abyde tyll dreadfull death you take
As the most part of [the] vnwytty doth I vndertake
O that ye wyll not this well vnderstande
Of fooles there is doubtles an infinite bande
Sythens then I do knowe and playnly se
120   This great planet howe fast it doth fle
Which tyme when I myght, by folye I haue not taken
But with muche great losse this tyme forsaken
I sawe amonge these vnwyse foles all
A nation that by theyr science lytle cared at all
Nor feared not oft tyme the course rabidouse
These I saye remoued and people most gloriouse
Whiche hystorians hath taken in theyr garde
And poetes also that wrote howe that they farde
Of this it semed then the Sonne had enuye
130   Whiche by them selfe so mounted [t]o hyghe glorye
Passyng awaye from the madde vulgar quyte
By the honorable vertuous wayes noble & right
He hasted then this sonne a wonders spedy pas
With moche more forse then euer there was

And to his swyft horses he doubled the meate
Passynge by the great beare this planet great
So that the quene of whom I haue sayde
Would haue departed from the sonne at [the] brayde
I haue hard say, I wote not well of whome
140   That euen as a wede wasteth our glory is goone
And that all our fame is but blynde and derke
And a perpetual forgetfulnes al our labor & werk
And he sayd further that all the longe yeares
And the processe also of the lusters and speares
And of worldes infinite hereafter for to come
Shall vanysh awaye our fame al and some
Doubtles of as many it is playne euen so
As are betwyxt these places Peneo and Hebro
Or as far a sunder as that ryuer of [Z]anto
150   Is distaunt by measure from the valey of Thebro
And that oure glory is to be sayde by ryght
Euen as we se the ayer fayre and bryght
Made darke and hydde with a mysty cloude
And breifly this alwayes note wel we should
A hasty longe rynnyng awaye of the tyme
Is a poyson to fame to cause it to declyne
Our Tryumphs shal passe our pompes shal decay
Our lordshyppes our kyngdomes shall all awaye
And al thynge also that we accompt mortall
160   Tyme at the length shal clene deface it al
And to this those that are but meanly good
They affirme and say playne [that] who so vnderstode
Not onely our bodyes sone away doth passe
But all our wyttes and eloquence in lyke case
Thus not goyng but flying the world doth go
Nor resysteth nor tarieth nor is it playne so
Tyl he haue brought al false worldly luste
To no better thynge but to bare ashes and duste
Why than hath humayne glory so much hy pryde
170   When that it is very playne sene on euery syde

Although the vulgar doth not this thinge marke
We shuld wel by ryght experie[n]ce know this wark
That these foles do bable they wote not what
If that the case were our short lyfe declyned not
So sone nor so swyftly vnto the last ende
Al the hye fame whereto that men pretende
Euen as the smoke doth vanyshe awaye
So at the last al thynges do playne decay
This hearing me think it standes [with] good reason
180   Not for to deny the truth at no season
But to agre to that thynge we do wel know
Euen by comparison as the sonne melteth [the] snow
So doth the tyme put awaye and shall
Not a thousande famouse but at the last them all
Though that the moost part thynke it be not so
O therfore I saye, howe blynde are they therto
That thynke it muche better for to die in age
Then lyinge in the cradle to go that passage
To how many men had it ben far passing better?
190   Yea: and I affyrme it a [thousand] tymes more sweter
To haue dyed beyng yonge then to haue died old
Many excellent clarckes doth it by reason holde
That muche more fortunate the vnborne chylder be
Then chyldren that be borne such payne to se
But the great number hath alway greatest error
If it were so certayne and thervnto so sure
That after a longe lyfe shuld come a longe fame
Who be they I pray you that wyll folow the same
The couetous time turneth al thinge vp so doune
200   And our great fame that doth so hyghly soune
It is no nother to be named but a second death
Nor stay is there none as the true truth sayth
Thus tryumpheth tyme and hasteth so a pace
That all our glory and fame it doth deface.

The Triumph of Eternity

ELIZABETH I (1533–1603)

Queen Elizabeth is not so well known as a translator, but she turned her hand to Psalm 13, the second chorus from Seneca's *Hercules Oetaeus*, some metres from Boethius's *Consolation of Philosophy*, a long section of Horace's *Art of Poetry*, Plutarch's *On Curiosity*, as well as some original poems. In this translation, she attempts to keep the metre and rhyme of the original *terza rima*, and the lines have been arranged in triplets to indicate this fact. Text from Ruth Hughey (ed.), *The Arundel Harington Manuscript of Tudor Poetry* (1960), vol. 1.

Triumphe Petrarcke (lines 1–88)

Amazed to see, nought vnder heavens cope
   steddie and fast, thus to my self I spake
   Advise the well: on whome doth hang thie hope,
On god (said I) that promyse never brake
   With those that trust in hym. But now I know
   how earst the fickle world abvsed me
eke what I am and was, and now to goe
   or rather flye the nimble tyme I see
   Blame wold I, wist I whome: for all the cryme
10 is myne that sholde (not slacking till the last)
   haue earst vnclosed myne eyes before this tyme
   for trouthe to say, olde waxe I all to fast
But overlate godes grace came never yet
   in me also I trust there shall be wrought
   works wonderfull and strange by meanes of it.
Theise sayed and answere made thus more I thought

If none of all theise thinges do stand in staye
that heaven turnes and guydes, what end at last
shall follow of their everturning swaye?
Whyle deeper yet my searching mynd I cast
20   a world all new even then it seemed me
in never chaunging and ever lyving age
the sonne, the skye with all her sterres to see
dissolved quite with earth and Seas that rage
one made more faire and pleasant in his place
when hym that never stayed but earst to chaunge
eache thing was wont wandring in divers race
stand on one foote I saw: how seemed it straunge
all his three partes, brought into onlye one
and that one fast so that as wont it was
30   no more so swifte it hasted to be gone
but had one shew as earth dispoiled of grasse
there were not shall be, hath bene, after earst
to irkesome weake and divers state that brought
our life. As Sonne dothe pearce the glasse so pearste
my thought, yea more, for nothing stoppith thought
What grace fynd I, to see if I attaine
even face to face the greattest god of all
(no ill whiche onlye tyme gieves and againe
as first it came with tyme eke parte it shall
40   the Bull or fishe lodge shall no more the Sonne
whose chaunge dothe make a toyle now dye now springe
now waste now growe. Oh happie spirites that wonne
or shall hereafter stand in the chief ring
Wose names aye memorie writes in her booke
Oh happie hee to fynde, whose happ shalbe
the deepe Chanell of this swift ronning brooke
whose name is life that manie wishe to see,
wretched and blynd the common sort that stay
50   their hope on things [which] tyme reaves in a trice
all deaff, naked and subiect to decaye
quite void of reason and of good advice

and wretchid mortall men throughout diseas'd)
whose beck doth guide the world by whome at iarre
are sett the elements and eake appeased
whose skill doth stretche beyond my reache so farr
that even the Angells are content and ioye
of thowsand partes but one to see, and bend
their witts to this; and this wishe to enioye
Oh happie wandring mynde; ay hungring to the end
60 What meane so manie thoughts? one howre dothe reave
that manye yeares gathered with moche a doe
To morrow, yesterdaye, morning and eve,
that presse our sowle and it encombre soe
before hym passe shade like at ones awaye
for was or shalbe no place shall be fownde
but for the tyme of is, now, and todaye
onlye eternitie knitt fast and sownde
Huge hills shalbe made plaine, that stopped cleane
70 our sight, ne shall there any thing remayne
where on may hope or our remembrance leane
whose chaunge make other doe that is but vaine
and lif to seeme a sporte. Even with this thought
what shall I be, what was I hearetofore
all shall be one, ne peese meale parted ought
Sommer shalbe, ne winter any more
but tyme shall dye, and place be chang'd with all
and yeares shall beare no rule on mortall fame
but his renome for ever florishe shall
80 that once atchiev'd to be of flowring name
Oh happie soules that now the path dothe treade
or henceforth shall when so it happs to be
whiche, to the end whearof I speake doth leade
of faire and wandring sprights yet happiest shee
Whome deathe hath slayne farr shortt of natures bounde
the heavenlye talke good words and thoughts so chaste
Open shall lye vnfolded in that stounde
Whiche kinde within a youthfull hart hath plaste:

REVEREND HENRY BOYD
(1748/9–1832)

Boyd was a clergyman of the Church of Ireland and the first to translate Dante's *Divine Comedy* into English (1802). His *Trionfi* appeared in 1807. Text from *Bohn's Illustrated Library* (1859).

The Triumph of Eternity

When all beneath the ample cope of heaven
I saw, like clouds before the tempest driven,
In sad vicissitude's eternal round,
Awhile I stood in holy horror bound;
And thus at last with self-exploring mind,
Musing, I asked, 'What basis I could find
To fix my trust?' – An inward voice replied,
'Trust to th' Almighty: He thy steps shall guide;
He never fails to hear the faithful prayer,
But worldly hope must end in dark despair.'

Now, what I am, and what I was, I know;
I see the seasons in procession go
With still increasing speed; while things to come,
Unknown, unthought, amid the growing gloom
Of long futurity, perplex my soul,
While life is posting to its final goal.
Mine is the crime, who ought with clearer light
To watch the winged years' incessant flight;
And not to slumber on in dull delay
Till circling seasons bring the doomful day.
But grace is never slow in that, I trust,
To wake the mind, before I sink to dust,
With those strong energies that left the soul
To scenes unhop'd, unthought, above the pole.

While thus I ponder'd, soon my working thought
Once more that ever-changing picture brought
Of sublunary things before my view,
And thus I question'd with myself anew: —
'What is the end of this incessant flight
30   Of life and death, alternate day and night?
When will the motion on these orbs imprest
Sink on the bosom of eternal rest?'

At once, as if obsequious to my will,
Another prospect shone, unmov'd and still;
Eternal as the Heavens that glow'd above,
A wide resplendent scene of light and love.
The wheels of Phœbus from the Zodiac turn'd;
No more the nightly constellations burn'd;
Green earth and undulating Ocean roll'd
40   Away, by some resistless power controll'd;
Immensity conceiv'd, and brought to birth
A grander firmament, and more luxuriant earth.
What wonder seiz'd my soul when first I view'd
How motionless the restless racer stood,
Whose flying feet, with winged speed before,
Still mark'd with sad mutation sea and shore.
No more he sway'd the future and the past,
But on the moveless present fixt at last;

As at a goal reposing from his toils,
50   Like earth uncloth'd of all its vernal foils.
Unvaried scene! where neither change nor fate,
Nor care nor sorrow, can our joys abate;
Nor finds the light of thought resistance here,
More than the sunbeams in a crystal sphere.
But no material things can match their flight,
In speed excelling far the race of light.
Oh! what a glorious lot shall then be mine
If Heaven to me these nameless joys assign!

For there the sovereign good for ever reigns,
60   Nor evil yet to come, nor present pains;
No baleful birth of time its inmates fear,
That comes, the burthen of the passing year;
No solar chariot circles through the Signs,
And now too near, and now too distant, shines;
To wretched man and earth's devoted soil
Dispensing sad variety of toil.
Oh! happy are the blessed souls, that sing,
Loud hallelujahs in eternal ring!

Thrice happy he, who late, at last shall find
70   A lot in the celestial climes assign'd!
He, led by grace, th' auspicious ford explores,
Where, cross the plains, the wintry torrent roars;
That troublous tide, where, with incessant strife,
Weak mortals struggle through, and call it life.
In love with Vanity, o doubly blind
Are they that final consolation find
In things that fleet on dissolution's wing,
Or dance away upon the transient ring
Of seasons, as they roll. No sound they hear
80   From that still voice that Wisdom's sons revere;
No vestment they procure to keep them warm
Against the menace of the wintry storm;
But all expos'd, in naked nature lie,
A shivering crowd beneath the inclement sky,
Of reason void, by every foe subdued,
Self-ruin'd, self-depriv'd of sovereign good;
Reckless of Him, whose universal sway,
Matter, and all its various forms, obey;

Whether they mix in elemental strife,
90   Or meet in married calm, and foster life.
His nature baffles all created mind,
In earth or heaven, to fathom, or to find.

One glimpse of glory on the saints bestow'd,
With eager longings fills the courts of God
For deeper views, in that abyss of light,
While mortals slumber here, content with night:
Though nought, we find, below the moon, can fill
The boundless cravings of the human will.
And yet, what fierce desire the fancy wings
100 To gain a grasp of perishable things;
Although one fleeting hour may scatter far
The fruit of many a year's corroding care;
Those spacious regions where our fancies roam,
Pain'd by the past, expecting ills to come,
In some dread moment, by the Fates assign'd,
Shall pass away, nor leave a rack behind;

And Time's revolving wheels shall lose at last
The speed that spins the future and the past;
And, sovereign of an undisputed throne,
110 Awful eternity shall reign alone.
Then every darksome veil shall fleet away
That hides the prospects of eternal day:
Those cloud-born objects of our hopes and fears,
Whose air-drawn forms deluded memory bears
As of substantial things, away so fast,
Shall fleet, that mortals, at their speed aghast,
Watching the change of all beneath the moon,
Shall ask, what once they were, and will be soon?

The time will come when every change shall cease,
120 This quick revolving wheel shall rest in peace:
No summer then shall glow, nor winter freeze;
Nothing shall be to come, and nothing past,
But an eternal now shall ever last.
Though time shall be no more, yet space shall give
A nobler theatre to love and live.

The winged courier then no more shall claim
The power to sink or raise the notes of Fame,
Or give its glories to the noontide ray:
True merit then, in everlasting day,
130   Shall shine for ever, as at first it shone
At once to God and man and angels known.
Happy are they who in this changing sphere
Already have begun the bright career
That reaches to the goal which, all in vain,
The Muse would blazon in her feeble strain:
But blest above all other blest is he
Who from the trammels of mortality,
Ere half the vital thread ran out, was free,
Mature for Heaven; where now the matchless fair
140   Preserves those features, that seraphic air,
And all those mental charms that rais'd my mind,
To judge of heaven while yet on earth confined.
That soft attractive glance that won my heart
When first my bosom felt unusual smart,
Now beams, now glories, in the realms above,
Fed by th'eternal source of light and love.
Then shall I see her as I first beheld,
But lovelier far; and by herself excell'd;
And I distinguish'd in the bands above
150   Shall hear this plaudit in the choirs of love.
'Lo! this is he who sung ill mournful strains
For many years a lover's doubts and pains;
Yet in this soul-expanding, sweet employ,
A sacred transport felt above all vulgar joy.'
She too shall wonder at herself to hear
Her praises ring around the radiant sphere:
But of that hour it is not mine to know;
To her perhaps, the period of my woe
Is manifest; for she my fate may find
160   In the pure mirror of th' eternal mind.

To me it seems at hand a sure presage,
Denotes my rise from this terrestrial stage;
Then what I gain'd and lost below shall lie
Suspended in the balance of the sky,
And all our anxious sublunary cares
Shall seem one tissue of Arachne's snares;
And all the lying vanities of life,
The sordid source of envy, hate, and strife,
Ignoble as they are, shall then appear
170 Before the searching beam of truth severe;
Then souls, from sense refin'd, shall see the fraud
That led them from the living way of God.
From the dark dungeon of the human breast
All direful secrets then shall rise confest,
In honour multiplied – a dreadful show
To hierarchies above, and saints below.
Eternal reason then shall give her doom;
And, sever'd wide, the tenants of the tomb
Shall seek their portions with instinctive haste,
180 Quick as the savage speeds along the waste.
Then shall the golden hoard its trust betray,
And they, that, mindless of that dreadful day,
Boasted their wealth, its vanity shall know
In the dread avenue of endless woe:
While they whom moderation's wholesome rule
Kept still unstain'd in virtue's heavenly school,
Who the calm sunshine of the soul beneath
Enjoy'd, will share the triumph of the Faith.

These pageants five the world and I beheld,
190 The sixth and last, I hope, in heaven reveal'd
(If Heaven so will), when Time with speedy hand
The scene despoils, and Death's funereal wand
The Triumph leads. But soon they both shall fall
Under that mighty hand that governs all,

While they who toil for true renown below,
Whom envious Time and Death, a mightier foe
Relentless plung'd in dark oblivion's womb,
When virtue seem'd to seek the silent tomb,
Spoil'd of her heavenly charms once more shall rise,
200   Regain their beauty, and assert the skies;
Leaving the dark sojourn of time beneath,
And the wide desolated realms of Death.
But she will early seek these glorious bounds,
Whose long-lamented fall the world resounds
In unison with me. And heaven will view
That awful day her heavenly charms renew,
When soul with body joins. *Gehenna's* strand
Saw me enroll'd in Love's devoted band.
And mark'd my toils through many hard campaigns
210   And wounds, whose scars my memory yet retains.
Blest is the pile that marks the hallow'd dust!
There, at the resurrection of the just,
When the last trumpet with earth-shaking sound
Shall wake her sleepers from their couch profound;
Then, when that spotless and immortal mind
In a material mould once more enshrin'd,
With wonted charms shall wake seraphic love,
How will the beatific sight improve
219   Her heavenly beauties in the climes above!

CANZONIERE

GEOFFREY CHAUCER
(*c.* 1343–1400)

The first fully recognizable adaptation of a Petrarch poem in English is Chaucer's rendition of P132 as *Canticus Troili*, the perplexed lament of the young Troilus about his love for Criseyde. Chaucer adapts Petrarch's sonnet to fill three of the rhyme royal stanzas of his *Troilus and Criseyde*, Book 1.400–421. That Chaucer should have chosen this particularly philosophic questioning of love as the first words his young hero speaks about his situation shows that Chaucer may have known Petrarch in the early Chigi form of the manuscript. There is even the possibility that the two poets might have met in 1368 since Chaucer was part of the entourage accompanying Prince Lionel to his wedding to Violante Visconti, daughter of the Duke of Milan; Petrarch was also in attendance at this wedding. Chaucer's diplomatic mission to Italy in 1372 is a less likely occasion for their meeting since Petrarch's presence in Arguà in the last years of his life was erratic owing to the war between Padua and Venice.

P132: *S'amor non è, che dunque è quel ch'io sento?*

Canticus Troili

'If no love is, O God, what fele I so?
And if love is, what thing and which is he?
If love be good, from whennes cometh my woo?
If it be wikke, a wonder thynketh me,
When every torment and adversite
That cometh of hym may to me savory thinke,
For ay thurst I, the more that ich it drynke.

'And if that ay myn owen lust I brenne,
From whennes cometh my waillynge and my pleynte?
If harm agree me, wherto pleyne I thenne?
I noot, ne whi unwery that I feynte.
O quike deth, O swete harm so queynte,
How may of the in me swich quantite,
But if that I consente that it be?

'And if that I consente, I wrongfully
Compleyne, iwis. Thus possed to and fro,
Al sterelees withinne a boot am I
Amydde the see, bitwixen wyndes two,
That in contrarie stonden evere mo.
Allas, what is this wondre maladie?
For hete of cold, for cold of hete, I dye.'

Sixteenth Century

The Tomb Sonnet

The Tomb Sonnet, which follows, comes with a strange story that predates the 'discovery' of Laura by the Abbé de Sade by two centuries. The sonnet first appears in a 1545 edition of Petrarch, published at Lyons for Giovanni di Tournes, a Frenchman writing and publishing in Italian, who had just published the *Délie* of Maurice Scève the year before. He dedicates the book to Scève:

A non men virtuoso che dotto M Mauritio Scæva, Giovanni di Tournes suo affettionatissimo

and proceeds to remind the dedicatee of a story told by him more than seventeen years before, when Scève was studying at Avignon. Two Italian friends came to him with a strange story of the tomb of Petrarch's

Laura. They went immediately to the Franciscan church, broke into the tomb of the de Sade family and discovered there only a few bones and a metal box, in which they found a medal of a woman ripping out her heart and this poem. The discovery must have spread quickly because François I, on his way to Rome, stopped at Avignon in order to visit the tomb and wrote a poem in praise of Laura, which is also included in di Tournes's preface:

Questo è quell'Epitaphio, ch' il Gran Re Francesco I fece di Madonna Laura

En petit lieu compris vous pouez voir
Ce, quicomprent beaucoup par renommée
Plume, labeur, la langue, & le devoir
Furent vaincuz par l'Aymant del'Aymee.
    O gentill' Ame, restant tant estimee,
Qui te pourra louer, qu'en se taisant?
Car la parole est toujours reprimee,
Quand le subiet surmonte le disant.

Di Tournes, needless to say, attributes the Tomb Sonnet to Petrarch. But this cannot be true because of the haste with which she was buried, on the very day of her death – 6 April 1348 – and the indisputable fact that Petrarch was in Verona and did not learn of her death until a month after the event, and the equally valid assumption of the utter inappropriateness of his putting any memorial in the tomb of the wife of another man. Who wrote this poem? It has been suggested that it was written by Scève himself. Who knows? – when the vandalism of these literary grave-robbers is never considered as any part of the story. Myth is being created, a myth that the eighteenth-century Abbé de Sade never alludes to. The sonnet is taken from the di Tournes edition of Petrarch and the three translations from *Bohn's Illustrated Library* (1859): the first is anonymous (1777), the second by Capel Lofft and the third by Lord Woodhouselee (see also their own sections).

Questo è il Sonnetto ritrouato nel sepulchro di Madonna Laura in questo modo

Qui reposan quei caste & felice ossa
  Di quella alma gentile & sola in terra.
  Aspro e dur sasso hor ben teco hai sotterra
  El vero honor, la fama, e belta scossa.
Morte hà del verde Lauro suelta e smossa
  Fresca radice, e il premio di mia guerra
  Di quatro lustri, e piu, s'ancor non erra
  Mio pensier tristo: e l' chiude in poca fossa.
Felice pianta in Borgo d'Auignone
  Nacque e mori: e qui con ella giace
  La penna, el stil, l'inchiostro, e la ragione.
O delicati membri, ô viva face,
  Ch' ancor mi cuoggi, e struggi, in genochione
  Ciascun preghi, il Signor t'accetti in pace
            O   S   E   V   L
  Vanne Mortal bellezza indarno si sospira:
  L'alma creata in ciel viura ineterno,
  Pianga il Presente, & il futur secol' priuo
  D'vna talluce, & io de gli occhi, e il tempo.

Sonnet Found in Laura's Tomb

Qui reposan quei caste e felice ossa

Here peaceful sleeps the chaste, the happy shade
Of that pure spirit, which adorn'd this earth:
Pure fame, true beauty, and transcendent worth,
Rude stone! Beneath thy rugged breast are laid.

Death sudden snatch'd the dear lamented maid!
Who first to all by tender woes gave birth,
Woes! That estranged my sorrowing soul to mirth,
While full four lustres times completely made.
Sweet plant! That nursed on Avignon's sweet soil,
There bloom'd, there died; when soon the weeping Muse
Threw by the lute, forsook her wonted toil.
Bright spark of beauty, that still fires my breast!
What pitying mortal shall a prayer refuse,
That Heaven may number thee amid the blest?

Here rest the chaste, the dear, the blest remains
Of her most lovely; peerless while on earth:
What late was beauty, spotless honour, worth,
Stern marble, here thy chill embrace retains.
The freshness of the laurel Death disdains;
And hath its root thus wither'd. – Such the dearth
O'ertakes me. Here I bury ease and mirth.
And hope from twenty years of cares and pains.
This happy plant Avignon lonely fed
With life, and saw it die. – And with it lies
My pen, my verse, my reason: – useless, dead.
O graceful form! – Fire, which consuming flies
Through all my frame! – For blessings on thy head
Oh, may continual prayers to heaven rise!

Here now repose those chaste, those blest remains
Of that most gentle spirit, sole in earth!
Harsh monumental stone, that here confinest
True honour, fame, and beauty, all o'erthrown!
Death has destroy'd that Laurel green, and torn
Its tender roots; and all the noble meed
Of my long warfare, passing (if aright

My melancholy reckoning holds) four lustres.
O happy plant! Avignon's favour'd soil
10   Has seen thee spring and die: – and here with thee
Thy poet's pen, and muse, and genius lies.
O lovely, beauteous limbs! O vivid fire,
That even in death hast power to melt the soul!
Heaven be thy portion, peace with God on high!

Richard Tottel, *Tottel's Miscellany*
(1557)

Richard Tottel's *Songes and Sonnettes, written by the ryght honorable Lorde Henry H[o]ward, late Earle of Surrey, and other* is the first and most important miscellany of poetry in the English Renaissance. Known today almost universally as *Tottel's Miscellany*, it printed for the first time the work of Sir Thomas Wyatt, Henry Howard, Earl of Surrey, and other poets who were writing during the reign of Henry VIII. It became a prime source of Petrarchanism in that Wyatt and Surrey translated so many of his poems.

HENRY HOWARD, EARL OF SURREY (1517?–47)

The poems of Henry Howard take pride of place in Tottel because of his social status. Maternally and paternally he was descended from British kings, and in his teens he was made the companion of Henry VIII's illegitimate son, Henry Fitzroy, Duke of Richmond, spent time with Richmond in the French court of Francis I, had spectacular successes as a military and naval commander, and was beheaded for quartering the arms of his ancestor Edward the Confessor with his own. He is the first English poet to use blank verse, in his translations of Books II and IV of Virgil's *Aeneid*, published by Tottel in 1557. He was very much influenced by the poetic example of Sir Thomas Wyatt, for whom he composed the most beautiful elegy in English before *Lycidas*, but Surrey wrote a smoother line.

P310: *Zefiro torna, e 'l bel tempo rimena*

2. Description of Spring, wherin eche thing renewes, saue onelie the louer

The soote season, that bud and blome furth bringes,
With grene hath clad the hill and eke the vale:
The nightingale with fethers new she singes:
The turtle to her make hath tolde her tale:
Somer is come, for euery spray nowe springes,
The hart hath hong his olde hed on the pale:
The buck in brake his winter cote he flinges:
The fishes flote with newe repaired scale:
The adder all her sloughe awaye she slinges:
The swift swalow pursueth the flyes smale:
The busy bee her honye now she minges:
Winter is worne that was the flowers bale:
And thus I see among these pleasant thinges
Eche care decayes, and yet my sorow springes.

P140: *Amor, che nel penser mio vive et regna*

6. Complaint of a louer rebuked

Loue, that liueth, and reigneth in my thought,
That built his seat within my captiue brest,
Clad in the armes, wherin with me he fought,
Oft in my face he doth his banner rest.

She, that me taught to loue, and suffer payne,
My doutfull hope, and eke my hote desyre,
With shamefast cloke to shadowe, and refraine,
Her smilyng grace conuerteth straight to yre.
And cowarde Loue then to the hart apace
10   Taketh his flight, whereas he lurkes, and plaines
His purpose lost, and dare not shewe his face.
For my lordes gilt thus faultlesse byde I paynes.
Yet from my lorde shall not my foote remoue.
Swete is his death, that takes his end by loue.

P164: *Or che 'l ciel e la terra e 'l vento tace*

10. A Complaint by night of the louer not beloued

Alas so all thinges nowe doe holde their peace.
Heauen and earth disturbed in nothing:
The beastes, the ayer, the birdes their song doe cease:
The nightes chare the starres aboute dothe bring:
Calme is the Sea, the waues worke lesse and lesse:
So am hot I, whom loue alas doth wring,
Bringing before my face the great encrease
Of my desires, whereat I wepe and syng,
In ioye and wo, as in a doutfull ease.
10   For my swete thoughtes sometyme doe pleasure bring:
But by and by the cause of my disease
Geues me a pang, that inwardly dothe sting,
When that I thinke what griefe it is againe,
To hue and lacke the thing should ridde my paine.

P145: *Ponmi ove 'l sole occide i fiori e l'erba*

12. Vow to loue faithfully howsoever he be rewarded

Set me wheras the sunne doth parche the grene,
Or where his beames do not dissolue the yse:
In temperate heate where he is felt and sene:
In presence prest of people madde or wise.
Set me in hye, or yet in lowe degree:
In longest night, or in the shortest daye:
In clearest skye, or where clowdes thickest be:
In lusty youth, or when my heeres are graye.
Set me in heauen, in earth, or els in hell,
In hyll, or dale, or in the fomyng flood:
Thrall, or at large, aliue where so I dwell:
Sicke, or in health: in euyll fame, or good.
Hers will I be, and onely with this thought
Content my selfe, although my chaunce be nought.

10

P11: *Lassare il velo o per sole o per ombra*

13. Complaint that his ladie after she knew of his loue kept her face alway hidden from him

I neuer sawe my Ladye laye apart
Her cornet blacke, in colde nor yet in heate,
Sith first she knew my griefe was growen so great,
Which other fansies driueth from my hart
That to my selfe I do the thought reserue,
The which vnwares did wounde my wofull brest:
But on her face mine eyes mought neuer rest,
Yet, sins she knew I did her loue and serue

Her golden tresses cladde alway with blacke,
10   Her smilyng lokes that hid thus euermore,
And that restraines whiche I desire so sore.
So dothe this cornet gouerne me alacke:
In somer, sunne: in winters breath, a frost:
Wherby the light of her faire lokes I lost.

SIR THOMAS WYATT (*c.* 1503–42)

Courtier, statesman and poet in the court of Henry VIII, Sir Thomas
Wyatt travelled to Italy in 1527 where he became fascinated by the
poetry of Petrarch. He was the first to write sonnets in English and the
first to attempt to deal poetically with the intricacies of Petrarch's
canzoni (P37 and P360). He is the most important crafter of English
verse in the early sixteenth century. His translation of P190 is perhaps
an autobiographical attempt to memorialize his purported affair with
Anne Boleyn. For Tottel's regularizing of his poetry in the *Miscellany*,
see the Introduction, pp. xix–xx. The Egerton Manuscript at the
British Library is Wyatt's autograph copybook (BL2711) and his trans-
lations of P190 and P199 are taken from it.

P140: *Amor, che nel penser mio vive e regna*

37. The louer for shamefastnesse hideth his desire within his faithfull hart

The longe loue, that in my thought I harber,
And in my hart doth kepe his residence,
Into my face preaseth with bold pretence,
And there campeth, displaying his banner.
She that me learns to loue, and to suffer,
And willes that my trust, and lustes negligence
Be reined by reason, shame, and reuerence,
With his hardinesse takes displeasure.

Wherwith loue to the hartes forest he fleeth,
10   Leauyng his enterprise with paine and crye,
And there him hideth and not appeareth.
What may I do? when my maister feareth,
But in the field with him to liue and dye,
For good is the life, endyng faithfully.

P82: *Io non fu' d'amar voi lassato unquanco*

38. The louer waxeth wiser, and will not die for affection

Yet was I neuer of your loue agreued,
Nor neuer shall, while that my life doth last:
But of hatyng my self, that date is past,
And teares continual sore haue me weried.
I will not yet in my graue be buried,
Nor on my tombe your name haue fixed fast,
As cruel cause, that did my sprite sone hast.
From thunhappy boones by great sighes stirred.
Then if an hart of amorous fayth and will
10   Content your minde withouten doyng grief:
Please it you so to this to do relief.
If otherwise you seke for to fulfill
Your wrath: you erre, and shal not as you wene,
And you your self the cause therof haue bene.

P258: *Vive faville uscian de' duo bei lumi*

40. The louer describeth his being striken with sight of his loue

The liuely sparkes, that issue from those eyes,
Against the which there vaileth no defence,
Haue perst my hart, and done it none offence,
With quakyng pleasure, more then once or twise.

Was neuer man could any thing deuise,
Sunne beames to turne with so great vehemence
To dase mans sight, as by their bright presence
Dased am I, much like vnto the gise
Of one striken with dint of lightenyng,
Blind with the stroke, and errying here and there.
So call I for helpe, I not when, nor where,
The payne of my fall paciently bearyng.
For streight after the blase (as is no wonder)
Of deadly noyse heare I the fearfull thunder.

P169: *Pien d'un vago penser che me desvia*

41. The waueryng louer wylleth, and dreadeth, to moue his desire

Such vain thought, as wonted to mislead me
In desert hope by well assured mone,
Makes me from company to liue alone,
In folowyng her whom reason bids me fle.
And after her my hart would faine be gone:
But armed sighes my way do stop anone,
Twixt hope and dread lockyng my libertie.
So fleeth she by gentle crueltie.
Yet as I gesse vnder disdainfull brow
One beame of ruth is in her cloudy loke:
Which comfortes the mind, that erst for fear shoke.
That bolded straight the way then seke I how
To vtter forth the smart I bide within:
But such it is, I not how to begyn.

P102: *Cesare, poi che 'l traditor d'Egitto*

45. Of others fained sorrow, and the louers fained mirth

Cesar, when that the traytour of Egypt
With thonorable hed did him present,
Coueryng his hartes gladnesse, did represent
Plaint with his teares outward, as it is writ.
Eke Hannibal, when fortune him outshyt
Clene from his reigne, and from all his entent,
Laught to his folke, whom sorow did torment,
His cruel despite for to disgorge and quit.
So chanceth me, that euery passion
10   The minde hideth by colour contrary,
With fayned visage, now sad, now mery.
Wherby, if that I laugh at any season:
It is because I haue none other way
To cloke my care, but vnder sport and play.

P19: *Son animali al mondo de sí altera*

47. How the louer perisheth in his delight, as the flie in the fire

Some fowles there be, that haue so perfit sight
Against the sunne their eies for to defend:
And some, because the light doth them offend,
Neuer appeare, but in the darke, or night.
Other reioyce, to se the fire so bryght,
And wene to play in it, as they pretend:
But find contrary of it, that they intend.
Alas, of that sort may I be, by right.

For to withstand her loke I am not able:
10   Yet can I not hide me in no dark place:
So foloweth me remembrance of that face:
That with my teary eyn, swolne, and vnstable,
My desteny to beholde her doth me lead:
And yet I knowe, I runne into the glead.

P49: *Perch'io t'abbia guardato di menzogna*

48. Against his tong that failed to vtter his sutes

Because I still kept thee fro lyes, and blame,
And to my power alwayes thee honoured,
Vnkind tongue, to yll hast thou me rendred,
For such desert to do me wreke and shame.
In nede of succour most when that I am,
To aske reward: thou standst like one afraied,
Alway most cold: and if one word be sayd,
As in a dreame, vnperfit is the same.
And ye salt teares, agaynst my wyll eche nyght,
10   That are wyth me, when I would be alone:
Then are ye gone, when I should make my mone.
And ye so ready sighes, to make me shright,
Then are ye slacke, when that ye should outstart.
And onely doth my loke declare my hart.

P134: *Pace non trovo e non ò da far guerra*

49. Description of the contrarious passions in a louer

I find no peace, and all my warre is done:
I feare, and hope: I burne, and frese like yse:
I flye aloft, yet can I not arise:
And nought I haue, and all the worlde I season.

That lockes nor loseth, holdeth me in pryson,
And holdes me not, yet can I scape no wise:
Nor lettes me lyue, nor dye, at my deuise,
And yet of death it geueth me occasion.
Without eye I se, without tong I playne:
10   I wish to perysh, yet I aske for helth:
I loue another, and thus I hate my selfe.
I fede me in sorow, and laugh in all my payne.
Lo, thus displeaseth me both death and life.
And my delight is causer of this strife.

PI89: *Passa la nave mia colma d'oblio*

50. The louer compareth his state to a shippe in perilous storme tossed on the sea

My galley charged with forgetfulnesse,
Through sharpe seas, in winter nightes doth passe,
Twene rocke, and rocke: and eke my fo (alas)
That is my lord, stereth with cruelnesse:
And euery houre, a thought in readinesse,
As though that death were light, in such a case.
An endlesse wynd doth teare the sayle apace
Of forced sighes, and trusty fearfulnesse.
A rayne of teares, a clowde of darke disdayne
10   Haue done the weried coardes great hinderance,
Wrethed with errour, and wyth ignorance.
The starres be hidde, that leade me to this payne.
Drownde is reason that should be my comfort:
And I remayne, dispearyng of the port.

P173: *Mirando 'l sol de' begli occhi sereno*

51. Of douteous loue

Avisyng the bright beames of those fayre eyes,
Where he abides that mine oft moistes and washeth:
The weried mynd streight from the hart departeth,
To rest within hys worldly Paradise,
And bitter findes the swete, vnder this gyse.
What webbes there he hath wrought, well he perceaueth
Wherby then with him self on loue he playneth,
That spurs wyth fire, and brydleth eke with yse.
In such extremity thus is he brought:
Frosen now cold, and now he standes in flame:
Twixt wo, and welth: betwixt earnest, and game:
With seldome glad, and many a diuers thought:
In sore repentance of hys hardinesse.
Of such a roote lo cometh frute frutelesse.

P360: *Quell'antico mio dolce empio signore*

64. Wiates complaint vpon Loue, to Reason: with Loues answer

Myne olde dere enmy, my froward maister,
Afore that Quene, I causde to be accited,
Which holdeth the diuine part of our nature,
That, like as golde, in fire he mought be tryed.
Charged with dolour, there I me presented
With horrible feare, as one that greatly dredeth
A wrongfull death, and iustice alway seketh.

And thus I sayd: once my left foote, Madame,
When I was yong, I set within his reigne:
Wherby other than fiersly burning flame I neuer felt,
But many a greuous pain. Torment I suffred, angre, and
    disdain:
That mine oppressed pacience was past,
And I mine owne life hated, at the last.
Thus hitherto haue I my time passed

In pain and smart. What wayes profitable:
How many pleasant dayes haue me escaped,
In seruing this false lyer so deceauable?
What wit haue wordes so prest, and forceable,
That may conteyn my great mishappinesse,
And iust complaintes of his vngentlenesse?
So small hony, much aloes, and gall,

In bitternesse, my blinde life hath ytasted.
His false semblance, that turneth as a ball:
With fair and amorous daunce, made me be traced,
And, where I had my thought, and mynde araced,
From earthly frailnesse, and from vayn pleasure,
Me from my rest he toke, and set in errour:

God made he me regard lesse, than I ought,
And to my self to take right litle hede:
And for a woman haue I set at nought
All other thoughtes: in this onely to spede.
And he was onely counseler of this dede:
Whettyng alwayes my youthly frayle desire
On cruell whetston, tempered with fire.

But (Oh alas) where, had I euer wit?
Or other gift, geuen to me of nature?
That sooner shalbe changed my weried sprite:
Then the obstinate wyll, that is my ruler.

So robbeth he my fredom with displeasure,
40 This wicked traytour, whom I thus accuse:
That bitter life hath turned in pleasant vse.

He hath me hasted, thorough diuers regions:
Through desert wodes, and sharp hye mountaines:
Through froward people, and through bitter passions:
Through rocky seas, and ouer hilles and plaines:
With wery trauell, and with laborous paynes:
Alwayes in trouble and in tediousnesse:
All in errour, and dangerous distresse,

But nother he, nor she, my tother fo,
50 For all my flight, dyd euer me forsake:
That though my timely death hath been to slow
That me as yet, it hath not ouertake:
The heauenly goddes of pity doe it slake.
And, note they this his cruell tiranny,
That fedes him, with my care, and misery.

Since I was his, hower rested I neuer,
Nor loke to do: and eke the waky nightes
The banished slepe may in no wise recouer.
By guile, and force, ouer my thralled sprites,
60 He is ruler: since which bel neuer strikes,
That I heare not as sounding to renue
My plaintes. Himself, he knoweth, that I say true.

For, neuer wormes olde rotten stocke haue eaten:
As he my hart, where he is resident,
And doth the same with death dayly threaten.
Thence come the teares, and thence the bitter torment:
The sighes: the wordes, and eke the languishment:
That noy both me, and parauenture other.
Iudge thou: that knowest the one, and eke the tother.

70   Mine aduersair, with such greuous reproofe,
      Thus he began. Heare Lady, thother part:
      That the plain troth, from which he draweth aloofe,
      This vnkinde man may shew, ere that I part.
      In his yong age, I toke him from that art,
      That selleth wordes, and makes a clatteryng Knight:
      And of my wealth I gaue him the delight.

      Now shames he not on me for to complain,
      That held him euermore in pleasant gain,
      From his desyre, that might haue been his payn.
80   Yet therby alone I brought him to some frame:
      Which now, as wretchednes, he doth so blame:
      And towarde honor quickned I his wit:
      Where: as a daskard els he mought haue sit.

      He knoweth, how grete Atride that made Troy freat,
      And Hanniball, to Rome so troubelous:
      Whom Homer honored, Achilles that great,
      And Thaffricane Scipion the famous:
      And many other, by much nurture glorious:
      Whose fame, and honor did bring them aboue:
90   I did let fall in base dishonest loue.

      And vnto him, though he vnworthy were:
      I chose the best of many a Milion:
      That, under sonne yet neuer was her pere,
      Of wisdom, womanhod, and of discrecion:
      And of my grace I gaue her such a facion,
      And eke such way I taught her for to teache,
      That neuer base thought his hart so hye might reche,

      Euermore thus to content his maistresse,
      That was his onely frame of honesty,
100   I stirred him still, toward gentlenesse:
      And causde him to regard fidelity.

Pacience I taught him in aduersity.
Such vertues learned, he in my great schole:
Wherof repenteth, now the ignorant foole.

These, were the same deceites, and bitter gall,
That I haue vsed, the torment, and the anger:
Sweter, then euer dyd to other fall,
Of right good sede yll frute loe thus I gather.
And so shall he, that the vnkinde dothe further.
A Serpent nourish I vnder my wing:
And now of nature, ginneth he to styng.

And for to tell, at last, my great seruise.
From thousand dishonesties haue I him drawen:
That, by my meanes, him in no maner wyse.
Neuer vile pleasure once hath ouerthrowen.
Where, in his dede, shame hath him alwaies gnawen:
Doutyng report, that should come to her care:
Whom now he blames, her wonted he to feare.

What euer he hath of any honest custome:
Of her, and me: that holdes he euerywhit,
But, lo, yet neuer was there nightly fantome
So farre in errour, as he is from his wit.
To plain on vs, he striueth with the bit,
Which may rule him, and do him ease, and pain:
And in one hower, make all his grief his gayn.

But, one thing yet there is, aboue all other:
I gaue him winges, wherwith he might vpflie
To honor, and fame: and if he would to higher
Than mortall thinges, aboue the starry skie:
Considering the pleasure, that an eye
Might geue in earth, by reason of the loue:
What should that be that lasteth still aboue?

And he the same himself hath sayd, ere this.
But, now, forgotten is both that and I,
That gaue her him, his onely wealth and blisse.
And, at this word, with dedly shreke and cry:
Thou gaue her once: quod I, but by and by,
Thou toke her ayen from me: that wo worth the.
Not I but price: more worth than thou (quod he.)

140   At last: eche other for himself, concluded:
I, trembling still: but he, with small reuerence.
Lo, thus, as we eche other haue accused:
Dere Lady: now we waite thyne onely sentence.
She smiling, at the whisted audience:
It liketh me (quod she) to haue hard your question:
But, lenger time doth ask a resolucion.

P121: *Or vedi, Amor, che giovenetta donna*

69. Request to Cupid, for reuenge of his vnkinde loue

Behold, Loue, thy power how she dispiseth:
My gretious payn how litle she regardeth,
The solemne othe, wherof she takes no cure
Broken she hath: and yet, she bideth sure,
Right at her ease, and litle thee she dredeth.
Weaponed thou art, and she vnarmed sitteth:
To the disdainful, all her life she leadeth:
To me spitefull, withoute iust cause, or mesure.
Behold, Loue, how proudly she triumpheth,
10   I am in hold, but if thee pitie the meueth:
Go, bend thy bow, that stony hartes breaketh:
And with some stroke reuenge the great displeasure
Of thee, and him that sorow doth endure,
And as his Lord thee lowly here entreateth.

P153: *Ite, caldi sospiri, al freddo core*

77. The louer sendeth his complaints and teares to sue for grace

Passe forth my wonted cryes,
Those cruell eares to pearce,
Which in most hateful wyse
Doe styll my plaintes reuerse.
Doe you, my teares, also
So wet her barrein hart:
That pitye there may grow,
And crueltie depart.

For though hard rockes among
10   She semes to haue bene bred:
And of the Tigre long
Bene nourished, and fed.
Yet shall that nature change
If pitie once win place.
Whom as vnknowen, and strange,
She now away doth chase.

And as the water soft,
Without forcyng or strength,
Where that it falleth oft,
20   Hard stones doth perse at length:
So in her stony hart
My plaintes at last shall graue,
And, rygour set apart,
Winne grant of that I craue.

Wherfore my plaintes, present
Styll so to her my sute,
As ye, through her assent,
May bring to me some frute.

And as she shall me proue,
30　So bid her me regarde,
And render loue for loue:
Which is a just reward.

P57: *Mie venture al venir son tarde e pigre*

94. How vnpossible it is to finde quiet in his loue

Euer my hap is slack and slowe in commyng
Desire encreasyng ay my hope vncertaine
That loue or wait it, alike doth me payne
And Tygre like so swift it is in partyng.
Alas the snow black shal it be and scalding,
The sea waterles, and fishe vpon the mountaine:
The Temis shal backe returne into his fountaine:
And where he rose the sunne shall take his lodgyng.
Ere I in this finde peace or quietnesse.
10　Or that loue or my lady rightwisely
Leaue to conspire against me wrongfully.
And if I haue after such bitternesse,
Any thing swete, my mouth is out of taste:
That all my trust and trauell is but waste.

P124: *Amor, Fortuna e la mia mente schiva*

95. Of Loue, Fortune, and the louers minde

Loue, Fortune, and my minde which do remember
Eke that is now, and that that once hath bene:
Torment my hart so sore that very often
I hate and enuy them beyonde all measure.
Loue sleeth my hart while Fortune is depriuer
Of all my comfort: the folishe minde than:

Burneth and playneth: as one that sildam
Liueth in rest. Still in displeasure
My pleasant daies they flete away and passe.
10   And dayly doth myne yll change to the worse.
While more than halfe is runne now of my course.
Alas not of stele, but of brittle glasse,
I se that from my hand falleth my trust:
And all my thoughtes are dasshed into dust.

P21: *Mille fiate, o dolce mia guerrera*

96. The Louer prayeth his offred hart to be receiued

How oft haue I, my deare and cruell fo:
With my great pain to get som peace or truce,
Geuen you my hart? but you do not vse,
In so hie thinges, to cast your minde so low.
If any other loke for it, as you trow,
Their vaine weake hope doth greatly them abuse.
And that thus I disdayne, that you refuse.
It was once mine, it can no more be so.
If you it chase, that it in you can finde,
10   In this exile, no manner of comfort:
Nor liue alone, nor where he is calde, resort,
He may wander from his naturall kinde.
So shall it be great hurt vnto vs twayne,
And yours the losse, and mine the deadly payne.

P224: *S'una fede amorosa, un cor non finto*

98. Charging of his loue as vnpiteous and louing other

If amourous fayth, or if an hart vnfained
A swete languor, a great louely desire:
If honest will, kindled in gentle fire:
If long errour in a blinde mase chained,
If in my visage ech thought distayned:
Or if my sparkelyng voyce, lower, or hier,
Which fear and shame, so wofully doth tyre:
If pale colour, which loue alas hath stayned:
If to haue another then my self more dere,
10 If wailyng or sighyng continually,
With sorowfull anger fedyng busily,
If burnyng a farre of, and fresyng nere,
Are cause that by loue my selfe I stroy:
Yours is the fault, and mine the great annoy.

P269: *Rotta è l'alta colonna e 'l verde lauro*

102. The louer lamentes the death of his loue

The piller perisht is wherto I lent,
The strongest stay of mine vnquiet minde:
The like of it no man again can finde:
From East to West still seking though he went.
To mine vnhappe for happe away hath rent,
Of all my ioy the very bark and rynde:
And I (alas) by chance am thus assinde.
Daily to moorne till death do it relent,

But since that thus it is by desteny,
10   What can I more but haue a wofull hart,
My penne, in plaint, my voyce in carefull crye:
My minde in wo, my body full of smart.
And I my self, my selfe alwayes to hate,
Till dreadfull death do ease my dolefull state.

p37: *Sí è debile il filo a cui s'attene*

104. Complaint of the absence of his loue

So feble is the threde, that doth the burden stay,
Of my poore life: in heauy plight, that falleth in decay:
That, but it haue elswhere some ayde or some succoours:
The running spindle of my fate anone shall end his course.
For since thunhappy hower, that dyd me to depart,
From my swete weale: one onely hope hath stayed my life,
        apart:
Which doth perswade such wordes vnto my sored mind:
Maintain thy self, O wofull wight, some better luck to finde.
For though thou be depriued from thy desired sight:
10   Who can thee tell, if thy returne be for thy more delight?
Or who can tell, thy losse if thou mayst once recouer?
Some pleasant hower thy wo may wrappe: & thee defend, &
        couer.
Thus in this trust as yet it hath my life sustained:
But now (alas) I see it faint: and I, by trust, am trayned.
The tyme doth flete, and I se how the howers, do bend
So fast: that I haue scant the space to mark my commying end.
Westward the sonne from out the East scant shewes his light:
When in the West he hides him strayt, within the dark of
        nyght.
And comes as fast, where he began, his path awry.
20   From East to West, from West to East so doth his iourney ly.

The life so short, so fraile, that mortall men liue here:
So great a weight, so heauy charge the bodies, that we bere:
That, when I think vpon the distaunce, and the space:
That doth so farre deuide me from my dere desired face:
I know not, how tattain the winges, that I require,
To lift me vp: that I might flie, to folow my desyre.
Thus of that hope, that doth my life somethyng sustayne,
Alas: I feare, and partly fele: full litle doth remain.
Eche place doth bring me griefe: where I do not behold
30   Those huey eyes: which of my thoughts were wont the keys to
          hold
Those thoughtes were pleasant swete: whilst I enjoyed that
          grace:
My pleasure past, my present pain, when I might well
          embrace.
And, for because my want should more my wo encrease:
In watch, and slepe, both day, and night, my will doth neuer
          cease
That thing to wish: wherof since I did lesse the sight:
Was neuer thing that mought in ought my woful hart delight,
Thunesy lyfe, I lead, doth teach me for to mete
The floodes, the seas, the land, the hylles: that doth the
          entermete
Twene me, and those shene lightes: that wonted for to clere
40   My darked panges of cloudy thoughts, as bright as Pheb spere,
It teacheth me, also, what was my pleasant state:
The more to fele, by such record, how that my wealth doth
          bate.
If such record (alas) prouoke thenflamed mynde:
Which sprong that day, that I did leaue the best of me
          behynde:
If loue forget himself, by length of absence, let:
Who doth me guyde (O wofull wretch) vnto this bayted net?
Where doth encrease my care: much better wer for me,
As dumme, as stone, all thyng forgot, still absent for to be.

Alas: the clere cristall, the bright transplendant glasse
50   Doth not bewray the colours didde, which vnderneth it hase:
As doth thaccumbred sprite the thoughtfull throwes discouer,
Of feares delite, of feruent loue: that in our hartes we couer.
Out by these eyes, it sheweth that euermore delight.
In plaint, and teares to seke redresse: and eke both day and
      night.
These kindes of pleasures most wherein men so reioyce,
To me they do redubble still of stormy sighes the voyce.
For, I am one of them, whom playnt doth well content:
It sits me well: myne absent wealth me semes for to lament:
And with my teares, tassay to charge myne eies twayn:
60   Lyke as my hart aboue the brink is fraughted full of payn.
And forbecause, therto, of those fair eyes to treate
Do me prouoke: I wyll returne, my plaint thus to repeate.
For, there is nothing els, that toucheth me so within:
Where they rule all: and I alone nought but the case, or skin.
Wherefore, I shall returne to them, as well, or spring:
From whom descendes my mortall wo, aboue all other thing.
So shall myne eyes in pain accompany my hart:
That were the guides, that did it lead of loue to fele the smart.
The crisped golde, that doth surmount Apollos pride:
70   The liuely streames of pleasant starres that vnder it doth glyde:
Wherein the beames of loue doe styll encrease theyr heate:
Which yet so farre touch me so nere, in colde to make me
      sweate.
The wise and pleasant talk, so rare, or els alone:
That gaue to me the curteis gift, that erst had neuer none:
Be farre from me, alas: and euery other thyng
I might forbeare with better wyll: then this that dyd me bryng,
With pleasant worde and chere, redresse of lingred pain:
And wonted oft in kindled will to vertue me to trayn.
Thus, am I forst to heare, and harken after newes.
80   My comfort scant my large desire in doutfull trust renewes.
And yet with more delite to mone my wofull case:
I must complain those handes, those armes: they firmely do
      embrace

Me from my self, and rule the sterne of my poore lyfe:
The swete disdaines, the pleasant wrathes, and eke the louely
    strife:
That wonted well to tune in temper iust, and mete,
The rage: that oft dyd make me erre, by furour vndiscrete.
All this is hydde me fro, with sharp, and ragged hylles:
At others will, my long abode my depe dispaire fullfils.
And if my hope sometime ryse vp, by some redresse:
It stumbleth straite, for feble faint: my feare hath such
90   excesse.
Such is the sort of hope: the lesse for more desyre:
And yet I trust ere that I dye to see that I require:
The restyng place of loue: where vertue dwelles and growes
There I desire, my wery life, somtime, may take repose.
My song: thou shalt attain to finde that pleasant place:
Where she doth lyue, by who I liue: may chance, to haue this
    grace
When she hath red, and sene the grief, wherin I serue:
Betwene her brestes she shall thee put: there, shall she thee
    reserue
Then, tell her, that I cumme: she shall me shortly see:
100   And if for waighte the body fayle, the soule shall to her flee.

P190: *Una candida cerva sopra l'erba*

7.   [From the Egerton MS]
Who so list to hounte I know where is an hynde
    but as for me helas I may no more:
    the vayne travaill hath weried me so sore,
    I ame of theim that farthest cometh behinde;
    yet may I by no meanes my weried mynde
    drawe from the Diere: but as she fleeth afore
    faynting I folowe; I leve of therefore,
    sethens in a nett I seke to hold the wynde.

Who list her hount I put him owte of dowbte,
10   as well as I may spend his tyme in vain:
    and graven with Diamond[es] in letters plain
There is written her faier neck rounde abowte:
    'Noli me tangere for Cesars I ame,
And wylde for to hold though I seme tame'.

P199: *O bella man, che mi destringi 'l core*

86.   [From the Egerton MS]
O goodely Hand
    wherein doeth stand
    my hert distraste in payne
    faire hand Alas
    in little spas
    my liff that doeth restrayne
O fingers slight
    dep[ar]ted right
    so long so small so rownd
10   goodely bygone
    and yet alone
    most cruell in my wound
W[ith] Lilis whight
    and Roses bright
    doth stryve they colo[ur] faire
    nature did lend
    eche fingers ende
    a perle for to repayre
Consent at last
20   syns that thou hast
    my hert in thy demayne
    for s[er]uice trew
    on me to rew
    and reche me love againe

And if not so
   then with more woo
     enforce thiself to strayne
   this simple hert
   that suffereth smart
30   and rid it owte of payne.

ANONYMOUS (from *Tottel's Miscellany*)

The interest of the following three anonymous poems lies less in what they achieve than in what they try to do with Petrarch. Tottel 185 is the first attempt in English to deal with the complexities of P23, the first *canzone* of the *Canzoniere*, which is a tissue of Ovidian metamorphoses in which the poet changes in rapid succession into a laurel (Daphne), a swan (Cygnus), a rock (Battus), a fountain (Byblis), flint (Echo) and a deer (Actaeon), indicating the psychological effects of Petrarch's being smitten by love. The translator avoids any use of the Ovidian metaphors but rationalizes all of them – in octosyllabic quatrains – into this bouncy jingle on the progress of love, an intellectual triumph but a poetic failure; he is all for *sentence* and nothing for *solas*. Tottel 276 and 277 (P1 and P3) similarly do not attempt to deal with the form of Petrarch's sonnets but with the substance of those poems in septenary couplets. These poets view Petrarch as meaning and not as form, a cautionary tale for all later translators.

P23: *Nel dolce tempo de la prima etade*

185. The louer here telleth of his diuers ioyes and aduersities in loue and lastly of his ladies death

Sythe singyng gladdeth oft the hartes
Of them that fele the panges of loue:
And for the while doth ease their smartes:
My self I shall the same way proue.

And though that loue hath smit the stroke,
Wherby is lost my libertie:
Which by no meanes I may reuoke:
Yet shall I sing, how pleasantly.

Ny twenty yeres of youth I past:
Which all in libertie I spent:
And so from fyrst vnto the last,
Er aught I knew, what louing ment.

And after shall I syng the wo,
The payne, the greefe, the deadly smart:
When loue this lyfe did ouerthrowe,
That hydden lyes within my hart.

And then, the ioyes, that I did feele.
When fortune lifted after this,
And set me hye vpon her whele:
And changed my wo to pleasant blisse,

And so the sodeyn fall agayne
From all the ioyes, that I was in.
All you, that list to heare of payne,
Geue care, for now I doe beginne.

Lo, fyrst of all, when loue began
With hote desyres my heart to burne:
Me thought, his might auailde not than
From libertie my heart to turne.

For I was free: and dyd not knowe,
How much his might mannes hert may greue.
I had profest to be his fo:
His law I thought not to beleue.

I went vntyed in lusty leas,
I had my wish alwayes at will:
Ther was no wo, might me displease:
Of pleasant ioyes I had my fill.

No paynfull thought dyd passe my hart:
I spilt no teare to wet my brest:
I knew no sorrow, sigh, nor smart.
My greatest grefe was quyet rest.

I brake no slepe, I tossed not:
Nor dyd delyte to syt alone.
I felt no change of colde, and hote:
Nor nought a nightes could make me mone.
  For all was ioy that I did fele:
And of voide wandering I was free.
I had no clogge tied at my hele:
This was my life at libertie.
  That yet me thinkes it is a blisse,
To thinke vpon that pleasure past.
But forthwithall I finde the misse,
For that it might no lenger last.
  Those dayes I spent at my desire,
Without wo or aduersitie:
Till that my hart was set a fire,
With loue, with wrath, and ielousie.
  For on a day (alas the while)
Lo, hear my harme how it began:
The blinded Lord, the God of guile
Had list to end my fredome than.
  And through mine eye into my hart,
All sodenly I felt it glide.
He shot his sharped fiery dart,
So hard, that yet vnder my side
  The head (alas) dothe still remaine,
And yet since could I neuer know,
The way to wring it out againe:
Yet was it nye three yere ago.
  This soden stroke make me agaist:
And it began to vexe me sore.
But yet I thought, it would haue past,
As other such had done before.
  But it did not that (wo is me)
So depe imprinted in my thought,
The stroke abode: that yet I see,
Me thynkes my harme how it was wrought.
  Kinde taught me streight that this was loue

50

60

70

And I perceiued it perfectlye.
Yet thought I thus: Nought shall me moue:
80 I will not thrall my libertie.

And diuers waies I did assay,
By flight, by force, by frend, by fo,
This fyrye thought to put away.
I was so lothe for to forgo
My libertie: that me was leuer,
Then bondage was, where I heard saie:
Who once was bounde, was sure neuer
Without great paine to scape away.

But what for that, there is no choyce,
90 For my mishap was shapen so:
That those my dayes that did reioyce,
Should turne my blisse to bitter wo.

For with that stroke my blisse toke ende.
In stede wherof forthwith I caught,
Hotte burnyng sighes, that sins haue brend,
My wretched hart almost to naught.

And sins that day, O Lord my life,
The misery that it hath felt.
That nought hath had, but wo and strife,
100 And hotte desires my hart to melt.

O Lord how sodain was the change
From such a pleasant liberty?
The very thraldome semed strange:
But yet there was not remedy.

But I must yeld, and geue vp all,
And make my guide my chiefest fo.
And in this wise became I thrall.
Lo loue and happe would haue it so.

I suffred wrong and helde my peace,
110 I gaue my teares good leaue to ronne:
And neuer would seke for redresse,
But hopt to liueas I begonne.

For what it was that might me ease,
He liued not that might it know.
Thus dranke I all mine owne disease:
And all alone bewailde my wo.

There was no sight that might mee please,
I fled from them that did reioyce.
And oft alone my hart to ease,
120 I would bewayle with wofull voyce
My life, my state, my miserie,
And curse my selfe and all my dayes.
Thus wrought I with my fantasie,
And sought my helpe none other waies.

Saue sometime to my selfe alone,
When farre of was my helpe God wot:
Lowde would I cry: My life is gone,
My dere, if that ye helpe me not.

Then wisht I streight, that death might end
130 These bitter panges, and all this grief.
For nought, methought, might it amend.
Thus in dispaire to haue relief,
I lingred forth: tyll I was brought
With pining in so piteous case:
That all, that saw me, sayd, methought:
Lo, death is painted in his face.

I went no where: but by the way
I saw some sight before mine eyes:
That made me sigh, and oft times say:
140 My life, alas I thee despyse.

This lasted well a yere, and more:
Which no wight knew, but onely I:
So that my life was nere forlore:
And I dispaired vtterly.

Tyll on a day, as fortune would:
(For that, that shalbe, nedes must fall)
I sat me down, as though I should
Haue ended then my lyfe, and all.

And as I sat to wryte my plaint,
150   Meaning to shew my great vnrest:
With quaking hand, and hart full faint,
Amid my plaintes, among the rest,

I wrote with ynk, and bitter teares:
I am not myne, I am not mine:
Behold my lyfe, away that weares:
And if I dye the losse is thyne.

Herewith a litle hope I caught:
That for a whyle my life did stay.
But in effect, all was for naught.
160   Thus liued I styll: tyll on a day,

As I sat staring on those eyes:
I meane, those eyes, that first me bound:
My inward thought tho cryed: Aryse:
Lo, mercy where it may be found.

And therewithall I drew me nere:
With feble hart, and at a braide,
(But it was softly in her eare)
Mercy Madame, was all, I sayd.

But wo was me, when it was tolde.
170   For therewithall fainted my breath.
And I sate still for to beholde,
And here the iudgement of my death.

But Loue nor hap would not consent,
To end me then, but welaway:
There gaue me blisse: that I repent
To thinke I liue to see this day.

For after this I playned still
So long, and in so piteous wise:
That I my wish had at my will
180   Graunted, as I would it deuise.

But Lord who euer heard, or knew
Of halfe the ioye that I felt than?
Or who can thinke it may be true,
That so much blisse had euer man?

Lo, fortune thus set me aloft:
And more my sorowes to releue,
Of pleasant ioyes I tasted oft:
As much as Loue or happe might geue.

The sorrowes olde, I felt before
190 About my hart, were driuen thence:
And for eche greefe, I felt afore,
I had a blisse in recompence.

Then thought I all the time well spent:
That I in plaint had spent so long.
So was I with my life content:
That to my self I sayd among.

Sins thou art ridde of all thine yll:
To showe thy ioyes set forth thy voyce.
And sins thou hast thy wish at will:
200 My happy hart, reioyce, reioyce.

Thus felt I ioyes a great deale mo,
Then by my song may well be tolde:
And thinkyng on my passed wo,
my blisse did double many folde.

And thus I thought with mannes blood,
Such blisse might not be bought to deare.
In such estate my ioyes then strode:
That of a change I had no feare.

But why sing I so long of blisse?
210 It lasteth not, that will away,
Let me therefore bewaile the misse:
And sing the cause of my decay.

Yet all this while there liued none,
That led his life more pleasantly:
Nor vnder hap there was not one,
Me thought, so well at ease, as I.

But O blinde ioye, who may thee trust?
For no estate thou canst assure?
Thy faithfull vowes proue all vniust:
220 Thy faire behestes be full vnsure.

Good proufe by me: that but of late
Not fully twenty dayes ago:
Which thought my life was in such state:
That nought might worke my hart this wo.

Yet hath the enemy of my ease,
Mishappe I meane, that wretched wight:
now when my life did moste me please:
Deuised me such cruel spight.

That from the hiest place of all,
230   As to the pleasying of my thought,
Downe to the deepest am I fall,
And to my helpe auaileth nought,

Lo, thus are all my ioyes gone:
And I am brought from happinesse,
Continually to waile, and mone.
Lo, such is fortunes stablenesse.

In welth I thought such suretie,
That pleasure should haue ended neuer.
But now (alas) aduersitie,
240   Doth make my singyng cease for euer.

O brittle ioye, o slidying blisse,
O fraile pleasure, o welth vnstable:
Who feles thee most, he shall not misse
At length to be make miserable.

For all must end as doth my blisse:
May well away with wretchednesse
But he shall finde that hath it sayd,
A paine to part from pleasantnesse:

As I doe now, for er I knew
250   What pleasure was: I felt no griefe,
Like vnto this, and it is true,
That blisse hath brought me all this mischiefe.

But yet I haue not songen, how
This mischief came: but I intend
With woftill voice to sing it now:
And therewithall I make an end.

But Lord, now that it is begoon,
I feele, my sprites are vexed sore.
Oh, geue me breath till this be done:
260   And after let me liue no more,
    Alas, the enmy of my life,
The ender of all pleasantnesse:
Alas, he bringeth all this strife,
And causeth all this wretchednesse.

    For in the middes of all the welth,
That brought my hart to happinesse
This wicked death he came by stelthe,
And robde me of my ioyfulnesse.

    He came, when that I little thought
270   Of ought, that might me vexe so sore:
And sodenly he brought to nought
My pleasantriesse for euermore,

    He slew my ioye (alas, the wretch)
He slew my ioye, or I was ware:
And now (alas) no might may stretch
To set an end to my great care.

    For by this cursed deadly stroke,
My blisse is lost, and I forlore:
And no help may the losse reuoke:
280   For lost it is for euermore.

    And closed vp are those faire eyes,
That gaue me first the signe of grace:
My faire swete foes, myne enemies,
And earth dothe hide her pleasant face.

    The loke which did my life vpholde:
And all my sorowes did confounde:
With which more blisse then may be tolde:
Alas, now lieth it vnder ground.

    But cease, for I will syng no more:
290   Since that my harme hath no redresse:
But as a wretche for euermore,
My life will waste with wretchednesse.

And ending thys my wofull song,
Now that it ended is and past:
I wold my life were but as long:
And that this work might be my last.

    For lothsome is that life (men saye)
That liketh not the liuers minde:
Lo, thus I seke myne owne decaye,
300   And will, till that I may it finde.

PI: *Voi ch'ascoltate in rime sparse il suono*

276. The louer asketh pardon of his passed follie in loue

You that in play peruse my plaint, and reade in rime the smart,
Which in my youth with sighes full cold I harbourd in my
    hart.
Know ye that Loue in that fraile age, draue me to that
    distresse,
When I was halfe an other man, then I am now to gesse.
Then for this worke of wauering words where I now rage
Tost in the toyes of troublous Loue, as care of comfort grew.
I trust with you that loues affaires by proofe haue put in vre:
Not onely pardon in my plaint, but pitie to procure.
For now I wot that in the world a wonder haue I be,
10 And where to log Loue made me blind, to late shame makes
    me se.
Thus of my fault shame is the fruite, and for my youth thus
    past,
Repentance is my recompence, and this I learne at last.
Looke what the world hath most in price, as sure it is to kepe,
As is the dreame which fansie driues, while sence and reason
    slepe.

P3: *Era il giorno ch'al sol si scoloraro*

277. The louer sheweth that he was striken by loue on good Friday

It was the day on which the sunne depriued of his light,
To rew Christs death amid his course gaue place vnto y night
When I amid mine ease did fall to such distemperate fits,
That for the face that hath my hart I was bereft my wits.
I had the bayte, the hooke and all, and wist not loues pretence,
But farde as one that fearde none yll, nor forst for no defence.
Thus dwelling in most quiet state, I fell into this plight,
And that day gan my secret sighes, when all folke wept in
    sight.
For Loue that vewed me moide of care, approcht to take his
    pray,
10 And stept by stelth from eye to hart, so open lay the way.
And straight at eyes brake out in teares, so salt that did declare,
By token of their bitter taste that they were forgde of care.
Now vaunt thee Loue which fleest a maid defenst [with]
    vertues rare,
And wounded has a wight vnwise, vnweaponed and vnware.

EDMUND SPENSER (1554?–99)

Spenser could only have been in his middle to late teens at the Merchant
Taylors' School when (as the story goes) Richard Mulcaster, his head-
master, conveyed these translations of P323 to the London publisher,
John Day, to be used in his edition of Jan van der Noot's *A Theatre
wherein be represented as wel the miseries & calamities that follow the voluptuous
Worldlings* . . . (1569), a work Day had previously published in Dutch
and French in 1568. That Petrarch's superbly emblematic love poem
should have become a vehicle for a Protestant polemic is a story that

perhaps only St Augustine could have told. Spenser later converted these *Epigrams* into sonnets, which he published as *The Vision of Petrarch* in his *Complaints* volume of 1591. Text from *A Theatre for Worldlings*.

P323: *Standomi un giorno solo a la fenestra*

Epigrams

1.

Being one day at my window all alone,
So many strange things hapned me to see,
As much it grieueth me to thinke thereon.
At my right hande, a Hinde appearde to me,
So faire as mought the greatest God delite:
Two egre Dogs dyd hir pursue in chace,
Of whiche the one was black, the other white.
With deadly force so in their cruell race
They pinchte the haunches of this gentle beast,

10 That at the last, and in shorte time, I spied,
Vnder a rocke, where she (alas) opprest,
Fell to the grounde, and there vntimely dide.
Cruell death vanquishing so noble beautie,
Oft makes me waile so harde a destinie.

2.

After at Sea a tall Ship dyd appere,
Made all of Heben and white Iuorie,
The sailes of Golde, of Silke the tackle were:
Milde was the winde, calme seemed the sea to be:
The Skie eche where did shew full bright and faire.

20 With riche treasures this gay ship fraighted was.
But sodaine storme did so turmoyle the aire,
And tombled vp the sea, that she, alas,

Strake on a rocke that vnder water lay.
O great misfortune, O great griefe, I say,
Thus in one moment to see lost and drownde
So great riches, as lyke can not be founde.

3.

Then heauenly branches did I see arise,
Out of a fresh and lusty Laurell tree
Amidde the yong grene wood. Of Paradise
30   Some noble plant I thought my selfe to see,
Suche store of birdes therein yshrouded were,
Chaunting in shade their sundry melodie.
My sprites were rauisht with these pleasures there.
While on this Laurell fixed was mine eye,
The Skie gan euery where to ouercast,
And darkned was the welkin all aboute,
When sodaine flash of heauens fire outbrast,
And rent this royall tree quite by the roote.
Which makes me much and euer to complaine,
40   For no such shadow shal be had againe.

4.

Within this wood, out of the rocke did rise
A Spring of water mildely romblyng downe,
Whereto approached not in any wise
The homely Shepherde, nor the ruder cloune,
But many Muses, and the Nymphes withall,
That sweetely in accorde did tune their voice
Vnto the gentle sounding of the waters fall.
The sight wherof dyd make my heart reioyce.
But while I toke herein my chiefe delight,
50   I sawe (alas) the gaping earth deuoure
The Spring, the place, and all cleane out of sight.
Whiche yet agreues my heart euen to this houre.

5.

I saw a Phœnix in the wood alone,
With purple wings and crest of golden hew,
Straunge birde he was, whereby I thought anone,
That of some heauenly wight I had the vew:
Vntill he came vnto the broken tree
And to the spring that late deuoured was.
What say I more? Eche thing at length we see
60   Doth passe away: the Phœnix there, alas,
Spying the tree destroyde, the water dride,
Himselfe smote with his beake, as in disdaine,
And so forthwith in great despite he dide.
For pitie and loue my heart yet burnes in paine.

6.

At last so faire a Ladie did I spie,
That in thinking on hir I burne and quake,
On herbes and floures she walked pensiuely.
Milde, but yet loue she proudely did forsake.
White seemed hir robes, yet wouen so they were,
70   As snowe and golde together had bene wrought.
Aboue the waste a darke cloude shrouded hir,
A stinging Serpent by the heele hir caught,
Wherewith she languisht as the gathered floure:
And well assurde she mounted vp to joy.
Alas in earth so nothing doth endure
But bitter griefe that dothe our hearts anoy.

7.

My Song thus now in thy Conclusions,
Say boldly that these same six visions
Do yelde vnto thy lorde a sweete request,
80   Ere it be long within the earth to rest.

SIR WALTER RALEGH
(c. 1552–1618)

Ralegh was an explorer, statesman, poet, favourite of Elizabeth I
and friend of Spenser. He wrote this commendatory sonnet for the
publication of *The Faerie Queene* (1590), in which it was published. It
may be the first mention in English literature of Laura's grave and
therefore merits inclusion in this collection.

A Vision Vpon This Conceipt of the Faery Queene

Me thought I saw the graue, where *Laura* lay,
Within that Temple, where the vestall flame
Was wont to burne, and passing by that way,
To see that buried dust of liuing fame,
Whose tumbe faire loue, and fairer vertue kept,
All suddeinly I saw the Faery Queene:
At whose approch the soule of *Petrarke* wept,
And from thenceforth those graces were not seene.
For they this Queene attended, in whose steed
Obliuion laid him downe on *Lauras* herse:
Hereat the hardest stones were seene to bleed,
And grones of buried ghostes the heuens did perse.
    Where *Homers* spright did tremble all for griefe.
    And curst th'accesse of that celestial theife.

Richard Edwards, *The Paradise of Dainty Devices* (1576)

This miscellany was clearly an attempt to compete with Tottel, and includes the writings of noblemen such as the Earl of Oxford, one of whose poems is presented below. It went through nine editions between 1576 and 1606. Edwards died in 1566.

EDWARD DE VERE, EARL OF OXFORD (1550–1604)

Edward de Vere, seventeenth Earl of Oxford, succeeded his father in 1562, but not being of age was assigned to the household of William Cecil, Lord Burghley, whose eldest daughter, Anne, he married. He led an extravagant and litigious life, including a duel with Sir Philip Sidney. He was a favourite of Queen Elizabeth and served as Lord Great Chamberlain at the coronation of James I. He was patron of a company of actors and was praised as a poet by the literati of the Elizabethan period.

P102: *Cesare, poi che 'l traditor d'Egitto*

84. Not attainyng to his desire, he complaineth

I am not as [I] seme to bee,
Nor when I smile, I am not glad:
A thrall although you count me free,
I moste in mirthe, moste pensiue sadd.
I smile to shade my bitter spight,
As *Haniball that* sawe in sight:
His countrey soile, with Carthage toune:
By Romaine force, defaced doune.

And *Caesar* that presented was,
10   With noble *Pompeyes* princely hedd,
As twere some iudge, to rule the case,
A floud of teares, he semde to shedd.
Although in deede, it sprong of ioye,
Yet others thought it was annoye:
Thus contraries be vsed I finde,
Of wise to cloke the couert minde.

I *Haniball* that smiles for grief,
And let you Caesars teares suffice:
The one that laughs at his mischief,
20   The other all for ioye that cries.
I smile to see me scorned so,
You wepe for ioye, to see me wo:
And I a harte by loue slaine dead,
Presents in place of *Pompeyes* head.

O cruell happ, and harde estate,
That forceth me to loue my foe:
Accursed be so foule a fate,
My choise for to profixe it so.
So long to fight with secret sore,
30   And finde no secret salue therefore:
Some purge their paine, by plaint I finde,
But I in vaine doe breathe my winde.

THOMAS WATSON (*c.* 1557–92)

Watson's *Hekatompathia, or a Passionate Century of Love* (1582) has been
advanced as a candidate for the first sonnet sequence in English, but
its typical 18-line sonnet form and its lack of poetic invention do not
steal the laurel from Sidney. His *Tears of Fancy* (1593) do not advance
his distinction as a sonneteer. He is mainly remembered for his Latin
hexameter poem, *Amyntas* (1585), an adaptation of Tasso's pastoral,

Aminta. Abraham Fraunce translated Watson into English (1587) without acknowledging his source, and this version gained some popularity and is mentioned by Spenser. Watson is also credited with *The First Sett of Italian Madrigalls Englished* (1590), from which the third poem (no. 4) in the selection comes; the first two poems are Sonnets 5 and 40 from *Hekatompathia*.

PI 32: *S'amor non è, che dunque è quel ch'io sento?*

If it bee not loue I feele, what is it then?
If loue it bee, what kind a thing is loue?
If good, how chance he hurtes so many men?
If badd, how happ's that none his hurtes disproue?
　　If willingly I burne, how chance i waile?
　　If gainst my will, what forrow will auaile?
O liuesome death, O sweete and pleasant ill,
Against my minde how can thy might preuaile?
If I bend backe, and but refraine my will,
10　If I consent, I doe not well to waile;
　　And touching him, whome will hath made a slaue,
　　The prouerbe saith of olde, Selfe doe, selfe haue.
Thus beeing tost with windes of sundry sorte
Through daung'rous Seas but in a slender Boat,
With errour stuft, and driu'n beside the porte,
Where voide of wisdomes fraight it lies afloate,
　　I waue in doubt what helpe I shall require,
　　In Sommer freeze, in winter burn like fire.

PI 34: *Pace non trovo e non ò da far guerra*

I ioy not peace, where yet no warre is found;
I fear, and hope; I burne, yet freeze withal;
I mount to heau'n, yet lie but on the ground;
I compasse nought, and yet I compasse all;

    I liue her bond, which neither is my foe,
      Nor frend; nor holdes me fast, nor lets me goe;
  Loue will not that I liue, nor lets me die;
  Nor lockes me fast, nor suffers me to scape;
  I want both eyes and tongue, yet see and cry;
10 I wish for death, yet after helpe I gape;
    I hate my selfe, but loue an other wight;
      And feede on greefe, in lieu of sweete delight;
  At selfe same time I both lament and ioy;
  I still am pleasd, and yet displeased still;
  Loue sometimes seemes a God, sometimes a Boy;
  Sometimes I sincke, sometimes I swimme at will;
    Twixt death and life, small difference I make
    All this deere Dame befals me for thy sake.

P310: *Zefiro torna e 'l bel tempo rimena*

Zephirus breathing, now calls nymfs from out their bowres,
To play and wanton, in roubes of sundry flow'rs:
Progne chirpeth, and sweet Philomele recordeth:
And Flora seeing what the spring affordeth
Smyleth so sweetly, that heauen itself inflamed,
Greatly reioyceth to but heare her named,
The welkin, water, and earth are full of pleasure,
All creatures ioy in loue, as Natures treasure.

Clement Robinson, *A Handful of Pleasant Delights* (1584)

A Handful of Pleasant Delights was a miscellany mainly of broadside ballads, collected by Clement Robinson, in whose name it was registered in 1566. It demonstrates that even broadside balladeers tried their hand at Petrarch.

P258: *Vive faville uscian de' duo bei lumi*

The Louer being wounded with his Ladis beutie, requireth mercy. To the tune of Apelles

The liuelie sparkes of those two eyes,
my wounded hart hath set on fire:
And since I can no way deuise,
To stay the rage of my desire,
with sighs and trembling tears I craue
my deare on me some pitie haue.
In vewing thee, I tooke such ioy,
As one that sought his quiet rest:
Vntill I felt the fethered boy,
Ay flickring in my captiue brest:
Since that time loe, in deepe dispaire,
all voide of ioy, my time I weare.
The wofull prisoner *Palemon*,
And *Troylus* eke kinge *Pyramus* sonne,
Constrained by loue did neuer mone:
As I my deer for thee haue done.
Let pitie then requite my paines,
My life and death in thee remaines.
If constant loue may reape his hire,
And faith vnfained may purchace:
Great hope I haue to my desire.
Your gentle hart wil grant me grace,
Til then (my deer) in few words plaine,
In pensiue thoughts I shall remaine.

HENRY CONSTABLE (1562–1613)

Like Barnabe Barnes, Constable wrote both a secular and a sacred sonnet sequence, the latter published only in the nineteenth century. His *Diana* appeared as a 22-sonnet sequence in 1592 and as a 76-sonnet sequence in 1594, containing eight of Sidney's *Certaine Sonnets*. A manuscript version containing 63 sonnets was edited by Joan Grundy. Constable was connected on both sides of his family to nobility, and served on diplomatic missions for Elizabeth I, James VI and Henry of Navarre. Although he began his career as a pro-Huguenot Protestant, he soon became an ardent defender of the Church of Rome, and used his social position to further the cause of a Roman Catholic ecumenism that failed. Sonnets 1, 3 and 6 from *Diana*.

P248: *Chi vuol veder quantunque pò Natura*

The second 7 of his Ladies prayse. An exhortation to the reader to come and see his Mistrisse beautie

Eyes curiouse to behold what nature can create
Come see come see and write what wonder yow doe see
Causing by true reporte oure next posteritye.
Curse fortune for that they were borne to late

Come then and come ye all, come soone least that
The tyme should be to shorte and men to few should be
For all be few to write her least parts historie
Though they should euer write and neuer write but that

millions looke on her eyes millions thinke on her witte
millions speake of her [lip] millions write of her hand
The whole eye or the lip I doe not vnderstand
Millions to few to prayse but some one parte of it
As eyther of her ey or lip or hand to write
The light or blacke the tast or red the soft or white

P84: *Occhi, piangete, accompagnate il core*

My reason absent did myne eyes require
To watch and ward and such foes to descrie
As neare my heart they should approaching spy
But traytoure eyes my hearts death did conspire

Corrupted with hopes guifts let in desire
To burne my heart and sought no remedie
Though store of water were in eyther eye
Which well employ'd might well haue quencht the fir,

Reason returned, loue and fortune made
Iudges, to iudge myne eyes to punishment
Fortune (sith they by sight my heart betrayd)
From wished sight adiudgd them banishment
Loue (sith by fire murdred my hearte was found)
Adiudged them in teares for to be drown'd

P334: *S'onesto amor pò meritar mercede*

If true loue might true loues reward obtayne
Dumbe wonder onlye could speake of my ioy
But to much worth hath made thee to much coy
And told me longe agoe I lou'd in vayne

Not then vayne hope of vndeserued gaine
Hath made me paint in verses myne annoye
But for thy pleasure that thow mightst enioy
Thy beauties sight in glasses of my payne

See then thy selfe though me thow wilt not heare
By looking on my verse (for payne in verse
Loue doth in payne, beautie in loue appeare)

So if thou wilt my verses meaning see
Expound them thus when I my loue rehearse
None loues like him that is none fayre like mee

SAMUEL DANIEL (c. 1562–1619)

Daniel was educated at Magdalen Hall, Oxford, and became tutor to
William Herbert, thus gaining access to the circle of the Countess of
Pembroke at Wilton. Twenty-eight of his sonnets appeared in the
surreptitious 1591 edition of Sidney's *Astrophil and Stella*, but in 1592
his *Delia . . . with the Complaint of Rosemond* appeared and was constantly
revised and augmented until 1601. Like Sidney, Daniel absorbed the
Petrarchan grammar and idiom without having to translate Petrarch.
The first sonnet selected here is as close to a translation as he gets, but
the second shows what Daniel can do on his own with the Petrarchan
language. Sonnets 6 and 7 from *Delia*.

P297: *Due gran nemiche inseme erano agiunte*

Faire is my Loue, and cruell as she's faire;
   Her browshades frownes, although her eyes are sunny;
   Her Smiles are lightning, though her pride dispaire,
   And her disdaines are gall, her fauours hunny.
A modest maide, deckt with a blush of honour,
   Whose feete doe tread greene pathes of youth and loue,
   The wonder of all eyes that looke vppon her:
   Sacred on earth, design'd a Saint aboue,
Chastitie and beautie, which were deadly foes,
10   Liue reconciled friends within her brow:
   And had she pittie, to conioine with those,
   Then who had heard the plaints I vtter now?
For had she not been faire, and thus vnkinde,
My Muse had slept, and none had knowne my minde.

For had she not bene faire and thus vnkinde,
  Then had no finger pointed at my lightnes:
  The world had neuer knowne what I do finde,
  And Clowdes obscure had shaded still her brightnes.
Then had no Censors eye these lines suruaid,
20   Nor grauer browes have judg'd my Muse so vaine;
  No sunne my blush and errour had bewraied,
  Nor yet the world had heard of such disdaine.
Then had I walkt with bold erected face,
  No downe-cast looke had signified my misse:
  But my degraded hopes, with such disgrace
  Did force me grone out griefes, and vtter this.
For being full, should I not then haue spoken:
My sence, oppress'd, had fail'd, and hart had broken.

THOMAS LODGE (c. 1558–1625)

Lodge may be the perfect exemplar of the Elizabethan litterateur. Educated at Merchant Taylors' School, Trinity College, Oxford, and Lincoln's Inn, he turned to literary productions, such as a reply to Stephen Gosson's School of Abuse in his Defense of Plays (1580), the epyllion, Scilla's Metamorphosis (1589), his prose romance, Rosalynde (1590; the source of Shakespeare's As You Like It), his sonnet sequence, Phillis (1593), and the satire, A Fig for Momus (1595). After 1600, he turned to the practice of medicine, with medical degrees from Avignon and Oxford. The first poem in this selection comes from Rosalynde, the second from Phillis and the last is after Ronsard's Amours, I.12.

P189: *Passa la nave mia colma d'oblio*

To this letter she annexed this sonnet:

My boat doth pass the straits
of seas incensed with fire,
Filled with forgetfulness;
Amidst the winter's night,
A blind and careless boy,
Brought up by fond desire,
Doth guide me in the sea
of sorrow and despite.

For every oar he sets
A rank of foolish thoughts,
And cuts, instead of wave,
A hope without distress;
The winds of my deep sighs,
That thunder still for noughts
Have split my sails with fear,
With care, with heaviness.

A mighty storm of tears
A black and hideous cloud,
A thousand fierce disdains
Do slack the halyards oft;
Till ignorance do pull,
And error hale the shrouds
No star for safety shines,
No Phoebe from aloft.

Time hath subdued art,
And joy is slave to woe
Alas, Love's guide, be kind;
What, shall I perish so?

PI34: *Pace non trovo e non ò da far guerra*

I wage the combat with two mighty foes
Which are more strong than I ten thousand fold;
The one is when thy pleasure I do lose,
The other, when thy person I behold.
In seeing thee a swarm of loves confound me
And cause my death in spite of my resist,
And if I see thee not, thy want doth wound me,
For in thy sight my comfort doth consist.
The one in me continual care createth,
The other doth occasion my desire;
The one the edge of all my joy rebateth,
The other makes me a phoenix in love's fire.
So that I grieve when I enjoy your presence,
And die for grief by reason of your absence.

I would in rich and golden-coloured rain,
With tempting showers in pleasant sort descend
Into fair Phillis' lap, my louely friend,
When sleep her slumber doth retrain,
    I would be changed to a milk-white bull,
When midst the gladsome field she should appear,
By pleasant fineness to surprise my dear,
Whilst from their stalks, she pleasant flowers did pull,
    I were content to weary out my pain,
To be Narcissus so she were a spring,
To drown in her those wose my heart do ring,
And more; I wish transformed to remain,
    That whilst I thus in pleasure's lap did lie,
    I might refresh desire, which else would die.

The Phoenix Nest (1593)

The Phoenix Nest was another popular anthology. T. L. Gent is undoubtedly Thomas Lodge; Sir W. H. has never been identified. I have included several Petrarchan virtuoso pieces, such as 'Hir face, Hir tong, Hir wit', which can be read from left to right as well as from top to bottom.

P189: *Passa la nave mia colmo d'oblio*

My fraile and earthly barke by reasons guide,
Which holds the helme, whilst will doth yeld the saile
By my desires the windes of bad betide,
Hath saild these worldly seas with small auaile,
Vaine obiects serue for dreadfull rocks to quaile,
　　My brittle boate, from hauen of life that flies,
　　To haunt the Sea of Mundane miseries.

My soule that drawes impressions from aboue,
And viewes my course, and sees the windes aspire,
Bids reason watch to scape the shoales of Loue
But lawles will enflamde with endles ire,
Doth steere in poope whilst reason doth retire:
　　The storms increase, my barke loues billowes fill
　　Thus are they wrackt, that guide their course by will.

T. L. Gent

P189: *Passa la nave mi colma d'oblio*

These lines I send by waues of woe,
And bale becomes my boate:
Which sighes of sorowes still shall keepe,
On floods of feare afloat.

My sighes shall serue me still for winde,
My lading is my smart:
And true report my pilot is,
My hauen is thy hart.

My keele is fram'd of crabbed care,
10   My ribs are all of ruthe:
My planks are nothing else but plants,
With treenailes ioinde with truthe.

My maine mast made of nought but mone,
My tackling trickling teares;
And Topyard like a troubled minde
A flagge of follie beares.

My Cable is a constant hart,
My Anckor luckles Loue:
Which Reasons Capstones from the ground,
20   Of griefe can not remoue.

My Decks are all of deepe disgrace,
My Compas discontent;
And perill is my Northern Pole,
And death my Orient.

My Saylers are my sorowing thoughts,
The Boateswane bitter sence:
The Master, miserie; his mate
Is dolefull diligence.

                                        Sir W. H.

Those eies which set my fancie on a fire,
Those crisped haires, which hold my hart in chains,
Those daintie hands, which conquer'd my desire,
That wit, which of my thoughts doth hold the rains.

Those eies for cleernes doe the starrs surpas,
Those haires obsure the brightnes of the Sunne,
Those hands more white, than euer Iourie was,
That wit euen to the skies hath glorie woon.

O eies that pearce our harts without remorse,
O haires of right that weares a roiall crowne,
O hands that conquer more than Caesars force,
O wit that turns huge kingdoms vpside downe.

Then Loue be Iudge, what hart may thee withstand:
Such eies, such haire, such wit, and such a hand.

Hir face,	Hir tong,	Hir wit,
So faine,	So sweete,	So sharpe,
First bent,	Then drew,	Then hit,
Mine eie,	Mine eare,	My hart.
Mine eie,	Mine eare,	My hart,
To like	To learne,	To loue,
Hir face,	Hir tong,	Hir wit,
Doth lead,	doth teach,	Doth moue.
Oh face,	Oh tong,	Oh wit,
With frownes	With checke	With smart,
Wrong not,	Vexe not,	Wound not,
Mine eie,	Mine eare,	My hart.
Mine eie,	Mine eare,	My hart,
To learne,	To knowe,	To feare,
Hir face,	Hir tong,	Hir wit,
Doth lead,	Doth teach,	Doth sweare.

What else is hell, but losse of blisfull heauen?
What darknes else, but lacke of lightsome day?
What else is death, but things of life bereauen?
What winter else, but pleasant springs decay?

Vnrest what else, but fancies hot desire,
Fed with delay, and followed with dispaire?
What else mishap, but longing to aspire,
To striue against, earth, water, fire, and aire?

Heauen were my state, and happie Sunneshine day,
And life most blest, to ioy one howres desire,
Hap, blisse, and rest, and sweete springtime of May,
Were to behold my faire consuming fire.

But loe, I feele, by absence from your sight,
Mishap, vnrest, death, winter, hell, darke night.

Would I were chaung'd into that golden showre,
That so diuinely streamed from the skies,
To fall in drops vpon the dainte floore,
Where in hir bed, she solitarie lies,
    Then would I hope such showres as richly shine,
    Would pearce more deepe than these wast tears of mine.

Or would I were, that plumed Swan, snowe white,
Vnder whose forme, was hidden heauenly power,
Then in that riuer would I most delite,
Whose waues doe beate, against hir stately bower,
    And in those banks, so tune my dying song,
    That hir deafe ears, would think my plaint too long.

Else would I were, Narcissus, that sweete boy,
And she hir selfe, the sacred fountaine cleere,
Who rauisht with the pride of his owne ioy,
Drenched his lims, with gazing ouer neere:
    So should I bring, my soule to happie rest,
    To end my life, in that I loued best.

P61: *Benedetto sia 'l giorno e 'l mese e l'anno*

The time, when first I fell in Loue,
Which now I must lament,
The yeere, wherein I lost such time,
To compasse my content.

The day, wherein I sawe too late,
The follies of a Louer,
The hower, wherein I found such losse,
As care cannot recouer.

And last, the minute of mishap,
10   Which makes me thus to plaine,
The dolefull fruits of Louers sutes,
Which labor lose in vaine:

Doth make me solemnly protest,
As I with paine doe proue,
There is no time, yeere, day, nor howre,
Nor minute, good to loue.

P310: *Zefiro torna e 'l bel tempo rimena*

The gentle season of the yeere,
Hath made my blouming branch appeere,
And beautified the land with flowres,
The aire doth fauor with delight,
The heauens doe smile, to see the sight,
And yet mine eies, augments their showres.

The meades are mantled all with greene,
The trembling leaues, haue cloth'd the treene,
The birds with feathers new doe sing,

10   But I poore soule, when wrong doth wrack,
        Attyres my selfe in mourning black,
        Whose leafe doth fall amid his spring.

        And as you see the skarlet Rose
        In his sweete prime, his buds disclose,
        Whose hewe is with the Sun reuiued,
        So in the Aprill of mine age,
        My liuely colours doe asswage,
        Because my Sun-shine is depriued.

        My hart that wonted was of yore,
20   Light as the winde abroad to sore,
        Amongst the buds when beautie springs,
        Now onely houers ouer you,
        As doth the birde thats taken new,
        And mourns when all hir neighbours sings.

        When euery man is bent to sport,
        Then pensiue I alone resort,
        Into some solitarie walke,
        As doth the dolefull Turtle doue,
        Who hauing lost hir faithfull loue,
30   Sits mourning on some withered stalke.

        There to my selfe, I doe recount,
        How far my woes, my ioyes surmount,
        How Loue requiteth me with hate:
        How all my pleasures end in paine,
        How hate doth say, my hope is vaine,
        How fortune frownes vpon my state.

        And in this moode, charg'd with despaire,
        With vapored sighes, I dim the aire,
        And to the Gods make this request:

40   That by the ending of my life,
        I may haue truce with this strange strife,
        And bring my soule to better rest.

        P145: *Ponmi ove 'l sole occide i fiori e l'erba*

        Set me where Phœbus heate, the flowers slaieth
        Or where continuall snowe withstands his forces,
        Set me where he his temprate raies displaieth,
        Or where he comes, or where he neuer courses.

        Set me in Fortunes grace, or else discharged,
        In sweete and pleasant aire, or darke and glooming,
        Where daies and nights, are lesser, or inlarged,
        In yeeres of strength, in failing age, or blooming.

        Set me in heauen, or earth, or in the center,
10   Lowe in a vale, or on a mountaine placed,
        Set me to daunger, perill, and aduenture,
        Graced by Fame, or infamie disgraced.

        Set me to these, or anie other triall,
        Except my Mistres anger and deniall.

        P5: *Quando io movo i sospiri a chiamar voi*

        Thinking vpon the name, by Loue engraued,
        Within my hart, to be my liues directer,
        The value of the whole entirely saued,
        I reade vpon the sillables this lecter,
        Maruell, the first into my spirits soundeth,
        And maruelling at hir, the maruell woundeth.

I seeke to Gaine, as by the second's ment,
An interest in this admired maruaile,
But cannot finde a meane sufficient,
10   So hie a rated Gem to counteruaile,
There is no weight in fire ordaind to shine,
Nor counterworth of any thing diuine.

The last doth giue me counsell to Retire,
And rest content, that Loue hath blest my sight,
And toucht my fancie with th' immortall fire,
Of this diuine, and precious Margaret,
And thanke my fortune of exceeding fauour,
As to be thralled to so sweete behauiour.

P21: *Mille fiate, o dolce mia guerrera*

To make a truce, sweete Mistres with your eies,
How often haue I proffred you my hart,
Which profers vnesteemed you despise,
As far to meane, to equall your desart,
Your minde wherein, all hie perfections flowe,
Deignes not the thought, of things that are so lowe.

To striue to alter his desires, were vaine,
Whose vowed hart, affects no other place,
The which since you despise, I doe disdaine
10   To count it mine, as erst before it was:
For that is mine, which you alone alow,
As I am yours, and onely liue for you.

Now if I him forsake, and he not finde,
His wretched exile, succord by your eies,
He can not yeeld, to serue anothers minde,
Nor liue alone, for nature that denies,

Then die he must, for other choise is none,
But liue in you, or me, or die alone.

20 Whose haples death, when Fame abroad hath blowne,
Blame and reproch, procures vnto vs both,
I, as vnkinde, forsaking so mine owne,
But you much more, from whom the rigour groweth,
And so much more, will your dishonor be,
By how much more, it loued you than me.

Sweete Ladie then, the harts misfortune rue,
Whose loue and seruice euermore was true.

WILLIAM SMITH (fl. 1596)

Of Smith, we know nothing except that he was acquainted with
Spenser because he makes reference to *Colin Clout*, and might have
been patronized by the Countess of Pembroke. His sonnet sequence,
Chloris, or the complaint of the passionate, despised shepheard, appeared in
1596. Here he returns Petrarch's first sestina to a sonnet. Sonnet 37
from *Chloris*.

P22: *A qualunque animale alberga in terra*

Each beast in field doth wish the morning light.
The birds to *Hesper* pleasant laies do sing:
The wanton kids, well fed, reioice in night;
Being likewise glad when day begins to spring.
But night, nor day, are welcome vnto me:
Both can beare witnes of my lamentation.
All day, sad sighing *Corine* you shall see;
All night he spends in teares and exclamation.

Thus still I lieu although I take no rest:
10   But liuing look as one that is a dying:
Thus my sad soule with care and griefe opprest,
Seems as a ghost to *Styx* and *Lethe* flying.
    Thus hath fond loue bereft my youthfull yeeres
    Of all good hap before old age appeeres.

ROBERT TOFTE (d. 1620)

Tofte travelled much in Italy, translated Boiardo and Ariosto, and here
turns Petrarch's mysterious deer poem into a game of hide-and-seek
in a park without even mentioning that the park and the deer belong
to Caesar. See Wyatt, p. 93. Sonnet III.xv from *Laura; the Toyes of a
Traveller* (1597).

P190: *Una candida cerva sopra l'erba*

A gentle tame deer am I, called a Hart:
The cruel huntress fierce my Mistress is.
With crossbow bent, she comes to me in Park;
Paled in with pleasant thoughts of wanton wish.
She shoots, and hits me; takes me for her prey:
And (having shot, hit, taken) flies her way.
Back she retires from me, with pleasant smile;
Unloosing me, and heals my wound and pain:
When, as afresh incensed (alack the while!)
10   'Gainst me, desirous me to plague again,
She turns towards me, o'ertakes me, strikes me sore:
And, binding up my wounds, makes deadly more.

Seventeenth Century

England's Helicon (1600)

This miscellany is almost a distillation of English lyric poetry from the sixteenth century, including selections from Spenser, Sidney, Shakespeare, and a host of lesser poets. It is one of the most tasteful anthologies ever assembled, and since many of its selections are already given in this anthology of Petrarchan translations, I give only one anonymous poem.

P310: *Zefiro torna, e 'l bel tempo rimena*

Zephirus brings the time that sweetly senteth
    with flowers and hearbs, which Winters frost elileth:
Progne now chirpeth, *Philomel* lamenteth,
    Flora the Garlands white and red compileth:
Fields doo rejoyce, the frowning skie relenteth,
    Jove to behold his dearest daughter smileth:
The ayre, the water, the earth to joy consenteth,
    each creature now to love him reconcileth.
But with me wretch, the stormes of woe persever,
    and heavie sighs which from my hart she straineth
That tooke the key thereof to heaven for ever,
    so that singing of birds, and spring-times flowring:
And Ladies love that mens affection gaineth,
are like a Desert, and cruell bests devouring.

SIR WILLIAM ALEXANDER, EARL OF STIRLING (*c.* 1567–1640)

Tutor to Prince Henry, Alexander came to England with James I. He was a friend of William Drummond (see next author). He wrote the sequence *Aurora* (1604) and a 12-book epic, *Doomsday* (1614). Alexander's attempt to reproduce Petrarch's first sestina, from *Aurora.*

P22: *A qualunque animale alberga in terra*

While as the day deliuers vs his light,
I wander through the solitarie fields,
And when the euening hath obscur'd the earth,
And hath with silence lull'd the world asleepe:
Then rage I like a mad-man in my bed,
Which being fir'd with sighes, I quench with teares.

But ere *Aurora* rise to spend her teares,
Still languishing againe to see the light,
As th' enemie of my rest, I flie my bed,
And take me to the most deserted fields:
There is no soule saue I but gets some sleepe,
Though one would seeke through all the peopled earth.

While th' *Aetna* of my fires affrights the earth,
And whiles it dreads, I drowne it with my teares:
And it's suspicious-like, I neither sleepe,
When *Phoebus* giues nor gathers in his light:
So many piles of grasse not cloath the fields,
As I deuise designes within my bed.

Vnto the time I find a frostie bed,
20 Digged within the bowels of the earth,
Mine eyes salt flouds shall still oreflow the fields:
I looke not for an abstinence from teares,
Till first I be secluded from the light,
And end my torments with an endlesse sleepe.

For now when I am purposed to sleepe,
A thousand thoughts assaile me in my bed,
That oft I do despaire to see the light:
O would to God I were dissolu'd in earth;
Then would the sauage beasts bemone with teares,
30 Their neighbours death through all th'vnpeopled fields.

Whil'st rauish'd whiles I walke alongst the fields,
The lookers on lament, I lose my sleepe:
But of the crocadiles those be the teares,
So to perswade me for to go to sleepe;
As being sure, when once I leaue the light,
To render me the greatest wretch on th'earth.

O happiest I in th'earth, if in the fields,
I might still see the light and neuer sleepe
Drinking salt teares, and making stones my bed.

WILLIAM DRUMMOND OF HAWTHORNDEN (1585–1649)

Laird of Hawthornden, Drummond took his MA from the University of Edinburgh in 1605 and went to France to study law. He abandoned that course after his father's death in order to remain in Hawthornden, collected a large library and befriended other poets, including Alexander, Drayton and Jonson. His *Conversations* record Jonson's first visit to him in 1619. His graceful verse depends much on French and Italian models. The selection prints Sonnets I.6, 9, 15, 50, 51 and II.7 from Parts I and II of *Poems* (1640).

P178: *Amor mi sprona in un tempo et affrena*

Faire is my Yocke, though grieuous be my Paines,
Sweet are my Wounds, although they deepely smart,
My Bit is Gold, though shortened be the Raines,
My Bondage braue, though I may not depart,
Although I burne, the Fire which doth impart
Those Flames, so sweet reuiuing Force containes,
That like *Arabia's* Bird my wasted Heart
Made quicke by Death, more liuely still remaines.
I joye though oft my waking Eyes spend Teares,
I neuer want Delight, euen when I grone,
Best companied when most I am alone,
A Heauen of Hopes I haue midst Hells of Feares:
    Thus euery way Contentment strange I finde,
    But most in Her rare Beautie, my rare Minde.

P164: *Or che 'l ciel e la terra e 'l vento tace*

Now while the *Night* her sable Vaile hath spred,
And silently her restie Coach doth rolle,
Rowsing with Her from *Tethis* azure Bed,
Those starrie *Nymphes* which dance about the Pole,
While *Cynthia*, in purest Cipres cled,
The *Latmian* Shepheard in a Trance descries,
And whiles lookes pale from hight of all the Skies,
Whiles dies her Beauties in a blushing Red,

Whiles *Sleepe* (in Triumph) closed hath all Eyes,
10   And Birds, and Beastes a Silence sweet doe keepe,
And *Proteus* monstrous People in the Deepe,
The Winds and Waues (husht vp) to rest entise,
     I wake, I turne, I weepe opprest with Paine,
     Toilde in the wayles *Labyrinthes* of my Braine.

P148: *Non Tesin, Po, Varo, Arno, Adige e Tebro*

Nor *Arne*, nor *Mincius*, nor stately *Tiber*,
Sebethus, nor the Flood into whose streames
He fel who burnt the World with borrowed beames,
Goldrolling *Tagus*, *Munda*, famous *Iber*,
Sorgue, *Rosne*, *Loire*, *Garron*, nor proud-banked *Seine*,
Peneus, *Phasis*, *Xanthus*, humble *Ladon*,
Nor *Shee* whose Nymphes excell her loued *Adon*,
Faire *Tamesis*, nor *Ister* large, nor *Rheine*,
Euphrates, *Tigris*, *Indus*, *Hermus*, *Gange*,
10   Pearlie *Hydaspes*, Serpent-like *Meander*,
The Golfe bereft sweet *Hero* her *Leander*,
Nile, that farre farre his hidden Head doth range
     Haue euer had so rare a cause of praise
     As *Ora* where this *Northerne Phoenix* stayes.

P112: *Sennuccio i'vo' che sappi in qual manera*

Alexis here *shee* stay'd; among these Pines
Sweet hermitresse did all alone repaire,
Here did *shee* spred the Treasure of her Haire,
More rich than that brought from the *Colchian* Mines.
Shee set her by these musket Eglantines,
The happie flowres seeme yet the print to beare,
Her voice did sweeten here thy sugred lines,
To which Windes, Trees, Beasts, Birdes did lend their Eare.

Me here *shee* first perceau'd, and here a Morne
Of bright *Carnations* did o'respred her Face;
Here did *shee* sigh, here first my Hopes were borne,
And I first got a Pledge of promis'd Grace:
    But *ah* what serues 't it to haue beene made happie so?
    Sith passed Pleasures double but new woe?

P145: *Ponmi ove 'l sole occide i fiori e l'erba*

Place me where angrie *Titan* burns the *More*,
And thirstie *Africke* fierie Monsters brings,
Or where the new-borne *Phoenix* spreads her Wings
And troupes of wondring Birds her flight adore.
Place me by *Gange* or *Indes* empampred shore,
Where smyling Heauens on Earth cause double Springs,
Place me where *Neptune's* Quire of *Syrens* sings,
Or where made hoarse through Cold, he leaues to roare.
Me place where *Fortune* doth her Darlings Crowne,
A *Wonder* or a *sparke* in *Enuies* Eye,
Or late outragious *Fates* vpon me frowne,
And *Pittie* wailing see disastred *Mee*,
Affections print my minde so deepe doth proue,
I may forget my Selfe; but not my Loue.

P310: *Zefiro torna e 'l bel tempo rimena*

Sweet *Spring* thou turnes with all thy goodlie traine,
Thy Head with Flames, thy Mantle bright with Flowres:
The *Zephires* curle the greene Lockes of the Plaine,
The Clouds for joy in Pearles weepe downe their Showres.
Thou turnes sweet Youth; but *ah* my pleasant Houres
And happie Dayes with thee come not againe,
The sad Memorialls onelie of my paine
Doe with thee turne, which turne my Sweets in Sowres.

Thou art the Same which still thou was before,
10   Delicious, wanton, amiable, faire;
But *shee* whose Breath embaulm'd thy wholesome Aire
Is gone; Nor Gold, nor Gemmes her can restore.
Neglected *Vertue* Seasons goe and come
While thine forgot lie closed in a Tombe.

THOMAS CAREW (1595?–1639?)

Thomas Carew was one of 'The Tribe of Ben' Jonson. He studied at
Merton College, Oxford, and later at Middle Temple. He performed
diplomatic service for Charles I. Text from *Poems* (1640).

P310: *Zefiro torna e 'l bel tempo rimena*

The Spring

Now that the winter's gone, the earth hath lost
Her snow-white robes, and now no more the frost
Candies the grasse, or castes an ycie creame
Vpon the silver Lake or Chrystall streame:
But the warme sunne thawes the benummed Earth,
And makes it tender, gives a sacred birth
To the dead Swallow; wakes in hollow tree
The drowzie Cuckow and the Humble-Bee.
Now doe a quire of chirping Minstrels bring
10   In tryumph to the world, the youthfull Spring.
The Vallies, hills, and woods in rich arraye,
Welcome the comming of the long'd for May.
Now all things smile; only my *Love* doth lowre;
Nor hath the scalding Noon-day-Sunne the power
To melt that marble yce, which still doth hold
Her heart congeald, and makes her pity cold.

The Oxe which lately did for shelter flie
Into the stall, doth now securely lie
In open fields; and love no more is made
20   By the fire side; but in the cooler shade.
Amyntas now doth with his *Cloris* sleepe
Vnder a Sycamoure, and all things keepe
Time with the season, only she doth carry
Iune in her eyes, in her heart *Ianuary*.

PI53: *Ite, caldi sospiri, al freddo core*

A Prayer to the Wind

Goe thou gentle whispering wind,
Beare this sigh; and if thou find
Where my cruell faire doth rest,
Cast it in her snowie brest;
So, enflamed by my desire,
It may set her heart a–fire.
Those sweet kisses thou shalt gaine,
Will reward thee for thy paine:
Boldly light upon her lip,
10   There suck odours, and thence skip
To her bosome; lastly fall
Downe, and wander over all:
Range about those Ivorie hills,
From whose every part distills
Amber deaw; there spices grow,
There pure streames of Nectar flow;
There perfume thy selfe, and bring
All those sweets upon thy wing:
As thou return'st, change by thy power,
20   Every weed into a flower;
Turn each Thistle to a Vine,
Make the Bramble Eglantine.

For so rich a bootie made,
Doe but this, and I am payd.
Thou canst with thy powerfull blast
Heat apace, and coole as fast:
Thou canst kindle hidden flame,
And ag'en destroy the same;
Then, for pittie, either stir
30   Vp the fire of love in her,
That alike both flames may shine,
Or else quite extinguish mine.

WILLIAM HABINGTON (1605–54)

A Jesuit-trained Catholic, Habington was the author of *Castara* (1634),
which is really the last of the Elizabethan-style sequences. His Castara
(Latin, 'chaste altar') was Lucy Herbert, whom he married sometime
between 1630 and 1633, and, in doing so, he domesticated the sonnet
sequence.

P145: *Ponmi ove 'l sole occide i fiori e l'erba*

Quoniam ego in flagella paratus sum. DAVID.

Fix me on some bleake precipice,
Where I ten thousand yeares may stand:
Made now a statue of ice,
Then by the sommer scorcht and tan'd!

Place me alone in some fraile boate
'Mid th' horrors of an angry Sea:
Where I while time shall move, may floate
Despairing either land or day!

Or under earth my youth confine
To th' night and silence of a cell:
Where Scorpions may my limbes entwine.
O God! So thou forgive me hell.

Aeternitie! when I thinke thee,
(Which never any end must have,
Nor knew'st beginning) and fore-see
Hell is design'd for sinne a grave.

My frighted flesh trembles to dust,
My blood ebbes fearefully away:
Both guilty that they did to lust
And vanity, my youth betray.

My eyes, which from each beautious sight
Drew Spider-like blacke venome in:
Close like the marigold at night
Opprest with dew to bath my sin.

My eares shut up that easie dore
Which did proud fallacies admit:
And vow to heare no follies more;
Deafe to the charmes of sinne and wit.

My hands (which when they toucht some faire,
Imagin'd such an excellence,
As th' Ermines skin ungentle were)
Contract themselves, and loose all sence.

But you bold sinners! still pursue
Your valiant wickednesse, and brave
Th' Almighty Iustice: hee'le subdue
And make you cowards in the grave.

Then when he as your judge appeares,
In vaine you'le tremble and lament.
And hope to soften him with teares,
40   To no advantage penitent.

Then will you scorne those treasures, which
So fiercely now you doate upon:
Then curse those pleasures did bewitch
You to this sad illusion.

The neighb'ring mountaines which you shall
Wooe to oppresse you with their weight:
Disdainefull will deny to fall;
By a sad death to ease your fate.

In vaine some midnight storme at sea
50   To swallow you, you will desire:
In vaine upon the wheele youle pray
Broken with torments to expire.

Death, at the sight of which you start,
In a mad fury then you'le Court:
Yet hate th' expressions of your heart,
Which onely shall be sigh'd for sport.

No sorrow then shall enter in
With pitty the great judges eares.
This moment's ours. Once dead, his sin
60   Man cannot expiate with teares.

JOHN MILTON (1608–74)

Vergine bella was not translated by any English poet before the eighteenth century. Milton is the only poet to attempt to reproduce the rhyme scheme (including the medial rhyme of line 13; shown below). That he should have used it for his 'Upon the Circumcision' must have satisfied his puritan instinct for taking from Mary to give to the Son. Text from *Poems* (1645).

P366: *Vergine bella, che di sol vestita*

Upon the Circumcision

Ye flaming Powers and winged Warriors bright,	*a*
That erst with Music and triumphant song	*b*
First heard by happy watchful Shepheards' ear,	*c*
So sweetly sung your Joy the Clouds along	*b*
Through the soft silence of the list'ning night,	*a*
Now mourn; and, if sad share with us to bear	*c*
Your fiery essence can distill no tear,	*c*
Burn in your sighs, and borrow	*d*
Seas wept from our deep sorrow:	*d*
10 He, who with all Heav'n's heraldry whilere	*c*
Enter'd the world, now bleeds to give us ease	*e*
Alas, how soon our sin	*f*
Sore doth begin	*f*
His Infancy to seize!	*e*
O more exceeding love or law more just?	*a*
Just law indeed, but more exceeding love!	*b*
For we by rightful doom remediless	*c*
Were lost in death, till he that dwelt above	*b*
High-thron'd in secret bliss, for us frail dust	*a*
20 Emptied his glory, ev'n to nakedness;	*c*
And that great Cov'nant which we still transgress	*c*

Entirely satisfi'd,   *d*
And the full wrath beside   *d*
Of vengeful Justice bore for our excess   *c*
And seals obedience first with wounding smart   *e*
This day; but Oh! Ere long   *f*
  Huge pangs and strong   *f*
    Will pierce more near his heart.   *e*

WILLIAM CARTWRIGHT
(1611–43)

Cartwright was one of 'The Tribe of Ben' Jonson. He was educated
at Westminster School and Christ Church, Oxford. He took Holy
Orders and was made Reader in Metaphysics at Christ Church. Text
from *Comedies, Tragi-comedies, with other Poems* (1651).

P153: *Ite, caldi sospiri, al freddo core*

Absence

Fly, O fly sad Sigh, and bear
These few Words into his Ear;
Blest where e'r thou dost remain,
Worthier of a softer chain,
Still I live, if it be true
The Turtle lives that's cleft in two
Tears and Sorrows I have store,
But O thine do grieve me more;
Dye I would, but that I do
10 Fear my Fate would kill thee too.

THOMAS STANLEY (1625–78)

After his education at Pembroke Hall, Cambridge, Stanley travelled before retiring to lodgings in the Middle Temple for a life of leisure and benevolence towards his literary friends. He was primarily a translator and imitator. In his later life, he returned to scholarship, and is credited with writing the first history of philosophy in English (1655–62). Text from *Poems and Translations* (1647).

P324: *Amor, quando fioria*

On His Mistresse's Death

Love the Ripe Harvest of my toils
Began to cherish with his Smiles
Preparing me to be indued
With all the Joyes I long pursued,
When my fresh Hopes fair and full blown
Death blasts ere I could call my own.

Malicious Death why with rude Force
Dost thou my fair from me divorce?
False Life why in this loathed Chain
Me from my fair dost thou detain?
In whom assistance shall I Finde?
Alike are life and Death unkinde.

Pardon me Love thy power outshines,
And laughs at their infirm designes.
She is not wedded to a Tomb,
Nor I to sorrow in her room.
They what thou joyn'st can nere divide:
She lives in me in her I dy'd.

JOHN DRYDEN (1631–1700)

Poet-laureate, dramatist, and the most financially successful poet before Alexander Pope, Dryden did not specifically translate Petrarch nor write sonnets, but these three songs are deeply entrenched in the Petrarchan mode, especially the 'wet dream' of the third. Text from *The Conquest of Granada* (1672).

Song

WHEREVER I am, and whatever I doe;
   My *Phillis* is still in my mind:
When angry I mean not to *Phillis* to goe,
   My Feet of themselves the way find:
Unknown to my self I am just at her door,
And when I would raile, I can bring out no more,
   Than *Phillis* too fair and unkind!

When *Phillis* I see, my Heart bounds in my Breast,
   And the Love I would stifle is shown:
But asleep, or awake, I am never at rest
   When from my Eyes *Phillis* is gone!
Sometimes a sweet Dream does delude my sad mind,
But, alas, when I wake and no *Phillis* I find
   How I sigh to my self all alone.

Should a King be my Rival in her I adore
   He should offer his Treasure in vain:
O let me alone to be happy and poor,
   And give me my *Phillis* again:
Let *Phillis* be mine, and for ever be kind
I could to a Desart with her be confin'd,
   And envy no Monarch his Raign.

Alas, I discover too much of my Love,
  And she too well knows her own power!
She makes me each day a new Martyrdom prove,
  And makes me grow jealous each hour:
But let her each minute torment my poor mind
I had rather love *Phillis* both False and Unkind,
  Then ever be freed from her Pow'r.

Song, *In Two Parts*

He. How unhappy a Lover am I
  While I sigh for my *Phillis* in vain;
All my hopes of Delight
Are another man's Right,
  Who is happy while I am in pain!

She. Since her Honour allows no Relief,
  But to pity the pains which you bear,
'Tis the best of your Fate,
(In a hopeless Estate,)
10   To give o're, and betimes to despair.

He. I have try'd the false Med'cine in vain;
  For I wish what I hope not to win:
From without, my desire
Has no Food to its Fire,
  But it burns and consumes me within.

She. Yet at least 'tis a pleasure to know
  That you are not unhappy alone:
For the Nymph you adore
Is as wretched and more,
20   And accounts all your suff'rings her own.

He. O ye Gods, let me suffer for both;
   At the feet of my *Phillis* I'le lye:
I'le resign up my Breath,
And take pleasure in Death,
   To be pity'd by her when I dye.

She. What her Honour deny'd you in Life
   In her Death she will give to your Love.
Such a Flame as is true
After Fate will renew,
30   For the Souls to meet closer above.

Song

   BENEATH a Myrtle shade
Which love for none but happy Lovers made,
I slept, and straight my Love before me brought
Phillis the object of my waking thought;
Undress'd she came my flames to meet,
While love strow'd flow'rs beneath her feet;
Flow'rs, which so press'd by her, became more sweet.

   From the bright Vision's head
A careless veil of lawn was loosely spread:
10   From her white temples fell her shaded hair,
Like cloudy sunshine not too brown nor fair:
Her hands, her lips did love inspire;
Her every grace my heart did fire:
But most her eyes which languish'd with desire.

   Ah, Charming fair, said I,
How long can you my bliss and yours deny?
By Nature and by love this lonely shade
Was for revenge of suffering Lovers made:

Silence and shades with love agree:
20   Both shelter you and favour me;
You cannot blush because I cannot see.

No, let me dye, she said,
Rather than loose the spotless name of Maid:
Faintly methought she spoke, for all the while
She bid me not believe her, with a smile.
Then dye said I, she still deny'd:
And is it thus, thus, thus she cried
You use a harmless Maid, and so she died!

I wak'd, and straight I knew
30   I lov'd so well it made my dream prove true:
Fancy, the kinder Mistress of the two,
Fancy had done what *Phillis* wou'd not do!
Ah, cruel nymph, cease your disdain,
While I can dream you scorn in vain;
Asleep or waking you must ease my pain.

PHILIP AYRES (1638–1712)

A friend of Dryden and 'prolific translator from several languages, and almost the only English translator from the *Canzoniere* in the period 1625–1765. His versions are loose and sentimental, and apparently designed to be sung' (Watson, *English Petrarchans*, p. 7). That he converted P19, a sonnet, into a sestina shows his interest in Petrarchan form for its own sake. From *Lyric Poems Made in Imitation of the Italians* (1687); text from *Bohn's Illustrated Library* (1859).

P132: *S'amor non è, che dunque è quel ch'io sento?*

A Sonnet. Of Love

If Love it be not, what is this I feel?
   If it be Love, what Love is, fain I'd know?
If good, why the effects severe and ill?
   If bad, why do its torments please me so?

If willingly I burn, should I complain?
   If 'gainst my will, what helps it to lament?
Oh living Death! oh most delightful pain!
   How comes all this, if I do not consent?

If I consent, 'tis madness then to grieve;
   Amidst these storms, in a weak Boat I'm tost
Upon a dangerous Sea, without relief
   No help from Reason, but in Error lost.

Which way in this distraction shall I turn,
That freeze in Summer, and in Winter burn?

P106: *Nova angeletta sovra l'ale accorta*

The Pleas'd Captive

A Glorious Angel coming on the Wing,
   From Heav'n descended near a River side,
Where me alone my Destiny did bring;
   To view the pleasant Fields without a Guide;
A Net she'd laid, drawn by a silken String,
   So hid in grass, it could not be espy'd,
   There was I captive taken in her snare,
   But *Cynthia's* chains who would not chuse to wear?

P121: *Or vedi, Amor, che giovenetta donna*

Revenge against Cynthia

See, Cupid, we have found our lovely foe,
  Who slights thy pow'r and does my flame despise,
Now thou art arm'd with all thy shafts and bow,
  And she at mercy 'twixt two enemies.

Asleep she's laid upon this bed of flowers,
  Her charms the sole defence to save her breast;
Thoughtless of injur'd me, or of thy powers;
  Oh, that guilty soul can take such rest!

Now may'st thou eas'ly with a single dart
10 Revenge thyself, and me, upon her heart.

P134: *Pace non trovo, e non ò da far guerra*

Love's Contrariety

I make no war, and yet no peace have found,
With heat I melt, when starv'd to death with cold.
I soar to heav'n, while grovelling on the ground,
Embrace the world, yet nothing do I hold.

I'm not confin'd, yet cannot I depart,
Nor loose the chain, tho' not a captive led;
Love kills me not, yet wounds me to the heart,
Will neither have m' alive, nor have me dead.

Being blind, I see; not having voice, I cry:
10 I wish for Death, while I of Life make choice:
I hate myself, yet love you tenderly;

Do feed of tears, and in my grief rejoice.
Thus, Cynthia, all my health is but disease;
Both life and death do equally displease.

P355: *O tempo, o ciel volubil, che fuggendo*

The Resolution

Oh Time! Oh rolling heavens, that fly so fast,
And cheat us mortals ignorant and blind!
Oh fugitive Day, swifter than bird or wind!
Your frauds I see, by all my suff'rings past.

But pardon me, 'tis I myself must blame,
Nature that spreads your wings, and makes you fly,
To me give eyes, that I my ills might spy:
Yet I retain'd them to my grief, and shame.

Time was I might, and Time is still I may
Direct my steps in a securer way,
And end this sad infinity of ill;
Yet 'tis not from thy yoke, O Love, I part,
But the effects; I will reclaim my heart:
Virtue's no chance, but is acquir'd by skill.

P19: *Son animali al mondo de sí altera*

A Sestina, in Imitation of Sig. Fra. Petrarca

So many creatures live not in the sea,
Nor e'er above the circle of the Moon,
Did man behold so many stars at night,
Nor little birds do shelter in the woods,
Nor herbs, nor flow'rs e'er beautified the fields;
As anxious thoughts my heart feels ev'ry day.

I, wishing Death, pray each may be the day,
And seek in vain for quiet in the fields,
My griefs succeed like waves upon the sea;
Such torments sure, no man beneath the Moon
E'er felt as I; 'tis known amongst the woods,
Where to complain I oft retire at night.

I never could enjoy a quiet night,
And do in pain and sorrow spend the day,
Since angry Cynthia drove me to the woods;
Yet e'er I quit my Love I'll weep a sea:
The Sun his light shall borrow of the Moon,
And May with flowers refuse to deck the fields.

Restless I wander up and down the fields,
And scarce can close my eyes to sleep at night:
So that my life's unstable as the moon,
The air I fill with sights both night and day;
My show'rs of tears seem to augment the sea,
make the herbs green, and to refresh the woods.

I hating cities, ramble in the woods,
And thence I shift to solitary fields,
I rove and imitate the troubled sea,
And hope most quiet in the silent night.
So that I wish at the approach of day,
The Sun would set, and give his place to th'Moon.

Oh, that like him who long had lov'd the Moon,
I could in dreams be happy in the woods;
I'd wish an end to this most glorious day,
Then should I meet my Cynthia in the fields,
Court her, and entertain her all the night;
The day should stop, and Sol swell in the sea.

By day nor night, sea, moon, nor wood, nor field
Now Cynthia frowns, can ease or pleasure yeild.

P275: *Occhi miei, oscurato è 'l nostro sole*

A Sonnet, of Petrarc, going to visit M. Laura

Oh eyes! Our Sun's extinct, and at an end,
or rather florified in Heav'n does shine;
There shall we see her, there does she attend,
And at our long delay perchance repine.

Alas, my ears, the voice you lov'd to hear,
Is now rais'd up to the cœlestial choir;
And you, my feet, she's gone that us'd to steer
Your course, where you till death can ne'er aspire.

Cannot my soul nor body yet be free?
'Twas not my fault, you this occasion lost;
That seeing, hearing, finding her y' are crost:
Blame Death, or rather blest be ever He,

who binds and looses, makes and can destroy,
And, when Life's done, crowns with Eternal joy.

P145: *Ponmi ove 'l sole occide i fiori e l'erba*

Constancy

Place me where Sol dries up the flow'ry fields,
or where he to the frosty winter yields:
Place me where he does mod'rate heat dispense,
And where his beams have a kind influence:

Place me in humble state, or place me high,
In a dark clime, or a serener sky;
Place me where days or nights are short or long,
In age mature, or be it old or young:

Place me in Heav'n, on earth, or in the main,
10   on a high hill, low vale, or level plain:
Let me have vigorous parts, or dullness have;
Place me in liberty, or as a slave:

Give me a black, or an illustrious fame:
As I have liv'd, I'll ever live the same;
Where I at first did fix my constant love,
Nothing from Cynthia can it e'er remove.

BASIL KENNET (1674–1715)

Kennet was Fellow of and, in his last years, President of Corpus Christi,
Oxford. He was named Chaplain to the British factory at Leghorn
(Livorno) in 1706, but ill health forced his return to England. He
published books on Roman antiquities, the lives of the Greek poets,
theological subjects and translations from the French. Text from *Bohn's
Illustrated Library* (1859).

P4: *Que' ch' infinita providenzia et arte*

He Celebrates the Birthplace of Laura

HE, that with wisdom, goodness, power divine,
Did ample Nature's perfect book design,
Adorn'd this beauteous world, and those above,
Kindled fierce Mars, and soften'd milder Jove:
When seen on earth the shadows to fulfill
Of the less volume which conceal'd his will,
Took John and Peter from their homely care,
And made them pillars of his temple fair.

Nor in imperial Rome would He be born,
Whom servile Judah yet received with scorn:
E'en Bethlehem could her infant King disown,
And the rude manger was his early throne.
Victorious sufferings did his pomp display,
Nor other chariot or triumphal way.
At once by Heaven's example and decree,
Such honour waits on such humility.

P99: *Poi, che voi et io più volte abbiam provato*

FRIEND, as we both in confidence complain
To see our ill-placed hopes return in vain,
Let that chief good which must for ever please
Exalt our thought and fix our happiness.
This world as some gay flowery field is spread,
Which hides a serpent in its painted bed,
And most it wounds when most it charms our eyes,
At once the tempter and the paradise.
And would you, then, sweet peace of mind restore,
And in fair calm expect your parting hour,
Leave the mad train, and court the happy few.
Well may it be replied, 'O friend, you show
Others the path, from which so often you
Have stray'd, and now stray farther than before.'

Eighteenth Century

JAMES CAULFEILD, EARL OF CHARLEMONT (1728–99)

Caulfeild was an Irish statesman; he translated 21 sonnets in *Select Sonnets of Petrarch* (1822). Text from *Bohn's Illustrated Library* (1859).

P218: *Tra quantunque leggiadre donne e belle*

WHENE'ER amidst the damsels, blooming bright,
She shows herself, whose like was never made,
At her approach all other beauties fade,
As at morn's orient glow the gems of night.
Love seems to whisper, – 'While to mortal sight
Her graces shall on earth be yet display'd,
Life shall be blest; 'till soon with her decay'd,
The virtues, and my reign shall sink outright.'
Of moon and sun, should nature rob the sky,
10   The air of winds, the earth of herbs and leaves,
Mankind of speech and intellectual eye,
The ocean's bed of fish, and dancing waves;
Even so shall all things dark and lonely lye,
When of her beauty Death the world bereaves!

P248: *Chi vuol veder quantunque pò, Natura*

Whoever Beholds Her Must Admit That His Praises Cannot Reach Her Perfection

WHO wishes to behold the utmost might
Of Heaven and Nature, on her let him gaze,
Sole sun, not only in my partial lays.
But to the dark world, blind to virtue's light!
And let him haste to view; for death in spite
The guilty leaves, and on the virtuous preys;
For this loved angel heaven impatient stays;
And mortal charms are transient as they're bright!
Here shall he see, if timely he arrive,
Virtue and beauty, royalty of mind,
In one bless'd union join'd. Then shall he say
That vainly my weak rhymes to praise her strive,
Whose dazzling beams have struck my genius blind. –
He must for ever weep if he delay!

P310: *Zefiro torna e 'l bel tempo rimena*

ZEPHYR returns and winter's rage restrains,
With herbs, with flowers, his blooming progeny!
Now Progne prattles, Philomel complains,
And spring assumes her robe of various dye;
The meadows smile, heaven glows, nor Jove disdains
To view his daughter with delighted eye;
While Love through universal nature reigns,
And life is fill'd with amorous sympathy!

But grief, not joy, returns to me forlorn,
10   And sighs, which from my inmost heart proceed
For her, by whom to heaven its keys were borne.
The song of birds, the flower-enamell'd mead,
And graceful acts, which most the fair adorn,
A desert seem, and beasts of savage prey!

P311: *Quel rosignuol che sì soave piagne*

THAT nightingale, who now melodious mourns
Perhaps his children or his consort dear,
The heavens with sweetness fills; the distant bourns
Resound his notes, so piteous and so clear;
With me all night he weeps, and seems by turns
To upbraid me with my fault and fortune drear,
Whose fond and foolish heart, where grief sojourns,
A goddess deem'd exempt from mortal fear.
Security, how easy to betray!
10   The radiance of those eyes who could have thought
Should e'er become a senseless clod of clay?
Living, and weeping, late I've learn'd to say
That here below – Oh, knowledge dearly bought! –
Whate'er delights will scarcely last a day!

JOHN LANGHORNE (1735–79)

According to Watson, *English Petrarchans*, p. 10, Langhorne was a
Somerset clergyman, who also translated Plutarch (1770). His *Poetical
Works*, from which these two poems come, was published in 1766.
Note that 'Where is that face . . .' contains only 12 lines.

P269: *Rotta è l'alta colonna e 'l verde lauro*

FALL'N the fair column, blasted is the bay,
That shaded once my solitary shore!
I've lost what hope can never give me more,
Though sought from Indus to the closing day.
My twofold treasure death has snatch'd away,
My pride, my pleasure, left me to deplore:
What fields far-cultur'd, nor imperial sway,
Nor orient gold, nor jewels can restore.
O destiny severe of human kind!
10   What portion have we unbedew'd with tears?
The downcast visage and the pensive mind
Through the thin veil of smiling life appears;
And in one moment vanish into wind
The hard-earn'd fruits of long laborious years.

P299: *Ov'è la fronte che con picciol cenno*

WHERE is that face, whose slightest air could move
My trembling heart, and strike the springs of love?
That heaven, where two fair stars, with genial ray,
Shed their kind influence on life's dim way?
Where are that science, sense, and worth confest,
That speech by virtue, by the graces drest?
Where are those beauties, where those charms combin'd,
That caus'd this long captivity of mind?
Where the dear shade of all that once was fair,
10   The source, the solace, of each amorous care;
My heart's sole sovereign, nature's only boast?
— Lost to the world, to me for ever lost!

REVEREND WILLIAM COLLIER (1743–1803)

Clergyman and Senior Fellow of Trinity College, Cambridge, Collier translated six of Petrarch's sonnets in the second volume of his *Poems on Various Occasions* (1800).

P263: *Arbor vittoriosa, triunfale*

Tree of triumphant victory! whose leaf
For bards and heroes forms the glorious crown,
How many days of blended joy and grief
Have I from thee, through life's short passage known?

Lady most noble! Who in Virtue's field
Reapest unrivall'd honour, all thy care;
To thee must Love his arts insidious yield,
Whose calm discretion sees, and scorns the snare.

The pride of birth, with all that here we hold
Most precious, sparkling gems or massy gold,
Abject alike in thy regard appear
Nay e'en thy charms, the world's fix'd wonder raise
No joy in thee, but as their splendours blaze
From Chastity's true light, serenely clear.

SIR BROOKE BOOTHBY
(1743–1824)

Boothby was a member of the literary society at Lichfield (including Anna Seward, Erasmus Darwin and the Edgeworths) and a friend of Rousseau, whom he defended against the attack of Edmund Burke. He translated Racine's *Britannicus*. Sonnet 21 from *Sorrows Sacred to the Memory of Penelope* (1796), written after his daughter Penelope died at the age of four. Poor Penelope must be the youngest Laura-surrogate in this volume.

P312: *Né per sereno ciel ir vaghe stelle*

Not silvery stars that gem the robe of night;
Nor painted vessels, bounding o'er the main;
Nor gallant bands of warriours on the plain;
Nor theatres, in gorgeous pomp bedight;
   Not labour's song, that makes the task sem light;
Nor tales of love, in high and artful strain;
Nor by fresh fountain's side, the virgin train,
Winning the ear with accents of delight;
   Can charm my sorrows: to these weary eyes,
The world is one vast desert, wild and drear;
Dead, like my hopes, all Nature's works appear;
   And sunk the sun of joy, no more to rise.
The step of Grace, and Beauty's radiant bloom,
Are but mementos of the mouldering tomb.

SIR WILLIAM JONES (1746–94)

Jones was the most noted Orientalist of his time and the first English scholar to master Sanskrit. He was a jurist in India, and was reputed to have known thirteen languages thoroughly and twenty-eight fairly well. Text from *Poems* (1772).

P126: *Chiare, fresche et dolci acque*

An Ode of Petrarch, to the Fountain of Valchiusa

Ye clear and sparkling streams,
    Warm'd by the sunny beams,
Through whose transparent crystal Laura play'd:
    Ye boughs, that deck the grove,
    Where Spring her chaplets wove,
While Laura lay beneath the quivering shade;
    Sweet herbs, and blushing flowers,
    That crown yon vernal bowers
For ever fatal, yet for ever dear;
10   And ye, that heard my sighs
    When first she charm'd my eyes,
Soft-breathing gales, my dying accents hear.
    If heaven has fix'd my doom,
    That Love must quite consume
My bursting heart, and close my eyes in death;
    Ah! grant this slight request,
    That here my urn may rest
When to its mansion flies my vital breath.
    This pleasing hope will smooth
20   My anxious mind, and sooth
The pangs of that inevitable hour;
    My spirit will not grieve
    Her mortal veil to leave

In these calm shades, and this enchanting bower.
   Haply the guilty maid
   Through yon accustom'd glade
To my sad tomb will take her lonely way;
   Where first her beauty's light
   O'erpower'd my dazzled sight,
30 When Love on this fair border bade me stray;
   There sorrowing shall she see,
   Beneath an aged tree,
Her true but hapless lover's lowly bier;
   Too late her tender sighs
   Shall melt the pitying skies,
And her soft veil shall hide the gushing tear.
   O! well-remember'd day,
   When on yon bank she lay,
Meek in her pride, and in her rigour mild;
40   The young and blooming flowers
   Falling in fragrant showers,
Shone on her neck, and on her bosom smil'd:
   Some on her mantle hung,
   Some in her locks were strung,
Like orient gems in rings of flaming gold;
   Some, in a spicy cloud
   Descending, call'd aloud
'Here Love and Youth the reins of empire hold.'
   I view'd the heavenly maid;
50   And, rapt in wonder, said
'The groves of Eden gave this angel birth;'
   Her look, her voice, her smile,
   That might all heaven beguile,
Wafted my soul above the realms of earth:
   The star-bespangled skies
   Were open'd to my eyes;
Sighing I said 'Whence rose this glittering scene?'
   Since that auspicious hour,
   This bank, and odorous bower,

60   My morning couch, and evening haunt, have been.
    Well mayst thou blush, my song,
    To leave the rural throng,
And fly thus artless to my Laura's ear;
    But were thy poet's fire
    Ardent as his desire,
Thou wert a song that heaven might stoop to hear.

ALEXANDER FRASER TYTLER, LORD WOODHOUSELEE (1747–1813)

Edinburgh judge and Augustan poet, Woodhouselee was prompted to translate some dozen sonnets to disprove the Abbé de Sade's contention that Laura was a married woman and the mother of eleven children (Watson, *English Petrarchans*, p. 13). The following poem is from *An Historical and Critical Essay on the Life and Character of Petrarch, with a Translation of a Few of his Sonnets* (1812); text from *Bohn's Illustrated Library* (1859).

P292: *Gli occhi di ch'io parlai sí caldamente*

Those eyes whose living lustre shed the heat
Of bright meridian day; the heavenly mould
Of that angelic form; the hands, the feet,
The taper arms, the crispèd locks of gold;
Charms that the sweets of paradise enfold;
The radiant lightning of her angel-smile,
And every grace that could the sense beguile
Are now a pile of ashes, deadly cold!
And yet I bear to drag this cumbrous chain,
10   That weighs my soul to earth – to bliss or pain

Alike insensible: − her anchor lost,
The frail dismantled bark, all tempest-toss'd,
Surveys no port of comfort − closed the scene
Of life's delusive joys; − and dry the Muse's vein.

CHARLOTTE TURNER SMITH
(1749−1806)

A Sussex poet and novelist, much admired by Elizabeth Barrett Browning, Smith's *Elegiac Sonnets* (1784), from which this poem is taken, ran through eleven editions by 1851, and was expanded into two volumes in 1797 (Watson, *English Petrarchans*, p. 12).

P90: *Erano i capei d'oro a l'aura sparsi*

LOOSE to the wind her golden tresses stream'd,
　　Forming bright waves with amorous Zephyr's sighs;
And, tho averted now her charming eyes
　　Then with warm Love, and melting Pity beam'd.
Was I deceiv'd? Ah! surely, Nymph divine,
　　That fine suffusion on thy cheek was Love;
What wonder then those beauteous tints should move,
　　Should fire, this Heart, this tender heart of mine?
Thy soft melodious voice, thy air, thy shape,
10　　Were of a Goddess − not a mortal Maid;
Yet though thy Charms, thy heavenly charms, should fade,
　　My Heart, my tender Heart, could not escape;
Nor cure for me in time or change be found:
The Dart extracted does not cure the Wound.

CAPEL LOFFT (1751–1824)

Laura, or an Anthology of Sonnets (5 vols., 1813–14) was the most ambitious collection of sonnets before Bohn: 250 sonnets in each of the four volumes of text, many of the translations by Capel Lofft himself, and his wife, Sarah Watson Finch. His inclusion of an original sonnet on the nature of women sonneteers indicates the degree to which sonneteering had recaptured the imagination of the early nineteenth century, and how closely this phenomenon still looked to Petrarch as its source. Lofft's talents as a translator have been undervalued. Text from *Laura*.

318. On the Sonnets by Female Authors

I CULL'D whate'er the TUSCAN MUSE had wove
  Of tenderest Elegance and highest Grace,
  In her bright Fane of Constancy to place
By SORGA'S Bank, VALCLUSA's aweful grove:
The Work and Triumph of mysterious LOVE;
  Poetic texture, which Time's chill embrace
  Robs not of gloss, nor Centuries efface
Its finest tints, but still their charms improve.

When from the Tomb the Shade of LAURA sigh'd
10   Most sweet – the heaven-breath'd Accents soothe my ear
With Melody to mortal sense denied.
  'Not PETRARCH only latest Times shall hear;
'His praise of LAURA shall her Sex inspire;
'They emulative wake the immortal TUSCAN LYRE.'

7 Aug 1805. C.L.

28. To Mrs. Lofft, on a sonnet compos'd by her on the day of Petrarch's birth, xxiv Jul.

LOV'D SONGSTRESS! who on PETRARCH's parting
    DAY
  Dear to the MUSE of the soft plaintive LYRE
  Hast breathed such strains as might his Dust inspire
With sense, – although his LAURA sleeps in clay, –
That *still* survives the pure celestial Ray
  Which in his breast waken'd the sacred Fire
  Of tender, elegant, and high Desire
And bade his numbers wing to Heaven their Way.

Dear be THAT DAY to us! – Oft as the Hours
  Bring its return, – if Heaven so will, – to me,
    May it remind me what to Heaven I owe
For thy mild sweetness, thy poetic Powers;
  For every source of purest Bliss in Thee:
    And never o'er this thought may chill Oblivion flow!

                     24 Jul. 1803. C.L.

Nacque PETRARCA à di xx dì LUGLIO; MCCCIV;
Passò poi a più felice Vita à dì xviii di LUGLIO;
MCCCLXXIV.

[Petrarch was born on the 20th day of July, 1304; he then
passed to a happier life on the 18th of July, 1374.]

p280: *Mai non fui in parte ove sì chiar vedessi*

Elegiac TRANSLATED: and Address'd to Miss Sarah Watson Finch

NEVER till now so clearly have I seen
   Her, whom my eyes desire, my Soul still views:
Never enjoy'd a freedom thus serene;
   Ne'er thus to Heaven breath'd my enamour'd Muse:
As in this Vale sequester'd, darkly green;
   Where my sooth'd heart [its] pensive thought pursues;
And nought intrusively may intervene;
   And all my sweetly tender sighs renews.

To Love and Meditation faithful Shade
     Receive the breathings of my grateful breast!
      Love not in Cyprus found so sweet a Nest
As this, by Pine and arching Laurel made!
The Birds, breeze, water, branches, whisper, LOVE;
Herb, flower, and verdant path the lay symphonious move.

                27 Aug. 1801. C.L.

10

JOHN NOTT (1751–1825)

Nott, a physician and classical scholar from Bristol, published his *Petrarch translated in a Selection of his Sonnets and Odes* in 1807–8. Text from *Bohn's Illustrated Library* (1859).

P7: *La gola e 'l sonno e l'oziose piume*

INTEMPERANCE, slumber, and the slothful down
Have chased each virtue from this world away;
Hence is our nature nearly led astray
From its due course, by habitude o'erthrown;
Those kindly lights of heaven so dim are grown,
Which shed o'er human life instruction's ray;
That him with scornful wonder they survey,
Who would draw forth the stream of Helicon.
'Whom doth the laurel please, or myrtle now?
Naked and poor, Philosophy, art thou!'
The worthless crowd, intent on lucre, cries.
Few on thy chosen road will thee attend;
Yet let it more incite thee, gentle friend,
To prosecute thy high-conceived emprize.

P156: *I' vidi in terra angelici costumi*

Yes, I beheld on earth angelic grace,
And charms divine which mortals rarely see,
Such as both glad and pain the memory;
Vain, light, unreal is all else I trace:
Tears I saw shower'd from those fine eyes apace,
Of which the sun ofttimes might envious be;
Accents I heard sigh'd forth so movingly,
As to stay floods, or mountains to displace.
Love and good sense, firmness, with pity join'd
And wailful grief, a sweeter concert made
Than ever yet was pour'd on human ear:
And heaven unto the music so inclined,
That not a leaf was seen to stir the shade;
Such melody had fraught the winds, the atmosphere.

MARY ROBINSON (1758–1800)

Pupil of David Garrick and mistress of George IV, Robinson's main claim to our attention is her sonnet sequence, *Sappho and Phaon* (1796), which tells the story of Sappho's rejected love for Phaon and her eventual suicide. Although no sonnet is a direct translation of any Petrarchan sonnet, Robinson 'regenders' the idea of the Petrarchan sequence with the added innovation of a suicide. Her sonnet of Laura to Petrarch expresses the reinvention of the lady's voice. She was the empress of the exclamation point! Text from *Sappho and Phaon*.

42. Her Last Appeal to Phaon

While from the dizzy precipice I gaze,
  The world receding from my pensive eyes,
  High o'er my head the tyrant eagle flies,
Cloth'd in the sinking sun's transcendent blaze!
The meek-ey'd moon, 'midst clouds of amber plays,
  As o'er the purpling plains of light she hies,
  Till the last stream of living lustre dies,
And the cool concave owns her temper'd rays!
  So shall this glowing, palpitating soul,
10 Welcome returning reason's placid beam,
  While o'er my breast the waves Lethean roll,
To calm rebellious fancy's fev'rish dream;
  Then shall my lyre disdain love's dread control,
And loftier passions prompt the loftier theme!

44. Conclusive

Here droops the Muse! while from her glowing mind,
  Celestial sympathy, with humid eye,
  Bids the light sylph, capricious fancy, fly,
Time's restless wings with transient flow'rs to bind!

For now, with folded arms and head inclin'd,
 Reflection pours the deep and frequent sigh,
 O'er the dark scroll of human destiny,
Where gaudy buds and wounding thorns are twin'd.
 O! sky-born VIRTUE! sacred is thy name!
10 And though mysterious Fate, with frown severe,
 Oft decorates thy brows with wreaths of fame,
Bespangled o'er with sorrow's chilling tear!
 Yet shalt thou more than mortal raptures claim,
The brightest planet of th' ETERNAL SPHERE!

Laura to Petrarch

O SOLITARY wand'rer! whither stray
 From the smooth path the dimpled pleasures love,
 From flow'ry meadow, and embow'ring grove,
Where hope and fancy smiling, lead the way!
To thee, I ween, full tedious seems the day;
 While lorn and slow the devious path you rove,
 Sighing soft sorrows on the garland wove
By young desire, of blossoms sweetly gay!
 Oh! blossoms! frail and fading! like the morn
10 Of love's first rapture! beauteous all, and pure,
 Deep hid beneath your charms lies mis'ry's thorn,
To bid the feeling breast a pang endure!
 Then check thy wand'rings, weary and forlorn,
And find in friendship's balm sick passions cure.

JOHN PENN (1760–1834)

John Penn, grandson of William Penn of Pennsylvania, became an
English MP. He was a litterateur and one of the most ardent translators
of Petrarch in the Regency period (Watson, *English Petrarchans*, pp. 11–
12). His *Poetical Miscellanies, including Translations from Petrarch*, from
which this sonnet is taken, came out in 1797.

P77: *Per mirar Policleto a prova fiso*

That master, Polycletus, and the rest
whom History boasts, exerting all their art
A thousand years, could only show a part
of the unrivalled grace that fires my breast;
But, surely, Simon, in the regions blessed,
Had seen the beauteous sovereign of my heart,
And thus, among the sons of earth, we start
To see her lineaments so fair expressed.
This face is of some being in the sky,
10   A semblance true; not one, like us, whose soul
Is veiled by cumbrous flesh from every eye:
My friend judged well, who could not form a whole
So various, where, less aided than on high,
The impediments of earth his sight control.

SIR SAMUEL EGERTON
BRYDGES (1762–1837)

Brydges, editor, printer, publisher of Lee Priory Press, caused much
trouble to Archdeacon Wrangham (see the next author), whose transla-
tions he published after a three year delay. Wrangham thought Brydges
plagiarized him in the 32 poems he translated. Brydges was proud of

his translations 'in Literal Prose', of which the following, from *Res Literariae* (vol. 1, 1821), is an example. Wrangham should never have complained.

P361: *Dicemi spesso il mio fidato speglio*

In Literal Prose

My faithful Mirror, my weary Spirit,
My altered countenance; my feeble address,
And my diminished strength, repeatedly say to me,
'Do not deceive yourself! Thou art no longer young!
It is better to obey Nature in every thing;
For, in disputing with her, we are overtaken by Time'
Then, as water extinguishes fire,
I awoke from my long, and heavy slumber,
And I clearly perceived that our life was passing away,
And that we can exist but once.
Sometimes from the inmost recesses of my heart I hear her
    voice,
Who is now free from her lovely earthly frame.
But whilst She dwelt among us, she was so preeminent that
(If I do not deceive myself,) She eclipsed all other women.

ARCHDEACON FRANCIS WRANGHAM (1767–1843)

Bookish clergyman and friend of Wordsworth, Archdeacon Wrangham had publishing difficulties with Sir Samuel Egerton Brydges (Watson, *English Petrarchans*, p. 13). These eight sonnets are taken from *A Few Sonnets Attempted from Petrarch in Early Life* (1817); text from *Bohn's Illustrated Library* (1859).

P12: *Se la mia vita da l'aspro tormento*

11. He Hopes That Time Will Render Her More Merciful

If o'er each bitter pang, each hidden throe
Sadly triumphant I my years drag on,
Till even the radiance of those eyes is gone,
Lady, which star-like now illume thy brow;
And silver'd are those locks of golden glow,
And wreaths and robes of green aside are thrown,
And from thy cheek those hues of beauty flown,
Which check'd so long the utterance of my woe,
Haply my bolder tongue may then reveal
10   The bosom'd annals of my heart's fierce fire,
The martyr-throbs that now in night I veil:
And should the chill Time frown on young Desire,
Still, still some late remorse that breast may feel,
And heave a tardy sigh – ere love with life expire.

P13: *Quando fra l'altre donne ad ora ad ora*

12. The Beauty of Laura Leads Him to the Contemplation of the Supreme Good

THRONED on her angel brow, when Love displays
His radiant form among all other fair,
Far as eclipsed their choicest charms appear,
I feel beyond its wont my passion blaze,
And still I bless the day, the hour, the place,
When first so high mine eyes I dared to rear;
And say, 'Fond heart, thy gratitude declare,
That then thou had'st the privilege to gaze.

'T was she inspired the tender thought of love,
10 Which points to heaven, and teaches to despise
The earthly vanities that others prize:
She gave the soul's light grace, which to the skies
Bids thee straight onward in the right path move;
Whence buoy'd by hope e'en now I soar to worlds above.'

P61: *Benedetto sia 'l giorno e 'l mese e l'anno*

47. He Blesses All the Circumstances of his Passion

BLEST be the day, and blest the month, the year,
The spring, the hour, the very moment blest,
The lovely scene, the spot, where first oppress'd
I sunk, of two bright eyes the prisoner:
And blest the first soft pang, to me most dear,
Which thrill'd my heart, when Love became its guest;
And blest the bow, the shafts which pierced my breast,
And even the wounds, which bosom'd thence I bear.
Blest too the strains which, pour'd through glade and grove,
10 Have made the woodlands echo with her name;
The sighs, the tears, the languishment, the love:
And blest those sonnets, sources of my fame;
And blest that thought – Oh! never to remove!
Which turns to her alone, from her alone which came.

P122: *Dicessette anni à già rivolto il cielo*

97. E'en in our Ashes Live our Wonted Fires

THE seventeenth summer now, alas! is gone,
And still with ardour unconsumed I glow;
Yet find, whene'er myself I seek to know,
Amidst the fire a frosty chill come on.

Truly 'tis said, 'Ere Habit quits her throne,
Years bleach the hair.' The senses feel life's snow,
But not less hot the tides of passion flow:
Such is our earthly nature's malison!
Oh! come the happy day, when doom'd to smart
10 No more from flames and lingering sorrows free,
Calm I may note how fast youth's minutes flew!
Ah! will it e'er be mine the hour to see,
When with delight, nor duty nor my heart
Can blame, these eyes once more that angel face may view?

P123: *Quel vago impallidir che 'l dolce riso*

98. Leave-Taking

THAT witching paleness, which with cloud of love
Veil'd her sweet smile, majestically bright,
So thrill'd my heart, that from the bosom's night
Midway to meet it on her face it strove.
Then learnt I how, 'mid realms of joy above,
The blest behold the blest: in such pure light
I scann'd her tender thought, to others' sight
Viewless! – but my fond glances would not rove.
Each angel grace, each lowly courtesy,
10 E'er traced in dame by Love's soft power inspired,
Would seem but foils to those which prompt my lay:
Upon the ground was cast her gentle eye,
And still methought, though silent, she inquired,
'What bears my faithful friend so soon, so far away?'

P163: *Amor, che vedi ogni pensero aperto*

130. He Cares Not for Sufferings, So That He Displease Not Laura

LOVE, thou who seest each secret thought display'd,
And the sad steps I take, with thee sole guide;
This throbbing breast, to thee thrown open wide,
To others' prying barr'd, thine eyes pervade.
Thou know'st what efforts, following thee, I made,
While still from height to height thy pinions glide;
Nor deign'st one pitying look to turn aside
On him who, fainting, treads a trackless glade.
I mark from far the mildly-beaming ray
To which thou goad'st me through the devious maze;
Alas! I want thy wings, to speed my way –
Henceforth, a distant homager, I'll gaze,
Content by silent longings to decay,
So that my sighs for her in her no anger raise.

P224: *S'una fede amorosa, un cor non finto*

188. The Misery of His Love

If fondest faith, a heart to guile unknown,
By melting languors the soft wish betray'd;
If chaste desires, with temper'd warmth display'd;
If weary wanderings, comfortless and lone;
If every thought in every feature shown,
Or in faint tones and broken sounds convey'd,
As fear or shame my pallid cheek array'd
In violet hues, with Love's thick blushes strown;

If more than self another to hold dear;
10 If still to weep and heave incessant sighs,
To feed on passion, or in grief to pine,
To glow when distant, and to freeze when near, –
If hence my bosom's anguish takes its rise,
Thine, lady, is the crime, the punishment is mine.

P243: *Fresco, ombroso, fiorito e verde colle*

205. He Congratulates His Heart on its Remaining With Her

O HILL with green o'erspread, with groves o'erhung!
Where musing now, now trilling her sweet lay,
Most like what bards of heavenly spirits say,
Sits she by fame through every region sung:
My heart, which wisely unto her has clung –
More wise, if there, in absence blest, it stay!
Notes now the turf o'er which her soft steps stray,
Now where her angel-eyes' mild beam is flung;
Then throbs and murmurs, as they onward rove,
10 'Ah! were he here, that man of wretched lot,
Doom'd but to taste the bitterness of love!'
She, conscious, smiles: our feelings tally not:
Heartless am I, mere stone; heaven is thy grove –
O dear delightful shade, O consecrated spot!

Nineteenth Century

BARBARINA OGLE BRAND,
LADY DACRE (1768–1854)

See headnote on p. 43. Text of P129 from Bohn; the others from the edition of her poems (1821).

P128: *Italia mia, benché 'l parlar sia indarno*

O MY own Italy! though words are vain
The mortal wounds to close,
Unnumber'd, that thy beauteous bosom stain,
Yet may it soothe my pain
To sigh forth Tyber's woes,
And Arno's wrongs, as on Po's sadden'd shore
Sorrowing I wander, and my numbers pour.
Ruler of heaven! By the all-pitying love
That could thy Godhead move
10   To dwell a lowly sojourner on earth,
Turn, Lord! on this thy chosen land thine eye:
See, God of Charity!
From what light cause this cruel war has birth;
And the hard hearts by savage discord steel'd,
Thou, Father! from on high,
Touch by my humble voice, that stubborn wrath may yield!

Ye, to whose sovereign hands the fates confide
Of this fair land the reins, –
(This land for which no pity wrings your breast) –
20   Why does the stranger's sword her plains invest?
That her green fields be dyed,
Hope ye, with blood from the Barbarians' veins?

Beguiled by error weak,
Ye see not, though to pierce so deep ye boast,
Who love, or faith, in venal bosoms seek:
When throng'd your standards most,
Ye are encompass'd most by hostile bands.
O hideous deluge gather'd in strange lands,
That rushing down amain
30   O'erwhelms our every native lovely plain!
Alas! if our own hands
Have thus our weal betray'd, who shall our cause sustain?

Well did kind Nature, guardian of our state,
Rear her rude alpine heights,
A lofty rampart against German hate;
But blind ambition, seeking his own ill,
With ever restless will,
To the pure gales contagion foul invites:
Within the same strait fold
40   The gentle flocks and wolves relentless throng,
Where still meek innocence must suffer wrong:
And these, – oh, shame avow'd! –
Are of the lawless hordes no tie can hold:
Fame tells how Marius' sword
Erewhile their bosoms gored, –
Nor has Time's hand aught blurr'd the record proud!
When they who, thirsting, stoop'd to quaff the flood,
With the cool waters mix'd, drank of a comrade's blood!

Great Caesar's name I pass, who o'er our plains
50   Pour'd forth the ensanguin'd tide,
Drawn by our own good swords from out their veins;
But now – nor know I what ill stars preside, –
Heaven holds this land in hate!
To you the thanks! – whose hands control her helm! –
You, whose rash feuds despoil
Of all the beauteous earth the fairest realm!

Are ye impell'd by judgment, crime, or fate,
To oppress the desolate?
From broken fortunes, and from humble toil,
60   The hard-earn'd dole to wring,
While from afar ye bring
Dealers in blood, bartering their souls for hire?
In truth's great cause I sing,
Nor hatred nor disdain my earnest lay inspire.

Nor mark ye yet, confirm'd by proof on proof,
Bavaria's perfidy,
Who strikes in mockery, keeping death aloof?
(Shame, worse than aught of loss, in honour's eye!)
While ye, with honest rage, devoted pour
70   Your inmost bosom's gore! –
Yet give one hour to thought,
And ye shall own, how little he can hold
Another's glory dear, who sets his own at nought
O Latin blood of old!
Arise, and wrest from obloquy thy fame,
Nor bow before a name
Of hollow sound, whose power no laws enforce!
For if barbarians rude
Have higher minds subdued,
80   Ours! ours the crime! – not such wise Nature's course.

Ah! is not this the soil my foot first press'd?
And here, in cradled rest,
Was I not softly hush'd? – here fondly rear'd?
Ah! is not this my country? – so endear'd
By every filial tie!
In whose lap shrouded both my parents lie!
Oh! by this tender thought,
Your torpid bosoms to compassion wrought,
Look on the people's grief!
90   Who, after God, of you expect relief;

And if ye but relent,
Virtue shall rouse her in embattled might,
Against blind fury bent,
Nor long shall doubtful hand the unequal fight;
For no, – the ancient flame
Is not extinguish'd yet, that raised the Italian name!

Mark, sovereign Lords! how Time, with pinion strong,
Swift hurries life along!
E'en now, behold! Death presses on the rear.
100 We sojourn here a day – the next, are gone!
The soul disrobed – alone,
Must shuddering seek the doubtful pass we fear.
Oh! at the dreaded bourne,
Abase the lofty brow of wrath and scorn,
(Storms adverse to the eternal calm on high!)
And ye, whose cruelty
Has sought another's harm, by fairer deed
Of heart, or hand, or intellect, aspire
To win the honest meed
110 Of just renown – the noble mind's desire!
Thus sweet on earth the stay!
Thus to the spirit pure, unbarr'd is Heaven's way!

My song! with courtesy, and numbers sooth,
Thy daring reasons grace,
For thou the mighty, in their pride of place,
Must woo to gentle ruth,
Whose haughty will long evil customs nurse,
Ever to truth averse!
Thee better fortunes wait,
120 Among the virtuous few – the truly great!
Tell them – but who shall bid my terrors cease?
Peace! Peace! on thee I call! return, O heaven-born Peace!

P129: *Di pensier in pensier, di monte in monte*

From hill to hill I roam, from thought to thought,
With Love my guide; the beaten path I fly,
For there in vain the tranquil life is sought;
If 'mid the waste well forth a lonely rill,
Or deep embosom'd a low valley lie,
In its calm shade my trembling heart is still;
And there, if Love so will,
I smile, or weep, or fondly hope, or fear,
While on my varying brow, that speaks the soul,
10   The wild emotions roll,
Now dark, now bright, as shifting skies appear;
That whosoe'er has proved the lover's state
Would say, He feels the flame, nor knows his future fate.

On mountains high, in forests drear and wide,
I find repose, and from the throng'd resort
Of man turn fearfully my eyes aside;
At each lone step thoughts ever new arise
Of her I love, who oft with cruel sport
Will mock the pangs I bear, the tears, the sighs;
20   Yet e'en these ills I prize,
Though bitter, sweet, nor would they were removed:
For my heart whispers me, Love yet has power
To grant a happier hour:
Perchance, though self-despised, thou yet art loved:
E'en then my breast a passing sigh will heave,
Ah! when, or how, may I a hope so wild believe?

Where shadows of high rocking pines dark wave
I stay my footsteps, and on some rude stone
With thought intense her beauteous face engrave;
30   Roused from the trance, my bosom bathed I find
With tears, and cry, Ah! whither thus alone

Hast thou far wander'd, and whom left behind?
But as with fixèd mind
On this fair image I impassion'd rest,
And, viewing her, forget awhile my ills,
Love my rapt fancy fills;
In its own error sweet the soul is blest,
While all around so bright the visions glide;
O! might the cheat endure, I ask not aught beside.

40   Her form portray'd within the lucid stream
Will oft appear, or on the verdant lawn,
Or glossy beech, or fleecy cloud, will gleam
So lovely fair, that Leda's self might say,
Her Helen sinks eclipsed, as at the dawn
A star when cover'd by the solar ray:
And, as o'er wilds I stray
Where the eye nought but savage nature meets,
There Fancy most her brightest tints employs;
But when rude truth destroys
50   The loved illusion of those dreamèd sweets,
I sit me down on the cold rugged stone,
Less cold, less dead than I, and think, and weep alone.

Where the huge mountain rears his brow sublime,
On which no neighbouring height its shadow flings,
Led by desire intense the steep I climb;
And tracing in the boundless space each woe,
Whose sad remembrance my torn bosom wrings,
Tears, that bespeak the heart o'erfraught, will flow:
While, viewing all below,
60   From me, I cry, what worlds of air divide
The beauteous form, still absent and still near!
Then, chiding soft the tear,
I whisper low, haply she too has sigh'd
That thou art far away: a thought so sweet
Awhile my labouring soul will of its burthen cheat.

Go thou, my song, beyond that Alpine bound,
Where the pure smiling heavens are most serene,
There by a murmuring stream may I be found,
Whose gentle airs around
70   Waft grateful odours from the laurel green;
Nought but my empty form roams here unblest,
There dwells my heart with her who steals it from my
        breast.

P292: *Gli occhi di ch'io parlai sí caldamente*

The eyes, the face, the limbs of heavenly mould,
So long the theme of my impassion'd lay,
Charms which so stole me from myself away,
That strange to other men the course I hold:
The crispèd locks of pure and lucid gold,
The lightning of the angelic smile, whose ray
To earth could all of paradise convey,
A little dust are now! – to feeling cold!
And yet I live! – but that I live bewail,
10   Sunk the loved light that through the tempest led
My shatter'd bark, bereft of mast and sail:
Hush'd be for aye the song that breathed love's fire!
Lost is the theme on which my fancy fed,
And turned to mourning my once tuneful lyre.

P312: *Né per sereno ciel ir vaghe stelle*

NOT skies serene, with glittering stars inlaid,
Nor gallant ships o'er tranquil ocean dancing,
Nor gay careering knights in arms advancing,
Nor wild herds bounding through the forest glade,
Nor tidings new of happiness delay'd,

Nor poesie, Love's witchery enhancing,
Nor lady's song beside clear fountain glancing,
In beauty's pride, with chastity array'd;
Nor aught of lovely, aught of gay in show,
10   Shall touch my heart, now cold within her tomb
Who was erewhile my life and light below!
So heavy – tedious – sad – my days unblest,
That I, with strong desire, invoke Death's gloom,
Her to behold, whom ne'er to have seen were best!

P315: *Tutta la mia fiorita e verde etade*

All my green years and golden prime of man
Had pass'd away, and with attemper'd sighs
My bosom heaved – ere yet the days arise
When life declines, contracting its brief span.
Already my loved enemy began
To lull suspicion, and in sportive guise,
With timid confidence, though playful, wise,
In gentle mockery my long pains to scan:
The hour was near when Love, at length, may mate
10   With chastity; and, by the dear one's side,
The lover's thoughts and words may freely flow:
Death saw, with envy, my too happy state,
E'en – its fair promise – and, with fatal pride,
Strode in the midway forth, an armèd foe!

THOMAS CAMPBELL (1777–1844)

Campbell was a prolific poet and essayist. He became the Rector of
Glasgow University. His biography of Petrarch, *Life of Petrarch* (1841),
promoted the Romantic image of Petrarch to an ever-widening audi-
ence, even in this 13-line sonnet.

P159: *In qual parte del ciel, in quale ydea*

In what ideal world or part of heaven
Did Nature find the model of the face
And form, so fraught with loveliness and grace,
In which, to our creation, she has given
Her prime proof of creative power above?
What fountain nymph or goddess ever let
Such lovely tresses float of gold refined
Upon the breeze, or in a single mind,
Where have so many virtues ever met,
10 E'en though those charms have slain my bosom's weal?
He knows not love who has not seen her eyes
Turn when she sweetly speaks, or smiles, or sighs,
Or how the power of love can hurt or heal.

SUSAN WOLLASTON (fl. 1841)

Wollaston published *One Hundred Sonnets Translated after the Italian of Petrarca* in 1841, claiming to be the first 'complete selection' from the *Canzoniere* in English (Watson, *English Petrarchans*, p. 13). She outdoes Mary Robinson in the use of exclamation marks!

P263: *Arbor victoriosa, triumfale*

Blest laurel! fadeless and triumphant tree!
Of kings and poets thou the fondest pride!
How much of joy and sorrow's changing tide
In my short breath hath been awaked by thee!
Lady, the will's sweet sovereign! thou canst see
No bliss but virtue, where thou dost preside;
Love's chain, his snare, thou dost alike deride;
From man's deceit thy wisdom sets thee free.

Birth's native pride, and treasure's precious store,
10   (Whose bright possession we so fondly hail)
That thee as burthens valueless appear:
Thy beauty's excellence – (none viewed before)
Thy soul had wearied – but thou lov'st the veil,
That shrine of purity adorneth here.

MAJOR ROBERT GUTHRIE MACGREGOR (1805–69)

Macgregor has the honour of being the first British person to translate all of the *Canzoniere*, with the exception of P105, which he considered 'almost untranslatable into English verse, possibly even into acceptable prose'. He spent his active life in India and describes himself as 'of the Bengal List retired'. In 1851 he brought out his *Odes of Petrarch*, but hearing of the impending Bohn Library edition hastened his complete translation into print as *Indian Leisure* (1854), a title that sums up the compartmentalization of his life. We do not know how he came to his passion for Petrarch, but he claims that he had 'much benefitted by reading with Professor Pistgrucchi, of King's College, somewhat more than one-third of the sonnets'. Although we do not know the circumstances, Bohn reprints 262 of his translations. Text from *Bohn's Illustrated Library* (1859).

P264: *I'vo pensando, e nel penser m'assale*

21. Self-Conflict

CEASELESS I think, and in each wasting thought
So strong a pity for myself appears,
That often it has brought
My harass'd heart to new yet natural tears;

Seeing each day my end of life draw nigh,
Instant in prayer, I ask of God the wings
With which the spirit springs,
Freed from its mortal coil, to bliss on high;
But nothing, to this hour, prayer, tear, or sigh,
Whatever man could do, my hopes sustain:
And so indeed in justice should it be;
Able to stay, who went and fell, that he
Should prostrate, in his own despite, remain.
But, lo! the tender arms
In which I trust are open to me still,
Though fears my bosom fill
Of others' fate, and my own heart alarms,
Which worldly feelings spur, haply, to utmost ill.

One thought thus parleys with my troubled mind –
'What still do you desire, whence succour wait?
Ah! wherefore to this great,
This guilty loss of time so madly blind?
Take up at length, wisely take up your part:
Tear every root of pleasure from your heart,
Which ne'er can make it blest,
Nor lets it freely play, nor calmly rest.
If long ago with tedium and disgust
You view'd the false and fugitive delights
With which its tools a treacherous world requites,
Why longer then repose in it your trust,
Whence peace and firmness are in exile thrust?
While life and vigour stay,
The bridle of your thoughts is in your power:
Grasp, guide it while you may:
So clogg'd with doubt, so dangerous is delay,
The best for wise reform is still the present hour.

'Well known to you what rapture still has been
Shed on your eyes by the dear sight of her
Whom, for your peace it were
40 Better if she the light had never seen;
And you remember well (as well you ought)
Her image, when, as with one conquering bound,
Your heart in prey she caught,
Where flame from other light no entrance found.
She fired it, and if that fallacious heat
Lasted long years, expecting still one day,
Which for our safety came not, to repay,
It lifts you now to hope more blest and sweet.
Uplooking to that heaven around your head
50 Immortal, glorious spread;
If but a glance, a brief word, an old song,
Had here such power to charm
Your eager passion, glad of its own harm,
How far 'twill then exceed if now the joy so strong.'

Another thought the while, severe and sweet,
Laborious, yet delectable in scope,
Takes in my heart its seat,
Filling with glory, feeding it with hope;
Till, bent alone on bright and deathless fame
60 It feels not when I freeze, or burn in flame,
When I am pale or ill,
And if I crush it rises stronger still.
This, from my helpless cradle, day by day,
Has strengthen'd with my strength, grown with my growth
Till haply now one tomb must cover both:
When from the flesh the soul has pass'd away
No more this passion comrades it as here;
For fame – if, after death,
Learning speak aught of me – is but a breath:
70 Wherefore, because I fear
Hopes to indulge which the next hour may chase,
I would old error leave, and the one truth embrace.

But the third wish which fills and fires my heart
O'ershadows all the rest which near it spring:
Time, too, dispels a part,
While, but for her, self-reckless grown, I sing.
And then the rare light of those beauteous eyes,
Sweetly before whose gentle heat I melt,
As a fine curb is felt,
80   To combat which avails not wit or force;
What boots it, trammell'd by such adverse ties,
If still between the rocks must lie her course,
To trim my little bark to new emprize?
Ah! wilt Thou never, Lord, who yet dost keep
Me safe and free from common chains, which bind,
In different modes, mankind,
Deign also from my brow this shame to sweep?
For as one sunk in sleep,
Methinks death ever present to my sight,
90   Yet when I would resist I have no arms to fight.

Full well I see my state, in nought deceived
By truth ill known, but rather forced by Love,
Who leaves not him to move
In honour, who too much his grace believed:
For o'er my heart from time to time I feel
A subtle scorn, a lively anguish, steal,
Whence every hidden thought,
Where all may see, upon my brow is writ.
For with such faith on mortal things to dote,
100   As unto God alone is just and fit
Disgraces worst the prize who covets most:
Should reason, amid things of sense, be lost,
This loudly calls her to the proper track:
But, when she would obey
And home return, ill habits keep her back,
And to my view portray
Her who was only born my death to be,
Too lovely in herself, too loved, alas! by me.

I neither know, to me what term of life
110　Heaven destined when on earth I came at first
To suffer this sharp strife.
'Gainst my own peace which I myself have nursed,
Nor can I, for the veil my body throws,
Yet see the time when my sad life may close.
I feel my frame begin
To fail, and vary each desire within:
And now that I believe my parting day
Is near at hand, or else not distant lies,
Like one whom losses wary make and wise,
120　I travel back in thought, where first the way,
The right-hand way, I left, to peace which led.
While through me shame and grief,
Recalling the vain past on this side spread,
On that brings no relief,
Passion, whose strength I now from habit, feel,
So great that it would dare with death itself to deal.

Song! I am here, my heart the while more cold
With fear than frozen snow,
Feels in its certain core death's coming blow;
130　For thus, in weak self-communing, has roll'd
Of my vain life the better portion by:
Worse burden surely ne'er
Tried mortal man than that which now I bear
Though death be seated nigh,
For future life still seeking councils new,
I know and love the good, yet, ah! the worse pursue.

P366: *Vergine bella, che di sol vestita*

Beautiful Virgin! clothed with the sun,
Crown'd with the stars, who so the Eternal Sun
Well pleasedst that in thine his light he hid;
Love pricks me on to utter speech of thee,

And – feeble to commence without thy aid –
Of Him who on thy bosom rests in love.
Her I invoke who gracious still replies
To all who ask in faith,
Virgin! if ever yet
The misery of man and mortal things
To mercy moved thee, to my prayer incline;
Help me in this my strife,
Though I am but of dust, and thou heaven's radiant Queen!

Wise Virgin! of that lovely number one
Of Virgins blest and wise,
Even the first and with the brightest lamp:
O solid buckler of afflicted hearts!
'Neath which against the blows of Fate and Death,
Not mere deliverance but great victory is;
Relief from the blind ardour which consumes
Vain mortals here below!
Virgin! those lustrous eyes,
Which tearfully beheld the cruel prints
In the fair limbs of thy beloved Son,
Ah! turn on my sad doubt,
Who friendless, helpless thus, for counsel come to thee!

O Virgin! pure and perfect in each part,
Maiden or Mother, from thy honour'd birth,
This life to lighten and the next adorn;
O bright and lofty gate of open'd heaven
By thee, thy Son and His, the Almighty Sire,
In our worst need to save us came below:
And, from amid all other earthly seats,
Thou only wert elect,
Virgin supremely blest!
The tears of Eve who turnedst into joy
Make me, thou canst, yet worthy of his grace,
O happy without end,
Who art in highest heaven a saint immortal shrined!

40   O holy Virgin! full of every good,
        Who, in humility most deep and true,
        To heaven art mounted, thence my prayers to hear,
        That fountain thou of pity didst produce,
        That sun of justice light, which calms and clears
        Our age, else clogg'd with errors dark and foul.
        Three sweet and precious names in thee combine,
        Of mother, daughter, wife,
        Virgin! with glory crown'd,
        Queen of that King who has unloosed our bonds,
50   And free and happy made the world again,
        By whose most sacred wounds,
        I pray my heart to fix where true joys only are!

        Virgin! of all unparallel'd, alone,
        Who with thy beauties hast enamour'd Heaven,
        Whose like has never been, nor e'er shall be;
        For holy thoughts with chaste and pious acts
        To the true God a sacred living shrine
        In thy fecund virginity have made:
        By thee, dear Mary, yet my life may be
60   Happy, if to thy prayers,
        O Virgin meek and mild!
        Where sin abounded grace shall more abound!
        With bended knee and broken heart I pray
        That thou my guide wouldst be,
        And to such prosperous end direct my faltering way.

        Bright Virgin! and immutable as bright,
        O'er life's tempestuous ocean the sure star
        Each trusting mariner that truly guides,
        Look down, and see amid this dreadful storm
70   How I am tost at random and alone,
        And how already my last shriek is near,
        Yet still in thee, sinful although and vile,
        My soul keeps all her trust;
        Virgin! I thee implore

Let not thy foe have triumph in my fall;
Remember that our sin made God himself,
To free us from its chain,
Within thy virgin womb our image on Him take!

Virgin! what tears already have I shed,
80   Cherish'd what dreams and breathed what prayers in vain
But for my own worse penance and sure loss;
Since first on Arno's shore I saw the light
Till now, whate'er I sought, wherever turn'd,
My life has pass'd in torment and in tears,
For mortal loveliness in air, act, speech,
Has seized and soil'd my soul:
O Virgin! pure and good,
Delay not till I reach my life's last year;
Swifter than shaft and shuttle are, my days
90   'Mid misery and sin
Have vanish'd all, and now Death only is behind!

Virgin! She now is dust, who, living, held
My heart in grief, and plunged it since in gloom;
She knew not of my many ills this one,
And had she known, what since befell me still
Had been the same, for every other wish
Was death to me and ill renown for her;
But, Queen of heaven, our Goddess – if to thee
Such homage be not sin
100   Virgin! of matchless mind,
Thou knowest now the whole; and that, which else
No other can, is nought to thy great power:
Deign then my grief to end,
Thus honour shall be thine, and safe my peace at last!

Virgin! in whom I fix my every hope,
Who canst and will'st assist me in great need,
Forsake me not in this my worst extreme,
Regard not me but Him who made me thus;

Let his high image stamp'd on my poor worth
110 Towards one so low and lost thy pity move:
Medusa spells have made me as a rock
Distilling a vain flood;
Virgin! my harass'd heart
With pure and pious tears do thou fulfil,
That its last sigh at least may be devout,
And free from earthly taint,
As was my earliest vow ere madness filled my veins!

Virgin! benevolent, and foe of pride,
Ah! let the love of our one Author win,
120 Some mercy for a contrite humble heart:
For, if her poor frail mortal dust I loved
With loyalty so wonderful and long,
Much more my faith and gratitude for thee.
From this my present sad and sunken state
If by thy help I rise,
Virgin! to thy dear name
I consecrate and cleanse my thoughts, speech, pen,
My mind, and heart with all its tears and sighs;
Point then that better path,
130 And with complacence view my changed desires at last.

The day must come, nor distant far its date,
Time flies so swift and sure,
O peerless and alone!
When death my heart, now conscience struck, shall seize:
Commend me, Virgin! then to thy dear Son,
True God and Very Man,
That my last sigh in peace may, in his arms, be breathed!

Bohn's Illustrated Library (1859)

Bohn's Illustrated Library: The Sonnets, Triumphs and other Poems of Petrarch, Now First Completely Translated into English Verse by Various Hands, with a Life of the Poet by Thomas Campbell. Of the three anonymous authors of sonnets in Bohn we know almost nothing, and of the first nothing at all. *The Dictionary of National Biography* attributes the second, Anon. 1777, *Sonnets and Odes Translated from the Italian of Petrarch* (London, 1777), to Dr John Nott of Bristol (see his section, above). The third, Anon. Ox. 1795, *Translations Chiefly from the Italian of Petrarch and Metastasio* (Oxford, 1795), is attributed by the British Museum catalogue to Thomas Le Mesurier of Guernsey (1757–1822), clergyman, Fellow of New College, Oxford, and anti-Catholic polemicist (Watson, *English Petrarchans*, pp. 10–11).

ANON.

P5: *Quando io movo i sospiri a chiamar voi*

5. He Plays Upon the Name Laureta or Laura

IN sighs when I outbreathe your cherish'd name,
That name which love has writ upon my heart,
LAUd instantly upon my doting tongue,
At the first thought of its sweet sound, is heard;
Your **RE**gal state, which I encounter next,
Doubles my valour in that high emprize:
But **TA**cit ends the word; your praise to tell
Is fitting load for better backs than mine.
Thus all who call you, by the name itself,
10   Are taught at once to LAUd and to REvere,

O worthy of all reverence and esteem!
Save that perchance Apollo may disdain
That mortal tongue of his immortal boughs
Should ever so presume as e'en to speak.

P51: *Poco era ad appressarsi agli occhi miei*

42. Such are his Sufferings that he Envies the Insensibility of Marble

Had but the light which dazzled them afar
Drawn but a little nearer to mine eyes,
Methinks I would have wholly changed my form,
Even as in Thessaly her form she changed:
But if I cannot lose myself in her
More than I have — small mercy though it won —
I would to-day in aspect thoughtful be,
Of harder stone than chisel ever wrought,
Of adamant, or marble cold and white,
10   Perchance through terror, or of jasper rare
And therefore prized by the blind greedy crowd.
Then were I free from this hard heavy yoke
Which makes me envy Atlas, old and worn,
Who with his shoulders brings Morocco night.

P159: *In qual parte del ciel, in quale ydea*

126. He Extols the Beauty and Virtue of Laura

In what celestial sphere — what realm of thought,
Dwelt the right model from which Nature drew
That fair and beautous face, in which we view
Her utmost power, on earth, divinely wrought?

What sylvan queen — what nymph by fountain sought,
Upon the breeze such golden tresses threw?
When did such virtues one sole breast imbue?
Though with my death her chief perfection's fraught.
For heavenly beauty he in vain inquires,
Who ne'er beheld her eyes, celestial stain,
Where'er she turns around their brilliant fires:
He knows not how Love wounds, and heals again,
Who knows not how she sweetly smiles, respires
The sweetest sighs, and speaks in sweetest strain!

P232: *Vincitore Alessandro l'ira vinse*

196. The Evil Results of Unrestrained Anger

What though the ablest artists of old time
Left us the sculptured bust, the imaged form
Of conq'ring Alexander, wrath o'ercame
And made him for the while than Philip less?
Wrath to such fury valiant Tydeus drove
That dying he devour'd his slaughter'd foe;
Wrath made not Sylla merely blear of eye,
But blind to all, and kill'd him in the end.
What Valentinian knew that to such pain
Wrath leads, and Ajax, he whose death it wrought,
Strong against many, 'gainst himself at last.
Wrath is brief madness, and, when unrestrain'd,
Long madness, which its master often leads
To shame and crime, and haply e'en to death.

ANONYMOUS 1777

P108: *Aventuroso píu d'altro terreno*

85. He Apostrophizes the Spot Where Laura First Saluted him

AH, happiest spot of earth! in this sweet place
Love first beheld my condescending fair
Retard her steps, to smile with courteous grace
On me, and smiling glad the ambient air.
The deep-cut image, wrought with skilful care,
Time shall from hardest adamant efface,
Ere from my mind that smile it shall erase,
Dear to my soul! which memory planted there.
Oft as I view thee, heart-enchanging soil!
With amorous awe I'll seek – delightful toil!
Where yet some traces of her footsteps lie.
And if fond Love still warms her generous breast,
When'er you see her, gentle friend! request
The tender tribute of a tear – a sigh.

P112: *Sennuccio, i'vo' che sappi in qual manera*

89. He Relates to his Friend Sennuccio His Unhappiness and the Varied Mood of Laura

To thee, Sennuccio, fain would I declare,
To sadden life, what wrongs, what woes I find:
Still glow my wonted flames; and, though resign'd
To Laura's fickle will, no change I bear.
All humble now, then haughty is my fair;
Now meek, then proud; now pitying, then unkind:
Softness and tenderness now sway her mind;
Then do her looks disdain and anger wear.

Here would she sweetly sing, there sit awhile,
10　Here bend her step, and there her step retard;
Here her bright eyes my easy heart ensnared;
There would she speak fond words, here lovely smile;
There frown contempt; – such wayward cares I prove
By night, by day; so wills our tyrant Love!

ANON. OX. 1795

P90: *Erano i capei d'oro a l'aura sparsi*

69.　He Paints the Beauties of Laura, Protesting his Unalterable Love

LOOSE to the breeze her golden tresses flow'd
Wildly in thousand mazy ringlets blown,
And from her eyes unconquer'd glances shone,
Those glances now so sparingly bestow'd.
And true or false, meseem'd some signs she show'd
As o'er her cheek soft pity's hue was thrown;
I whose whole breast with love's soft food was sown,
What wonder if at once my bosom glow'd?
Graceful she moved, with more than mortal mein,
10　In form an angel: and her accents won
Upon the ear with more than human sound.
A spirit heavenly pure, a living sun,
Was what I saw; and if no more 'twere seen,
T' unbend the bow will never heal the wound.

LEIGH HUNT (1784–1859)

Voluminous poet, liberal political and literary essayist, Hunt was the friend of Hazlitt, Byron, Shelley, Keats and Carlyle. He was present at the cremation of Shelley and composed the epitaph for his tomb at Rome. He was the quintessential Romantic. Text from *Poetical Works of Leigh Hunt* (1844).

P126: *Chiare, fresche et dolci acque*

Petrarch's Contemplation of Death in the Bower of Laura

Clear, fresh, and dulcet streams,
Which the fair shape, who seems
To me sole woman, haunted at noon-tide;
Fair bough, so gently fit
(I sigh to think of it.)
Which lent a pillar to her lovely side;
And turf, and flowers bright-eyed,
O'er which her folded gown
Flow'd like an angel's down
And you, O holy air and hush'd,
Where first my heart at her sweet glances gush'd;
Give ear, give ear, with one consenting,
To my last words, my last and my lamenting.

If 'tis fate below,
And Heaven will have it so,
That Love must close these dying eyes in tears,
May my poor dust be laid
In middle of your shade,

While my soul, naked, mounts to its own spheres
20   The thought would calm my fears,
When taking, out of breath,
The doubtful step of death;
For never could my spirit find
A stiller port after the stormy wind;
Nor in more calm, abstracted bourne,
Slip from my travail'd flesh, and from my bones outworn.

Perhaps, some future hour,
To her acustom'd bower
Might come the untamed, and yet the gentle she;
30   And where she saw me first,
Might turn with eyes athirst
And kinder joy to look again for me;
Then, oh! The charity
Seeing amidst the stones
The earth that held my bones,
A sigh for very love at last
Might ask of Heaven to pardon me the past;
And Heaven itself could not say nay,
As with her gentle veil she wiped the tears away.

40   How well I call to mind
When from those boughs the wind
Shook down upon her bosom flower on flower;
And there she sat, meek-eyed,
In midst of all that pride,
Sprinkled and blushing through an amorous shower
Some to her hair paid dower,
And seem'd to dress the curls,
Queenlike, with gold and pearls;
Some, snowing on her drapery stopp'd,
50   Some on the earth, some on the water dropp'd;
While others, fluttering from above,
Seem'd wheeling round in pomp, and saying, 'Here reigns
    Love.'

How often then I said,
Inward, and fill'd with dread,
'Doubtless this creature came from Paradise!'
For at her look the while,
Her voice, and her sweet smile,
And heavenly air, truth parted from my eyes;
So that, with long-drawn sighs,
60   I said, as far from men,
'How came I here, and when?'
I had forgotten; and alas!
Fancied myself in heaven, not where I was;
And from that time till this, I bear
Such love for this green bower, I cannot rest elsewhere.

FELICIA DOROTHEA
HEMANS (1793–1835)

Hemans was a prolific poetess, admired by Shelley, Byron and Words-
worth. She translated only two sonnets, P248 and P279. Text from
The Complete Poems of Felicia Hemans (1844).

P248: *Chi vuol veder quantunque pò Natura*

Thou that wouldst mark, in form of human birth,
All heaven and nature's perfect skill combined,
Come gaze on her, the day-star of the earth,
Dazzling not me alone, but all mankind:

And haste! for death, who spares the guilty long,
First calls the brightest and the best away;
And to her home, amidst the cherub-throng
The angelic mortal flies, and will not stay!

Haste! and each outward charm, each mental grace,
10   In one consummate form thine eye shall trace,
Model of loveliness, for earth too fair!
Then thou shalt own, how faint my votive lays,
My spirit dazzled by perfection's blaze –
But if thou still delay for long regret prepare.

P279: *Se lamentar augelli, o verdi fronde*

If to the sighing breeze of summer-hours
Bend the green leaves; if mourns a plaintive bird
Or from some fount's cool margin, fringed with flowers,
The soothing murmur of the wave is heard;

Her, whom the heavens reveal, the earth denies,
I see and hear: though dwelling far above,
Her spirit, still responsive to my sighs,
Visits the lone retreat of pensive love.

'Why thus in grief consume each fruitless day,
10   (Her gentle accents thus divinely say,)
'While from thine eyes the tear unceasing flows.
Weep not for me, who, hastening on my flight,
Died, to be deathless; and on heavenly light
Whose eyes but opened, when they seemed to close!'

THOMAS WENTWORTH
HIGGINSON (1823–1911)

Minister, social and political radical, abolitionist, commander of a Black
regiment in the American Civil War, and early feminist, Higginson
wrote frequently for the *Atlantic Monthly*. In response to one of his

articles urging women to write, Emily Dickinson sent him four of her poems. He became her mentor and her first publisher. He wrote more than thirty books, among which is his stylish *Fifteen Sonnets of Petrarch* (1903), from which sonnet 8 is selected.

P294: *Soleasi nel mio cor star bella e viva*

She ruled in beauty o'er this heart of mine,
A noble lady in a humble house,
And now her time for heavenly bliss has come,
'T is I am mortal proved, and she divine.
The soul that all its blessings must resign,
And love whose light no more on earth finds room
Might rend the rocks with pity, for their doom,
Yet none their sorrows can in words enshrine;
They weep within my heart; no ears they find
10 Save mine alone, and I am crushed with care,
And naught remains to me save mournful breath.
Assuredly but dust and shade we are;
Assuredly desire is mad and blind;
Assuredly its hope but ends in death.

CHARLES BAGOT CAYLEY
(1823–83)

Cayley, rejected suitor of Christina Rossetti, translated Homer, Aeschylus and Dante, and was the first man to translate all of Petrarch himself, beating Major Macgregor by doing P105. Text from *The Sonnets and Stanzas of Petrarch* (1879).

P119: *Una donna più bella assai che 'l sole*

Ode 12: Glory and Virtue

I

A lady brighter far than is the sun,
   And fairer, and of equal age thereto,
   Had drawn me with her crew,
     By her famed beauties, in my youth's raw day.
She, 'mid all thoughts, and words, and acts begun
   (Because of things like her the world had few),
   Met constantly my view,
     With lofty, graceful air in many a way.
     She did alone my altered nature sway,
Since closely first I dared her eyes to scan;
For her love I began
   Betimes, in faith, a stubborn enterprise.
Hence, if I reach the port I've coveted,
   From her I hope a prize
Of lasting life, when some will think me dead.

II

This lady-love for years my steps controlled
   While yet with longings of my youth I burned;
   And afterwards I learned
     That but to try me thus she meant in sooth.
Nought showed she but a shadow, garment's fold,
   Or veil oft; but aloof her face was turned;
   Nor yet had I discerned,
     Alack! how little I saw; but through my youth
     I passed content, and loved my past in truth.
But when in front I'd penetrated more,
Beyond her wont of yore

She raised her veil, and so much of her face
Revealed, that to my heart flew cold alarms,
    Which still possess the place,
30   And will, until I've held her in my arms.

III

Yet heart I lost not quite by fear or cold,
    But roused its vigour, and pressed near her feet,
    So that a sweet more sweet
        To draw forth from her eyes I might attain:
But, when the veil, that foiled my eyes, was rolled
    Aside, she said, 'My loveliness complete
    Thou seest; and now entreat,
        My friend, for what thy youth might fitly gain.'
        'Lady,' said I, 'my love doth long remain
40 Fast fixed on you – the love I now feel hot;
    Hence, in my present lot,
        I cannot choose aught else, or aught forswear.'
She answered with so admirably strung
    A voice, and such an air,
That thereto endless hope and fear have clung.

IV

'Few have been found on earth, in all its host,
    That, having heard discourse about my parts,
    Have not thence felt their hearts
        Touched with a spark, though it might last not long.
50 But mine antagonist, by whom is crossed
    All good, soon quells it; virtue thus departs;
    And up a new lord starts,
        Who calleth to an easier life the throng.
        New Love such things, which to thy mind belong,
Hath told me truly, that I thence descry,
    Thy aspirations high

Will fit for paths of honour render thee.
Now, since thou art my friend in rarest guise,
   To prove my words, thou'lt see
60 A lady, that will happier make thine eyes.'

V

I would have said, 'Impossible's the event;'
  She said, 'Now somewhat lift thy eyes, and view,
    In more retired purlieu,
      A lady, that was ne'er by many seen.'
That way forthwith my bashful brows I bent,
  And in me felt a heat increased and new;
    which thing to mirth she drew,
      And said, 'I see well what thy case hath been;
      For as the sun, with his more powerful sheen,
70 Suddenly quencheth every other star,
So seems my face now far
  Less lovely, by that grander light subdued.
Yet from my crew thou never shalt be torn,
  Since from the selfsame brood
First she, then I, at one same birth were born.'

VI

Now by this time the bond of shame was rent,
  Which round my tongue so closely bounden lay,
    Since I was mocked, I say,
      And her observance when I first descried.
80 I answered, 'If the truth you represent,
Oh blessed be the hour, blessed be the day,
    Which decked the world's array
      With you, and blessed all the time I hied
      To view you; for if aught I swerved aside
This grieves me more than I could demonstrate.
If then about your state

I could deserve more knowledge, this I crave.'
Full thoughtfully she answered, and so fast
  Fixed the sweet look she gave,
90 That in my heart her face and words were cast.

VII

'As pleased the Eternal Sire from whom we sprung,
  We both were born for endless permanence.
  Alack, what gain we thence?
    'Twere better, if to us the fault were owed!
Beloved and beautiful, winsome and young
  We've been, but have so lost our confidence,
  That now my sister hence
    Hath raised the wing, to seek her first abode.
    I am a shadow merely; now I've showed
100 Whate'er thou couldst be taught by speedy word.'
Then, when her feet she'd stirred,
  She said, 'Now fear not lest afar I stand.'
A garland of green laurel then she knit,
  And took with either hand,
And close about my temples fastened it.

P325: *Tacer non posso, e temo non adopre*

Ode 25

I

I cannot hold my peace, but am afraid
  My tongue my heart's intention may belie –
  That she, who from on high
    Is hearkening, might in honour more abound.
  But who, if Love instruct him not, can vie
By mortal words with beauties of a grade
Divine, and overlaid
    With self-collected lowliness profound?
    This gracious soul in the sweet prison's bound

10   Whence now 'tis freed, had had not long to bide,
        When I discerned her; and because the time
            Was in the May and prime
Of the year's course and mine, I forthwith hied
        To gather flowers in the meadows nigh,
            Hoping, thus decked, that I might please her eye.

        II
    Lo alabaster walls, a roof of gold,
        Windows of sapphire, gate of ivory,
            From which my earliest sigh
                Reached, and the latest hath to reach my heart!
20   From these appeared Love's messengers to fly,
With laurel crowned, and each of them to hold
        (Methinks, I yet behold
            And tremble at their host) a fiery dart.
        A stately throne was in the midmost part,
Compact of native diamond unwrought,
        Where the bright lady sate in solitude;
            And full before her stood
A crystal column, wherein every thought
            Was written, and appeared so plain outside,
30   That oft it made me blithe, and oft I sighed.

        III
By all those weapons keen, and bright, and hot,
        And that triumphant ensign green, which field
            Of battle scorns to yield
                To god, or giant, or to Jove most high,
        The place, wherein I'd entered, was revealed,
Where weeping still is fresh, and slackens not.
All helpless on the spot
            They took me; where or how was I to fly?
            But as one weeping while he goes, may spy
40   One thing, that draws his eyne and heart away,
        So tow'rd a window, where she stood, for whom
            I bear a captive's doom,

And who was singly perfect in her day,
    I began gazing with such eagerness,
    That I forgot myself and my distress.

IV

I was on earth, my heart in heav'n was set,
    In sweet obliviousness of every care.
    I felt to marble there
        My living shape turned, and imbued with awe.
50   A lady then, with prompt and dreadless air,
Ancient, but in complexion youthful yet,
When me so rapt she met,
        As by my forehead and my brows one saw,
        Said, 'Thou shouldst hither for advice withdraw,
For powers are in me, which thy thought transcend;
        And lighter than the wind, I make men glad
        By moments and then sad,
And all thou see'st on earth I rule and bend.
        But on yon sun fix eagle-like thy gaze,
60   Hearkening meanwhile to what my speech conveys.

V

'The day when she was born, those planets whence
    Proceed the effects most happy for thy race,
    In highest, choicest place,
        One tow'rd another looked with loving ray.
    Venus and Jove with their aspects of grace
Possessed a fair and noble residence;
All stars that work offence
        And bale, thro' heav'n were scattered far away.
        Ne'er had the sun disclosed so sweet a day;
70 The air and earth were glad, the seas at rest,
        And quiet all the waters of the streams.
        Amid these friendly beams
    I was but by one distant cloud distressed;
        Because in tears, should Pity not withdraw
        The hand of heav'n, I fear that it will thaw.

VI

'When first to this low state she was conveyed,
   Which ill deserved her, if the truth be told –
   A marvel to behold
    In that raw age, so hallowed and so sweet –
80   She seemed a white pearl set in finest gold;
And when she crept, or trembling footsteps laid,
Green, bright, and soft she made
   Wood, water, earth, and stone; yea with conceit
   The grasses freshened 'neath her palms and feet,
And her fair eyes the fields around her dressed
   With flowers; and the winds and storms she stilled
   With utterance unskilled,
As from a tongue that seeketh yet the breast.
   So well to this deaf, eyeless world she showed
90   That now it was a heav'nly light's abode.

VII

'But when, new years and new perfections gained,
   She entered her third age's flowery space,
   Such loveliness and grace,
    I trow, did never yet the sun delight.
   Such blameless gladness in her eyes found place,
So sweet a comeliness her speech maintained,
That every tongue's refrained
   From uttering what thou only know'st aright.
   Her aspect is with heav'nly rays so bright,
100 That from it soon your glances must be turned;
   And through those dungeon-walls, her earthly part,
   Such fire has reached thy heart,
That never yet a man more sweetly burned.
   But thee to live in bitterness she'll cause,
   Methinks, when on a sudden she withdraws.'

VIII

This said, she turned to guide her nimble wheel,
   On which our lives are spun; thus were divined
     My coming hurts in language sad and true;
     For then the years were few
110   Before the lady, for whose sake I pined
To die, was seized by stern and eager Death,
Who could not rob a fairer shape of breath.

RICHARD GARNETT (1835–1906)

Garnett was Keeper of Printed Books at the British Museum. Two
sonnets, 25 and 26, from his *Dante, Petrarch, Camoens: CXXIV Sonnets*
(1896).

P181: *Amor fra l'erbe una leggiadra rete*

Love spread a dainty net in grassy glade
   Woven from gold and pearl, 'neath fadeless boughs
   Of laurel, shrine of my enamoured vows,
Though gloomy more than gladsome be its shade.
Bait of the sweet and bitter seed was laid
   That I desire and dread, he reaps and sows;
   Never, since mortal eye did first unclose,
Music breathed sweetly as the strain he made.
And that bright light whereby the sun is dim
10   Flashed round me, and the cord by hand was held
   Whose snow doth snow and ivory reprove:
Thus the snare thralled me, captivate and quelled
   By gracious gest, accent of Seraphim,
   And pleasure and desire and hope of Love.

P185: *Questa fenice de l'aurata piuma*

This Phoenix, from her wealth of aureate plumes
   Sheathing her snowy neck in splendid dyes,
   Hath natural necklace fashioned in a wise
That softens other hearts, and mine consumes.
And all around this diadem illumes
   The airy space, while Love his bellows plies,
   And silent bids the subtle flame arise
That scorches me mid winter's chills and glooms.
A purple scarf, with fringing roses sown
   O'er bordering blue, her snowy shoulders veils;
   Garb like her beauty to none other given;
In aromatic Araby alone
   Fame plants this prodigy, with idle tales
   Concealing that she soars in our own heaven.

JOHN ADDINGTON SYMONDS (1840–93)

Symonds, the famous scholar, aesthete and historian of the Italian Renaissance, included 'Eight Sonnets of Petrarch' at the end of his *Sketches in Italy and Greece* (1874), of which this is the first of three excoriating the absence of the papacy from Rome.

P138: *Fontana di dolore, albergo d'ira*

On the Papal Court at Avignon

FOUNTAIN of woe! Harbour of endless ire!
   Thou school of errors, haunt of heresies!
   Once Rome now Babylon, the world's disease,
   That maddenest man with fears and fell desire!

O forge of fraud! O prison dark and dire,
  Where dies the good, where evil breeds increase!
  Thou living Hell! Wonders will never cease
  If Christ rise not to purge thy sins with fire.
Founded in chaste and humble poverty,
  Against thy founders thou dost raise thy horn,
  Thou shameless harlot! And whence flows this pride?
Even from foul and loathed adultery,
  The wage of lewdness. Constantine, return!
  Not so: the felon world its fate must bide.

Twentieth Century

AGNES TOBIN (1864–1939)

A wealthy San Franciscan, Tobin was the third of twelve children born
to an itinerant Irish father who was secretary to the first Archbishop of
California. She was a friend of Yeats, Synge, Shaw and the Meynells.
Conrad dedicated *Under Western Eyes* to her. These two sonnets are
taken from *On the Death of Madonna Laura by Francesco Petrarca, Rendered
into English* (1906).

P280: *Mai non fui in parte ove sí chiar vedessi*

I do not think that I have ever seen
   So many times in one short afternoon
   The Lady they call dead: I did nigh swoon
When she came running towards me through the green,
Laughing and calling out, 'Where have you been?
   Did you not know it was the first of June?'
   She faded on the sunny air too soon:
A long hour later and I saw her lean
Against a flowering hedge full drowsily.
10   And though this land is balmier than the nest
     That Cypris made for Eros, and there be
     Maids here most fair, how strange it seems to me
Here, here, where late the heart stirred in her breast,
   That men should think of aught that is not she.

P353: *Vago augelletto che cantando vai*

O lovely little bird, so heavenly gay
    You singing go, and then so mournful sweet!
    Dawn in a rosy tide broke at our feet;
But, oh, the twilight fields are very grey!
If I but knew a literal, soft way
    Like yours for telling of old wounds that beat,
    And sobs that I remember and repeat,
Straight to my breast you would come and, piteous, say:
'Doth not our plaining stir the stones?' And still
10   We share unlike; may be she is but late:
A bruisèd wing, perhaps, mourn if you will,
But do not doubt she comes. O Twilight! – gate
Wide open for the things Time cannot kill –
    The phantom Things that by the fences wait!

JOHN MILLINGTON SYNGE
(1871–1909)

Synge was an Irish poet and dramatist, who discovered Petrarch on his
visit to Italy in 1896 after a conspicuously unsuccessful courtship of a
Miss Cherry Matheson. Text from *Poems and Translations* (1909).

P300: *Quanta invidia io ti porto, avara terra*

He is jealous of the Heavens and the earth

What a grudge I am bearing the earth that
has its arms about her, and is holding that
face away from me, where I was finding peace
from great sadness.

What a grudge I am bearing the Heavens
that are after taking her, and shutting her in
with greediness, the Heavens that do push
their bolt against so many.
What a grudge I am bearing the blessed
10　saints that have got her sweet company, that
I am always seeking; and what a grudge I am
bearing against Death, that is standing in her
two eyes, and will not call me with a word.

HELEN LEE PEABODY (1879–?)

Peabody was an American artist and poet. Text from *Madrigals and Odes from Petrarch* (1940).

P366: *Vergine bella, che di sol vestita*

　　Fair Virgin,
　　　　Vestured with the sun!
　　Bright shining one,
　　　　Star-crowned;
　Who such sweet ultimate favor found
　　　From all eternity
　With the great primal Sun
　　　That from His height
　He stooped in thee to hide the light
10　　　Of His Divinity:
　　Now shall my love upraise
　　New measures in thy praise,
　Though to begin without thy aid were vain
　　　And without His,
　Who, joined with thee in love, shall ever reign.

When ardent faith called to thee without fear.
   Virgin, if our poor misery,
     Our trafficking with pain,
   In thy deep heart stir pity,
20   Incline to me again;
Once more on thy sure succour now I lean,
   Though of base clay am I
    And thou be Heaven's queen.

O Virgin wise,
    Of prudent virgins blest,
   Foremost and best
    Beyond compare,
With shining lamp most clear,
   Bright shield of the oppressed,
30   With thee we know
Not mere escape from evil fortune's blow
    Or bitter death;
   But triumph o'er the foe –
   Thou who dost cool this flame
Which, blazing among mortals, love we name.
   Virgin, turn thou thine eyes,
   Sad eyes that watched beside
The piteous body of thy Son that died,
   Unto my dubious state;
40 Thy counsel now I seek,
    Disconsolate.

Pure Virgin, without stain,
   God's daughter meet,
And by conception sweet
   His mother too,
Thou, a keen brightness to our dark world sent,
   Art high Heaven's ornament.
    Through thee alone,

O lofty window gleaming with heavenly light,
50   Came God's Son and thine own,
To save us mortals from our desperate plight.
    Among all dusty toilers of the earth,
        Virgin most blessed,
    Chosen wert thou, pure gold without alloy,
To turn Eve's sorrow into joy.
    O make me of God's grace to worthy be,
Thou who art crowned in heaven eternally.

    Virgin most holy, filled with every grace,
Who are the sure path of true humility did'st trace
60   To the bright heavens where my prayers ascend,
Thou did'st achieve the much-desired end
        That springs from fairest root.
    Of Justice and of Piety art thou
        The ripened fruit.
    Three sweetest names unite
        In thee alone,
Mother and spouse and daughter, all in one.
    O Virgin glorious,
    Sweet spouse of our high King
70   Who gloriously reigns,
        Who freed us from our chains,
By His most sacred wounds – His love's unerring dart,
    O soften thou my heart.

    Virgin, in all this world unparalleled,
        Heaven enamoured is
    Of thy pure bliss.
O thou, the living temple of high God,
    Who thy virginity did fruitful make,
Most joyful for thy sake,
80   In spite of inner strife,
        Is all my life.

Virgin most pious, sweet,
     In whom all graces meet,
My spirit flows to thee,
     Praying that thou wilt bend
The twisted fragments of my broken life
     Unto a perfect end.

O Virgin, bathed in ever-living light,
Bright star of our tempestuous dark sea,
90   Thou faithful guide
     To mariners that trust in thee,
Behold in what dread tempest I am tossed,
          Rudderless and alone,
     Fearing myself for lost.
With sinful soul I still in thee confide.
     Virgin, I pray
Let not our common enemy deride
     My bitter woe.
     Remember that for man's sin
100   God took upon Himself our human flesh,
     To thy sweet virgin cloister entering in.

Virgin, how many tears have I not shed,
What prayers have I not offered and in vain!
     Sorrow and loss and fear of future pain,
          All these have compassed me
Since my first breath I drew by Arno's side;
          My searchings far and wide,
My acts, my words and mortal beauty have undone
          me quite.
110   Virgin, sacred of soul,
          Do not delay,
          For who can say

That I approach not to life's end.
 And the long swiftly flowing years,
  Swift as an arrow's dart,
 Filled to the brim with bitter loss and tears,
 Have left no other trace
Than a sure death which looks me in the face.

 Virgin, she whom I mourn is now dry dust,
120 Who, living, caused me full a thousand woes,
  But of my bitter throes
  She knew not one,
Else had she honor lost, and I had been undone.
 But thou, O heavenly Lady fair,
  Our Goddess rare,
 (If to speak thus of thee is meet)
Virgin of delicate high sentiment.
  Thou see'st all.
 Others have failed to end my misery;
130 But now through thy great power can be wrought
 Health to my soul, and honor unto thee.

Virgin, with whom my hope is most secure,
 In need my refuge sure,
  Let not thy gaze
 Rest on unworthy me.
  But rather see
Him who in likeness to Himself did raise
 My fallen nature base,
  Enduing it with grace;
140 Else might my eyes of error take their fill.
  Medusa-like,
 My heart would turn to stone
And evil humors on the air distill.
 O Virgin, thou of pious, saintly tears,

Rid then my soul of cowardly fears,
   That my last hours devout may be,
Not mixed as heretofore with earthly mire,
   But tinged with heavenly fire.

Virgin, with human heart devoid of pride,
150   Humanity thou too did'st take
   By primal Love's decree.
With contrite heart I pray you pity me.
   I that so faithful proved
To mortal lady, greatly, vainly loved,
   So gentle art thou, shall I not love thee?
If from my sad and miserable state
   By thy sweet hands I rise,
Virgin, I consecrate to thee
   All my most treasured enterprise.
160   My dear imaginings,
My language and my thoughts, my pen, my heart,
   My tears and sighs;
Be thou my guide to Heaven, nor fail to weigh
   Celestial desires when I pray.

The day approaches now, so swift time flies,
   Virgin, uniquely one,
     Of my last end.
Pierced is my heart with thought of death;
   Now to thy Son, true Man, true God, commend
170   My parting soul, that He may give release,
Receiving my last breath in peace.

MORRIS BISHOP (1893–1973)

Poet and Professor of Romantic Languages at Cornell University, Bishop was a popularizer of Petrarch. Text from *Petrarch and His World* (1963).

P16: *Movesi il vecchierel canuto e bianco*

The ancient graybeard shoulders on his load
and quits the home of all his many days,
under the silent loving-fearful gaze
of eyes forfending what the hearts forebode.
Thence in life's wane his old ambitious goad
his quaking shanks into long longed-for ways.
Only the burning of his will upstays
him, by years broken, spent by the long road.
But so at last his longing brings him nigh
to Rome, to look upon the painted face
of Him whom soon in heaven he hopes to view.
Ah, Donna, Donna, even so go I,
seeking forever in whatever place
some much-desirèd shadowy hint of you.

P54: *Perch'al viso d'Amor portava insegna*

Because she bore Love's mark, a Wanderer
suddenly struck my heart, one youthful day,
and all my praise and honor turned to her.
And hunting her through the green wilderness,
I heard a voice cry, high and far away:
'All your pursuit is vain and purposeless!'

And then I sank in the shade of a beechen tree,
and gazed about, perceiving none too soon
the forest menace that encompassed me.
10   And I turned back, about the hour of noon.

P365: *I' vo piangendo i miei passati tempi*

Now I go grieving for the days on earth
I passed in worship of a mortal thing,
heedless to fledge the spiritual wing,
careless to try the measure of my worth.
Thou who dost know my every sin from birth,
invisible, immortal heavenly king,
help Thou my soul, so weak and wandering,
pour Thy abundant grace upon its dearth.
Out of the battle, out of the hurricane
10   I come to harbor; may my passing be
worthy, as all my dwelling here was vain.
And may Thy hand be quick to comfort me
in death, and in the scant hours that remain.
Thou knowest, I have no other hope but Thee.

JOSEPH AUSLANDER (1897–1965)

Poet and anti-Nazi activist, Auslander was a consultant in English poetry
at the Library of Congress. Text from *The Sonnets of Petrarch* (1931).

P344: *Fu forse un tempo dolce cosa amore*

Perhaps there was a time when love was sweet –
Though when, I scarce remember; now it grows
Bitter as gall. Who learns from living knows,
As I have learned, that grief is stubborn meat.

Ah, she, who was our era's Paraclete,
Who now adorns the beatific Rose,
Has cheated weariness of the one repose
It knew alive – now fled on phantom feet!
Remorseless Death has stripped and left me stark;
10   Nor can her liberated spirit heal
With its large bliss the agony I feel.
I wept and sang, who now must mutely mark
By day and night despair with eyes of steel,
The tears, the tortured words, the torturing dark.

THOMAS G. BERGIN (1904–89)

Bergin was Professor of Italian Literature at Yale University. Two
poems from *Petrarch: Selected Sonnets, Odes, Letters* (1966).

PI: *Voi ch'ascoltate in rime sparse il suono*

O ye who in these scattered rhymes may hear
The echoes of the sighs that fed my heart
In errant youth, for I was then, in part
Another man from what I now appear,
If you have learned by proof how Love can sear,
Then for these varied verses where I chart
Its vain and empty hope and vainer smart
Pardon I may beseech, nay, Pity's tear.
For now I see how once my story's spread
10   And I became a wonder to mankind
So in my heart I feel ashamed – alas,
That nought but shame my vanities have bred,
And penance, and the knowledge of clear mind
That earthly joys are dreams that swiftly pass.

P30: *Giovene donna sotto un verde lauro*

I saw beneath the shade of a green laurel
A lady fair and purer than the snow –
And colder too than snow which for long years
Has known no sun. And still that golden hair
And lovely face haunt my enraptured eyes
Where'er I wander, on whatever shore.

The ship of my desires will come to shore
Only alas when brown leaves spring from laurel,
When still shall be my heart and dry my eyes;
10   Nay, first we'll see cold fire and flaming snow:
A year shall pass for every thread of hair
Upon my head – and still there will be years.

Aye, but since time so hurries on the years
And soon we all must fare to Charon's shore –
What matter if with blonde or hoary hair?
I'll follow faithfully my tender laurel
Through scorching heat or freezing ice and snow
Until the last day close these anxious eyes.

Never has earth beheld such radiant eyes –
20   Nor in our days nor in the ancient years –
As those that vanquish me as summer snow.
A flood of tears, as swollen stream to shore,
Flows from my heart to lave that cruel laurel
Of gleaming limbs and precious golden hair.

Sooner, I fear, shall I change mien and hair
Than find some look of pity in the eyes
Of my fair idol, my sweet living laurel.

Today – well counts the heart! – marks seven years
I've wended sighing over sea and shore
30 By night and day, through rain and sleet and snow.

Within afire, without as white as snow
With constant thought though sadly fading hair
I'll go my restless way from shore to shore
Bringing perhaps compassion to some eyes
Who'll read my sorry plaint in future years –
If lives the glory of my mortal laurel.

For Laura'll melt my soul as sun melts snow –
Oh hair of gold above bright sapphire eyes! –
And bring my ship of years too soon ashore.

GRAHAM HOUGH (1908–90)

Hough was Professor of English at Cambridge University and Fellow of Christ's College. Sonnet from *Legends and Pastorals* (1961).

P62: *Padre del ciel, dopo i perduti giorni*

Sonnet for Good Friday

Father of heaven, after the lost days,
After the nights eaten with desire,
Wondering at the fire
That dries my heart of all enterprise,
Please you to pour new grace
Into my veins empty of all power;
Please you to let my adversary tire
Of digging pitfalls for me, go his ways.

Lord, unpitied ten years I have served
10   This tyrant. I who dare
Nothing against him feel him the more harsh.
Pity this misery no man deserved,
Teach my thoughts how to forget their care,
Forget their care, remembering your cross.

JAMES WYATT COOK (1932–   )

James Wyatt Cook was Professor of English Literature at Albion College, Michigan. From his *Petrarch's Songbook Rerum Vulgarium Fragmenta: A Verse Translation* (1995) the series that runs from P23 – the first and longest *canzone* in the sequence – until the second sestina (P30) has been chosen to give some sense of the enormous variety of subjects in any sample group of Petrarch's poetry.

P23: *Nel dolce tempo de la prima etade*

In the sweet season of my early youth
That saw break forth, almost in grasstime still,
The passion wild that grew into my bane –
Because my singing sweetens bitter grief,
I'll sing how once I lived in liberty
While in my dwelling place Love was disdained.
Next I shall tell how scorn vexed Love too sorely;
Recount, in turn, what chance befell and why,
How I was made a warning to the world.
10   Although elsewhere my torture
Cruel is penned – indeed, it's wearied now
A thousand quills – in almost every vale
The sound of my grave sighs reverberates
And testifies my life is full of pain.
And if my memory fails to serve me here

As well as once it used to do, let my
Woes pardon that, and one thought that alone
So grieves it that I'm made to turn my back
On all thoughts else, forget myself perforce;
20   That thought my being holds, and I the husk.

Since that day Love at first laid siege to me,
Indeed, I tell you, many years had passed
So that my youthful countenance was changed,
And frozen thoughts had hardened round my heart
To make an almost adamantine glaze
That would not let the hard effect abate.
No tear yet bathed my breast; none slumber broke,
And that which in myself I could not find,
In others' seemed a miracle to me.
30   Woe: What I am: What I was:
Praise life at end; at evening praise the day.
The cruel one of whom I tell, aware
That, after all, no arrow's point of his
Had even penetrated past my robe,
A powerful lady took into his train
'Gainst whom not skill, nor strength, nor begging grace,
Availed me then nor yet avails me now.
Those two transformed me into what I am,
Turned me a man alive, to laurel green
40   That shed no leaf for all the winter's chill.

What I became when first awareness dawned
Of this transfiguration of my self:
I saw my locks become that laurel frond
That I had hoped, indeed, would be their crown;
The feet I stood and walked and ran upon,
As to the spirit every limb responds
I sensed become two roots beside the waves –
Not of Peneus – of a statelier stream;
Felt arms transmute themselves, become two boughs:

50   My blood runs no less cold
     Than did it when, arrayed in plumage white,
     My hope plunged stricken by a thunderbolt,
     Lay dead because he'd risen far too high.
     Thus, since I knew not where or when I might
     Recover him, by night and day, in tears,
     Where hope was reft from me, I went alone,
     Searching along the banks and in the deeps,
     And never more did my tongue cease to tell,
     While it could do so, of his dreadful fall.
60   Hence I, with the swan's song, its color took.

     Thus I drifted past those banks well-loved,
     And though I wished to speak, went singing ever,
     Crying "Mercy" in that alien voice;
     Nor could I ever harmonize the notes –
     Now sweet, now soft – of amorous lament
     So that her stern, fierce heart would yield to me.
     For what was there to hear? How memory sears me:
     But even more of this – or rather more
     About that sweet and bitter foe of mine
70   Necessity bids me tell,
     Though such as she transcends the power of speech.
     That girl, who with a look rips souls away,
     Unsealed my breast, seized with her hand my heart,
     Instructing me: 'Breathe not a word of this:'
     I saw her next in altered guise, alone
     So that, mistaking her – oh human sense
     I, fearful, spoke the truth to her instead,
     At once, then, she resumed her former face
     And made of me – alas, poor wretch – a stone,
80   One half alive, disheartened and dismayed.

     She spoke with such a troubled countenance,
     It made me tremble there within that rock
     To hear: 'I am perhaps, not whom you think;'
     And to myself I said: 'If she frees me

From stone, no life can sadden or annoy.'
(To make me weep, my Lord, return, I pray)
I know not how, but thence I dragged my feet,
Accusing no one other than myself,
Suspended between life and death all day.
90   But, since my time grows short,
And with desire my pen cannot keep pace,
Much written in my mind I shall omit,
And only speak of certain things that will
Be wonders to whoever hears of them.
Death was within me, coiled about my heart;
Nor could my silence free it from her hand,
Nor succor give to my enfeebled powers;
To speak aloud had been forbidden me,
So I cried out with paper and with ink:
100   'No: I'm not mine; if I die, yours the cost.'

I thought in her eyes surely I would change
From one disdained to one deserving grace,
And this hope had made me presumptuous.
But humbleness will sometimes blow out scorn,
Sometimes inflame it: this I quickly learned
In darkness shrouded for a season long,
For at those prayers my candle had gone out,
And I could not recover anywhere
Her shadow or some vestige of her feet.
110   Like one who sleeps along
His way, one day I weary fell upon
The grass; accusing there that ray of light
Which fled, I gave free rein to woeful tears,
Allowing them to fall just as they would.
And never did snow melt beneath the sun
The way I felt myself grow faint and change
Into a fountain underneath a beech.
A long and tearful time I held that course.
Who's heard of fountains born from mortal man?
120   I speak of things undoubted and well known.

God only shapes the soul's nobility;
From no one else can she attain such grace.
She keeps her likeness to her Maker's state;
And thus she's never weary of forgiving
Whoever with a contrite mien and heart
Comes seeking mercy after many faults.
And if against her nature she endures
Long importunity, she mirrors Him –
Does so that sin may be more greatly feared;
130   One does not honestly repent
Of one ill-deed who's ready to do more.
Since, by compassion touched, my lady deigned
To look on me, she saw and understood
My penance had been equal to my sin;
Benign, she led me back to my first state.
But nothing on this earth a wise man trusts:
For when I pled once more, my nerves and bones
Were turned to hardest flint; and, shaken thus,
I lived a voice, still burdened as of old,
140   Calling on Death, and her alone by name.

An errant, doleful spirit (I recall)
Through caverns tenantless, unvisited
I wept my uncurbed daring many years
And found at length the end of that disease,
And turned again from flint to earthly limbs –
To make me feel the sorrow more, I think.
How far afield my passion I pursued:
One day, as usual, I went to hunt;
There that untamed one, lovely and severe,
150   Stood naked in a fount,
While down on her the sun burned, ardently.
Because no other sight contented me,
I paused to gaze on her, and she, ashamed,
Whether in vengeance or to hide herself,
With her hands splashed the water in my face.

The truth I'll tell (though it may falsehood seem):
I felt myself drawn forth from my own shape,
And to a stag, alone and wandering
From wood to wood, I swiftly was transformed,
160   And still I flee the baying of my hounds.
     O song, I never was that cloud of gold
Which in a priceless rain came falling once –
The one in which Jove's fire, in part, was spent –
But, lit by one sweet look, I've been a flame,
Yes, and that bird which shears the upper air,
Bearing her high whom my words celebrate;
Nor could I for a new form learn to part
From that first laurel whose sweet shade yet sweeps
Every delight less lovely from my heart.

P24: *Se l'onorata fronde che prescrive*

     Had not those honored leaves that tame the wrath
Of heaven when high Jove thunders, not denied
To me that crown which customarily
Adorns one who, while shaping verses, writes,
     I'd be a friend to these your goddesses,
The ones this age abandons wretchedly;
But far that wrong already drives me off
From the inventress of the olive tree.
     Indeed, no Ethiopic dust boils up
10   Beneath the hottest sun the way I blush
At losing such a treasured gift of mine.
     Search out, therefore, a fountain more serene,
For mine of every cordial stands in need,
Save only that which I well forth in tears.

P27: *Il successor di Carlo, che la chioma*

Charles' successor who now adorns his head
With his forefather's crown has seized, indeed,
Weapons to crush the horns of Babylon
And all of those who take their name from her.
    Christ's vicar, laden with his keys and cloak
Returns to his own seat; and so, unless
Some misadventure hinders him, he'll view
Bologna first, and then see noble Rome.
    Your mild and gentle lamb has beaten down
10 The savage wolves; and thus will meet their end
Whoever puts asunder lawful loves.
    Console her, therefore – she who yet stands guard –
And comfort Rome who for her spouse laments;
Gird on the sword at last for Jesus now.

P28: *O aspettata in ciel beata e bella*

O fair and blessed soul whom Heaven awaits
You go arrayed in our humanity
Not cumbered by the flesh as others are;
Henceforth those roads will seem less hard to you
By which you pass to His realm from below –
God's chosen one, handmaid obedient:
Behold afresh your vessel that has now
Already put behind it this blind world
To steer for the best harbor,
10 Solaced by a sweet wind from the west.
That breeze, amidst this dark and shadowy vale
Where we lament our own and others', woes
Will pilot you, freed from your ancient bonds,
Along the straightest course
To that true orient, where she is bound.

Perhaps the loving and devoted prayers
Of mortal beings, and their sacred tears,
Have gone before supernal mercy's throne;
But maybe they were not enough, nor such
20 That by their merit, one jot they might turn
Aside eternal justice from its course.
But in His grace that kindly King who rules
In Heaven looks toward that sacred place
Where he hung on the cross;
Hence in the breast of this new Charlemagne
That vengeance breathes which, tardy, saps our strength —
Because through long years Europe sighed for it.
Thus Christ brings succor to His cherished spouse
So that his voice alone
30 Makes Babylon stand quaking and afraid.
    All dwellers from the mountains to Garonne,
Between the Rhone, and Rhine, and salty waves,
To those most Christian banners rally now;
And all who ever prized true valor, from
The far horizon to the Pyrenees
Will empty Spain to follow Aragon;
From England, with the isles that ocean bathes
Between the Oxcart and the Pillars — from,
In short, wherever sounds
40 The teaching of most sacred Helicon —
All varied in their tongues and arms and dress,
Divine love spurs them to high enterprise.
Indeed, what love so lawful, of such worth?
What sons, what women ever
Have been the grounds for such a righteous wrath?
    There is a region of the world that lies
In ice forever, under freezing snow
Far distant from the pathway of the sun.
There, subject to days overcast and short,
50 There teems a folk by nature foes of peace,
A people that is not bereaved by death.

Should these prove more devout than usual
And with Teutonic rage take up the sword,
Then without doubt you'll learn
How much to prize Chaldeans, Arabs, Turks,
And all who place their hopes in pagan gods
From here to that sea red with bloody waves –
An unclothed, frightened, backward people who
Never close with swords; instead
60   They trust the wind to guide their every shot.
       The time has therefore come to draw our necks
From out the ancient yoke, to tear away
The veil that has been wound around our eyes.
Show noble genius, which, by Heaven's grace
From Apollo, the immortal one, is yours;
And here let eloquence display its power,
Now with the tongue, now celebrated script;
For if you do not wonder, reading of
Orpheus and Amphion,
70   Then marvel not when Italy, with all
Her sons, by your clear sermon's note is so
Aroused that she takes up the lance for Christ.
For if this ancient matriarch sees truth,
She'll find no cause of hers
Was ever so appropriate or fair.
       To profit from rich treasures you have turned
The ancient pages and the modern too,
And flown to Heaven, though in earthly form;
You know how, from the reign of Mars, own son
80   To great Augustus, who – thrice triumphing
Three times adorned his locks with laurel green,
Rome oftentimes, because of others' wounds,
Gave liberally so much of its own blood.
Then why is Rome not now –
Not 'liberal' – but thankful and devout
In taking vengeance for these cruel affronts
In company with Mary's glorious Son?
How in defences human can the foe

Repose his hope, when Christ
90   Stands firm in the opposing company?
        Consider Xerxes' reckless impudence;
When with ingenious bridges, he outraged
The sea so he could trample on our shores;
And you will see those Persian women who
Were draped in brown to mourn their husbands' deaths,
The sea of Salamis all red with blood.
Not only does the miserable ruin
Of that unhappy people of the East
Foretell your victory;
100 But Marathon, that deadly pass as well
The Lion held with such a tiny band,
And countless frays of which you've heard and read.
Most meet it is, therefore, that you subject
Both knee and mind to God
Who now preserves your life for such great good.
        Song, Italy you'll see, and see the shore
Revered, which neither stream nor sea nor hill
Can keep from me nor from my eyes conceal,
But only Love who, with his lofty lamp,
110 Attracts me more, the more that I catch fire
To habit Nature cannot stand opposed;
Now, Song, go forth; lag not behind your fellows,
Not just under kerchiefs
Does Love reside, who makes us laugh and weep.

P29: *Verdi panni, sanguigni oscuri o persi*

Green fabrics, blood-red, dark or violet,
You never gowned a lady
Nor ever in a blond tress wound gold hair
As fair as this that strips free will from me;
It draws me in such fashion from the path
Of liberty that no less heavy yoke
Can I endure to bear.

Yet if the soul to which ill counsel comes
Still sometimes takes up arms
10   To grieve when suffering leads it to doubt,
The sudden sight of her will call it back
From its unchecked desire, will rid my heart
Of frenzied schemes, since seeing her makes sweet
All my indignity.

For all my former sufferings for Love,
For those I still must bear
Till she who gnaws my heart shall make it whole —
She rebel 'gainst the mercy it still craves —
Let vengeance come; save only that against
20   Humility, let pride and wrath not block
Nor bar my passage fair.

The day and hour I gazed upon the lights
In that fair black and white
Which drove me from the place where love rushed in —
Of this new grievous life, that time was root,
And she in whom our age admires itself;
Whoever looks upon her unafraid
Is surely lead or wood.

No teardrop, then, caused by *her* eyes yet spills
30   From mine to bathe my heart,
Which felt that arrow first on my left side;
None causes me to shun my own desire,
For on the proper part this sentence falls;
For her, my soul sighs, and how meet it is
That she should wash my wounds.

My thoughts to me contrary have become:
Once one, like me exhausted,
Turned the beloved sword upon herself;
I don't ask this one, though, to set me free
40   For every other road to heaven's less straight;
Yes, to that glorious realm one can't aspire
In a more steady ship.

O stars benign that were companions of
That blessed womb when its
Fair issue slipped into this world below:
An earthly star is she; as laurel leaf
Its green, so she the prize of chastity
Preserves; there strikes no lightning, never blows
Base wind to bend her low.
50   I know well that my wish to catch in verse
Her praises would exhaust
Whoever, worthiest, set his hand to write.
What cell of memory is there to hold
Such virtue, such great beauty as one sees
Who gazes in those eyes – mark of all worth
And sweet key of my heart.
While the sun wheels,
Love will not have a pledge
Lady, more dear than you.

p30: *Giovene donna sotto un verde lauro*

A youthful lady under a green laurel
I saw once, whiter and more cold than snow
Untouched by sun for many, many, years;
I liked her speech, fair features, and her hair
So much that I keep her before my eyes –
And ever shall, though I'm on hill or shore.
    And thus my thoughts will stay along the shore,
Where no green leaf is found upon the laurel;
When I have stilled my heart and dried my eyes,
10   We'll see fire freeze and into flame burst snow;
I don't have strands as many in this hair
As, waiting for that day, there would be years.
    Because time flies, however, and since years
Soon flee until one fetches on death's shore –
Whether with locks of brown or with white hair –

I'll follow still the shade of that sweet laurel
Through the most parching sun and through the snow
Until the final day shall close these eyes.
    Never before were seen such lovely eyes
20 Not in our age nor in man's pristine years;
They make me melt just as the sun does snow,
From whence a tearful river floods the shore –
Love leads it to the foot of that hard laurel
Whose branches are of diamond, gold its hair.
I fear the changing of my face and hair
Before, with pity true, she shows her eyes –
My idol, sculpted in the living laurel;
For if my count errs not, it's seven years
Today that I have sighed from shore to shore
30 By night and day, in heat and in the snow.
    Still fire within, though outside whitest snow
With these thoughts only, though with altered hair,
Ever in tears, I'll wander every shore,
Perhaps creating pity in the eyes
Of persons born from hence a thousand years –
If, tended well, so long can live a laurel.
    In sun, the gold and topaz on the snow
Are conquered by blond hair close by those eyes
That lead my years so swiftly towards the shore.

MARK MUSA (1934–)

Musa was Professor of French and Italian Literature at Indiana University. P70 is a bravura piece in which Petrarch uses as the last line of succeeding stanzas the first line of the famous poems by his predecessors – Arnaut Daniel, Guido Cavalcanti, Dante and Cino da Pistoia – and ends with the first line of his own Canzone 23, the first *canzone* in the collection. P71–P73 are called the 'tre sorelle' because they have the same stanza and rhyme scheme. Text from *Petrarch: The Canzoniere, or, Rerum vulgarium fragmenta* (1996).

P50: *Ne la stagion che 'l ciel rapido inchina*

It is the time the rapid heavens bend
toward the West, the time our own day flees
to some expectant race beyond, perhaps,
the time an old and weary pilgrim-woman
feeling the loneliness of foreign lands,
doubles her pace, hastening more and more;
and then at her day's end,
though she is all alone,
at least she is consoled
10   by resting and forgetting for awhile
the labour and the pain of her past road.
But, oh, whatever pain the day brings me
grows more and more the moment
the eternal light begins to fade from us.

When the sun's burning wheels begin to flame,
in order to give way to night, and shadows
are now cast deeper by the highest mountains,
the avid workman packs away his tools
and with the words of mountain songs he clears
20   the weight of that day's labour from his chest;
and then he spreads his table
all full of meager food
like acorns of whose praises
the whole world sings and manages to shun.
But let who will find joy from time to time,
for I've not had, I will not say a happy,
but just one restful hour,
for all the turning of the sky and stars.

And when the shepherd sees the great sphere's rays
30   are falling toward the nest in which it dwells
and in the east the country turning dark,
he stands up straight and with his trusty crook,

he leaves the grass and springs and beech's shade,
moving his flock quietly on its way;
then far away from people
a hut or kind of cave
he weaves out of green leaves,
and there without a care he lies and sleeps.
But, ah, cruel Love, you drive me on to chase
40   the voice, the steps, the prints of a wild beast
who is destroying me;
you do not catch her: she crouches and she flees.

And sailors on their ship when sun is set
in some protected cove let their limbs drop
upon hard boards and sleep beneath coarse canvas.
But I, though sun may dive into the waves
and leave behind his back all that is Spain,
Granada and Morocco and the Pillars,
and though all men and women,
50   animals and the world
may come to calm their ills —
yet I cannot end my insistent anguish;
it pains me that each day augments my grief,
for here I am still growing in this love
for nearly ten years now,
wondering who will ever set me free.

And (to relieve my pain a bit by talking)
I see at evening oxen coming home,
freed from the fields and furrows they have ploughed —
60   why, then, must I not be free of my sighs
at least sometimes? Why not my heavy yoke?
Why day and night must my eyes still be wet?
Oh what I did that time
when I fixed them upon
the beauty of her face
to carve it in my heart's imagination

whence neither by coercion nor by art
could it be moved — not till I am the prey
of one who all does part!
70   And could she even then I am not sure.

My song, if being with me
from morning until night
has made you join my party,
you will not show yourself in any place
and will care little to be praised by others —
it will suffice to think from hill to hill
how I have been consumed
by fire of the living stone I cling to.

P52: *Non al suo amante più Diana piacque*

Diana never pleased her lover more,
when just by chance all of her naked body
he saw bathing within the chilly waters,

than did the simple mountain shepherdess
please me, the while she bathed the pretty veil
that holds her lovely blonde hair in the breeze.

So that even now in hot sunlight she makes me
tremble all over with the chill of love.

P53: *Spirto gentil che quelle membra reggi*

Noble spirit, you who informs those members
inside of which there dwells in pilgrimage
a lord of valor who is keen and wise:
now that you have achieved the honored staff
with which you guide Rome and its erring people

and call her back to her old way of life,
to you I speak for I see nowhere else
that virtuous ray extinguished in the world
and find no one ashamed of doing wrong.
10   For what Italy waits or yearns I know not,
for she does not appear to feel her woes —
she's idle, slow, and old;
will no one wake her, will she sleep forever?
If only I could grab her by the hair!

I have no hope she'll ever move her head
in sluggish sleep, loud as the shouts may be,
so gravely she's oppressed and by such weight;
but destiny now places in your arms,
that can shake her with strength and wake her up,
20   the head of all of us, the city Rome.
Now get your hands into those venerable locks
with confidence, into her unkept hair,
and pull the lazy one out of the mud.
I who all night and day weep for her torment
have placed almost all of my hope in you
for if Mars' progeny
should ever raise their eyes to their own honor,
it seems such grace will come in your own times.

The ancient walls which all the world still fears
30   and loves and trembles, every time it thinks
of turning back to look at those past times,
recalling those tombstones which hold the bodies
of men who will not be without great fame
until our universe dissolves away,
and everything involving this one ruin,
through you they hope to mend all of the faults.
O great Scipioni, O faithful Brutus,
how pleased you must be now if news reached you
down there of how well placed this office is!

40   To think how very glad
      Fabricius must have been to hear such news;
      he says: 'My Rome you shall once more be lovely.'

      And if the heavens care for things down here,
      then all those citizen-souls who dwell up there
      whose bodies were abandoned here on earth,
      pray that you end this lengthy, civil hatred
      because of which the people are not safe
      and which has closed the pathway to their temples,
      so well attended once, and now in war
50   have been transformed into a den of thieves,
      whose doors are closed only to men of good,
      and there among their altars and bare statues
      all kinds of cruel activity takes place –
      ah, how diverse those acts –
      nor do they start attacking without bells
      placed there on high to give thanks to our God.

      Women in tears and the defenseless throng
      of all the young and all the old and tired
      who hate themselves and their lives overlived
60   and the black friars and the grey, the white,
      and all the other groups of sick and weary
      cry out: 'O Lord of ours, help us, help us!'
      and all of these poor people in bewilderment,
      thousands and thousands show you all their wounds
      which would make even Hannibal feel pity.
      And if you take a good look at God's house
      that's all aflame today, by putting out a few
      sparks you could calm these wills
      that show that they are so enflamed today;
70   whereby your good works will be praised in Heaven.

The bears and wolves, the lions, eagles, and snakes
to a great column that is made of marble
give trouble, and they often harm themselves;
because of them that noble lady weeps
that called for you to uproot from herself
all those bad plants that know not how to flower.
More than a thousand years have now gone by
since all those noble souls did pass away
that made her what she was in their own day.
80   Ah, you newcomers haughty beyond limits,
irreverent to a mother great as she!
Be husband, be her father!
All help we wait to come from your own hand –
the greater Father is fixed on other work.

Rarely it happens that injurious Fortune
is not in conflict with high undertakings
for she does not agree with daring deeds.
Now, having cleared the way by which you entered,
she leads me to forgive all her misdeeds,
90   for here, at least, she differs from herself;
in all the time this world of ours remembers
was the way not clear to mortal man as now
it is to you, to reach eternal fame,
for you can raise that monarchy most noble
up on its feet, if I am not mistaken.
What glory to hear said:
'The others helped her in her youth and strength,
but he saved her from death when she was old.'

Upon Tarpeian Mount, my song, you'll see
100   a knight to whom all Italy pays honor,
who thinks of others more than of himself.
Tell him: 'One who's not seen you yet up close,
but only as one falls in love through fame,

says Rome keeps begging you
with eyes all wet and dripping with its pain,
from all her seven hills to show her mercy.'

P70: *Lasso me, ch'i' non so in qual parte pieghi*

Oh what to do with all that hope of mine
by now betrayed so many, many times!
since no one offers me an ear of pity,
why cast so many prayers into the air?
But should it be that I not be denied
an end to my poor words,
before my end has come,
I beg my lord it please him let me say
again one day, free in the grass and flowers:
'It's right and just that I sing and be joyful.'

There is good reason that I sing sometimes,
since for so long a time I have been sighing
that I could never start too soon to make
my smiling equal to my many woes.
If I could only make those holy eyes
receive delight somehow
from some sweet words of mine,
how blessèd would I be above all lovers!
But more so if in truth I were to say:
'A lady begs me, so I wish to speak.'

My yearning thoughts, that step by step have led
my reasoning to heights unreachable,
you see my lady's heart is hard as stone,
and on my own I cannot enter it.
She does not deign to look down low enough
to care about our words;

it is not Heaven's will,
and I am weary now from opposition,
and since my heart is hard and bitter now,
30   'So in my speech I now wish to be harsh.'

What am I saying? Where am I? Who cheats
me more than I and my excessive wants?
My mind could run the heavens sphere to sphere
and find no star condemning me to tears;
if mortal veil it is that dulls my sight,
what fault is it of stars
or any lovely thing?
In me dwells one who night and day gives grief,
since she gave me the burden of the pleasure:
40   'Her sweet presence, her soft and lovely glance.'

All things adorning our world with their beauty
came forth in goodness from the Master's hand,
but I, who cannot see so deep in her,
am dazzled by the beauty on the outside;
should I ever again see the true light,
my eyes will not resist,
so weak have they become
by their own fault and not by that day's fault
when I turned them to her angelic beauty
50   'In the sweet season of my early age.'

P71: *Perché la vita è breve*

Because life is so short
and wit so fearful of so high a venture,
I have no confidence in either one;
I hope for understanding
there where I yearn it be, where it must be,
that pain of mine which I cry out in silence.

by nature lazy, but by great pleasure spurred;
and he who speaks of you
acquires from the subject gracious habit

10   which, with the wings of love
lifting him, part him from all thought that's vile;
raised by such wings, I now shall say the things
my heart has carried hidden for so long.

Not that I do not see
how much my praise falls short of honoring you,
but I cannot resist the great desire
inside me since the time
that I saw what no thought can hope to equal,
let alone words, my own or any others.

20   Source of my sweet condition that is bitter
I know no one but you can understand:
when in your burning rays I turn to snow,
that kind disdain of yours
perhaps then my unworthiness offends.
Oh, if such fear as this
were not to temper flame that burns in me,
then, happy death! for I would in their presence
rather die happily than live without them.

That I am not destroyed,

30   so frail an object to so strong a fire,
is not because of my own worth that saves me;
but fear, that freezes blood
that runs through all my veins, strengthens the heart
a little so that it may burn for longer.
O hills, O vales, O streams, O woods, O fields,
O witnesses of this my heavy life,
how many times you've heard me call on Death!
Ah fate so dolorous,
staying destroys me, fleeing is no help!

40   But if a greater fear

did not stop me, a short and quicker way
would end this suffering, bitter and hard –
it is the fault of one who does not care.

Sorrow, why lead me off
the path to say what I would rather not?
Let me go where my pleasure urges me.
For I do not complain
about you, eyes serene beyond man's reach,
nor about him who binds me in this knot.
50   Take a good look at all the colors Love
will often paint right there upon my face,
then you can guess what he does inside me,
where day and night he rules
me with the force that he's gathered from you,
you holy lights and happy –
except that you cannot observe yourselves,
but every time you turn to look at me
you see in someone else what you are like.

Were you as well aware
60   of that beauty, divine, incredible
of which I speak, as is the one who sees it,
a measured happiness
your heart could not possess; perhaps, then, beauty
is separate from the natural face that moves you.
Happy the soul who sighs because of you,
celestial lights for which I thank my life
which for no other reason I find pleasant.
Ah, why do you so rarely
give me that which I never have enough of?
70   Why don't you look more often
at the destruction Love is causing me?
Why do you strip me without hesitation
of all the good my soul feels now and then?

I must say that sometimes,
with thanks to you, I feel within my soul
a sweetness that's unusual and new
which every other burden
of painful thoughts it then expels from there,
so of a thousand only one remains.

80 This bit of life and no more gives me pleasure;
and if this good of mine could last a while
no other life could ever equal it.
Perhaps it would make others
envious, and me proud from so much honor;
and so, alas, it's fated
that laughter's limits be assailed by tears,
and interrupting all those burning thoughts,
that I return to me, to think of me.

The amorous thought that dwells
90 inside of you reveals itself to me
and draws out of my heart all other joys;
whereby such words and deeds
come out of me that I hope to become
immortal through them though the flesh may die.
Before your presence, harm and anguish flee,
and when you leave the two of them return;
but since my memory, so much in love,
will not allow them entrance,
they get no further than the surface parts.
100 So if some lovely fruit
grows out of me, from you first comes the seed;
I see myself an arid piece of land
that's tilled by you – the praise all goes to you.

Song, you instead of calming make me burn
to tell about what steals me from myself;
and so be sure that you are not alone.

P72: *Gentil mia donna, i' veggio*

I see, my gracious lady,
when your eyes move, the sweetness of a glow
that lights the way for me that leads to Heaven;
and there, as is its custom,
within, where I sit all alone with Love,
your heart shines through – and I can almost see it.
This is the sight that leads me to do well
and shows me how to reach the goal of glory,
and this alone sets me apart from others.
10   There is no human tongue
that ever could explain what those divine
two lights can make me feel,
neither when winter scatters all the frost
nor later when the year grows young again
as it was at the time of my first yearning.

I think: if up above,
where the eternal Mover of the stars
deigned to display this work of His on earth,
there be more works so lovely,
20   then let the prison I am locked in open
which keeps me from the way to such a life!
Then I return to my accustomed war,
grateful to Nature and my day of birth
which have reserved for me so great a good,
and her who, to such hope,
raised up my heart (for until then I lay
heavy and hard to bear
but from then on a pleasure to myself)
filling with high and gracious thought that heart
30   for which those lovely eyes possess the key.

Never such happiness
did Love or ever-changing Fortune give
to those who were their closest friends in life
that I would not exchange
for one glance of those eyes where all my rest
comes from, as every tree comes from its roots.
Angelic sparks of loveliness, the blessers
of all my life, wherein flares up the pleasure
sweetly consuming and destroying me:
40   as every other light
will flee and fade whenever yours shines forth,
just so from my own heart,
when so much sweetness pours down into it,
all else, all of my other thoughts depart
and left there all alone with you is Love.

All sweetness ever found
in hearts of lucky lovers and collected
all in one place, is nothing next to what
I feel when you, at times,
50   sweetly within the lovely black and white,
make move the light in which Love takes delight.
And I believe from swaddling clothes and crib
that for my imperfection and bad fortune
this remedy the heavens have provided.
Your veil does me a wrong
as does your hand that often comes between
my highest of all pleasures
and my own eyes, so night and day pours forth
my great desire to relieve my heart
60   which takes its shape from your own changing look.

Since I can see, with sorrow,
that all my natural gifts are not enough
to make me worthy of so dear a glance,

I force myself to be
what is becoming to so high a hope
and noble fire in which all of me burns.
If swift to good and slow to what is ill,
condemner of what all the world desires,
I could become through persevering toil,
70   perhaps such reputation
could help me in her kind consideration.
Surely, an end to tears
my grieving heart invokes from that place only
will come at last from fair eyes sweetly trembling,
ultimate hope of every noble lover.

Song, just behind you is one of your sisters,
and in the same place I can feel the other
getting ready, and so I rule more paper.

P73: *Poi che per mio destino*

Since it has been my fate
for my own burning wish to make me write
the wish that forced me to eternal sighing,
Love, you who makes me want this,
show me the way to go and be my guide
and keep my verse in tune with my desire,
but not so that my heart is out of tune
with sweetness overflowing, as I fear
from what I feel where no eye ever reaches;
10   for my words burn and urge me,
nor does my talent (whence I fear and tremble),
as oftentimes it happens,
diminish the great fire of my mind;
rather, I melt when I hear my own words,
as if I were a snowman in the sun

When I began I thought
to find some brief repose, some kind of truce
for my inflamed desire through my words;
this hope of mine made me
20   daring enough to speak of what I felt,
now in my need it leaves me and dissolves.
But still I must pursue this lofty venture,
continuing to write my loving notes,
so powerful the will that transports me;
and dead is Reason now
who held the reins and cannot fight against it.
At least let Love show me
what I must say so that if by some chance
it strike the ears of my sweet enemy
30   it may make her, not mine, but pity's friend.

I say, if in that age
when souls burned so in search of the true honor,
the industry of some men took them round
and through the different countries
past hills and seas in search of honored things
and plucked from them their loveliest of flowers;
since it was wished by God and Love and Nature
to fill most perfectly with every virtue
those lovely lights by which I live in joy,
40   there is no need for me
to change countries or pass from shore to shore:
to them I always go
as to the source of all of my well-being –
and when I run desirous toward death,
with their sight only do I help my state.

Just as the helmsman tired
by furious winds will lift his head at night
to those two lights that our pole always holds,
so in the storm of love

50   which I endure, those shining eyes of hers
are my sole comfort and my constellation.
Alas, but much more do I steal from them
now here, now there, as Love suggests I do,
than what comes from them as a gracious gift;
the little worth I have
I have from them as my perpetual norm;
from the first time I saw them
I took no step toward good without them there,
so I have placed them at my very summit,
60   for my own worth alone is valueless.

Never could I imagine,
and no less tell about, all the effects
those gentle eyes produce within my heart;
all of the other pleasures
found in this life I hold to be far less,
and every other beauty falls behind.
A tranquil peace without a single worry
like that which reigns eternally in Heaven
moves from their smile that holds and makes one love.
70   Could I but see fixedly
how Love in all his sweetness governs them
up close, for just one day,
with none of the celestial spheres in motion,
nor think of anyone nor of myself,
without blinking my eyes too frequently!

Alas, I go in search
of what can never be in any way
and I live in desire beyond hope.
If only the tight knot
80   which Love ties round my tongue on the occasion
when too much light wins over human sight
were loosened, I would gather up the courage
right then and there to speak words so unusual
they would make anyone who hears them weep.

But those wounds deeply pressed
then force my wounded heart to turn away,
and from this I turn pale,
and my blood runs to hide, I know not where,
nor am I what I was; and I'm aware
90   this is the blow with which Love dealt me death.

Song, I can feel my pen already tired
from talking long and sweetly by its means,
but not of all my thoughts that speak to me.

ANTHONY MORTIMER (1936–   )

Professor of English Literature at the University of Fribourg, Switzer-
land, Mortimer has completed a translation for Penguin: *Petrarch's
Canzoniere: Selected Poems* (2002), from which these sixteen poems are
taken.

P34: *Apollo, s'ancor vive il bel desio*

Apollo, should the fair desire still last
that burned you where Thessalian waters flow,
if golden tresses loved so long ago
be not forgotten with the ages past;

from biting weather and from sluggish frost
that stays as long as you conceal your brow,
protect the honoured and the sacred bough
where you were first ensnared and I am lost;

and by the power of love's hope that then
10   sustained you in a hard and humble life,
dispel the noxious vapours that pervade;

so shall we both marvel to see again
our lady sit upon the grassy turf
and make with her own arms her own sweet shade.

P35: *Solo e pensoso i píu deserti campi*

Alone in thought, through the deserted fields
I wander with a slow and measured pace,
and eyes intent to flee from any trace
of human presence in the sand revealed.

For my defence I find no other shield
against the people's open knowing gaze,
for in my hearing and my cheerless ways
one reads the flame that burns in me concealed;

so that I think the mountain and the slope,
10   the wood and stream already understand
the temper of my life, from others hid.

But yet I cannot find a path so steep,
a way so wild that Love does not ascend,
discoursing with me still, and I with him.

P181: *Amor fra l'erbe una leggiadra rete*

Upon the grass Love spread a wanton net,
woven with gold and pearls, under a bough
of the dear evergreen I love, although
it holds more grief than gladness in its shade.

The seed he sows and gathers was the bait,
bitter and sweet, my fear and craving now;
never were notes so gentle and so low
since the first day when Adam raised his head.

And the clear light, forcing the sun to hide,
flashed all about, and in a hand more white
than ivory or snow was wound the rope.

So in the net I fell; here was I caught
by the fair motions and angelic words,
the pleasure, the desire, and the hope.

P192: *Stiamo, Amor, a veder la gloria nostra*

Love, let us stay, our glory to behold,
things passing nature, wonderful and rare:
see how much sweetness rains upon her there,
see the pure light of heaven on earth revealed,

see how art decks with scarlet, pearls and gold
the chosen habit never seen elsewhere,
giving the feet and eyes their motion rare
through this dim cloister which the hills enfold.

Blooms of a thousand colours, grasses green,
under the ancient blackened oak now pray
her foot may press or touch them where they rise;

and the sky, radiant with a glittering sheen,
kindles around, and visibly is gay
to be made cloudless by such lovely eyes.

P234: *O cameretta che già fosti un porto*

O little room that once a haven seemed
after the day when heavy tempests rave,
now you provoke the nightly grief I prove,
the tears that I by day must hide for shame.

O humble bed whence rest and solace came,
now are you bathed from grieving urns above
and watered by those ivory hands of Love,
that so unjustly mark me out for blame.

Not only from my solitude and rest,
10   but from myself I flee and from the thought
that gave me once the wings on which I've flown;

and now the crowd, the foe that I detest,
(who would have thought it?) is my last resort:
so much I fear to find myself alone.

P250: *Solea lontana in sonno consolarme*

In sleep my distant lady used to come,
consoling me with that angelic air,
but now she brings a sad foreboding there,
nor can the grief and dread be overcome:

for all too often in her face I seem
to see true pity blent with heavy care,
and hear those things that teach the heart despair,
since of all joy and hope it must disarm.

'Does our last evening not come back to you',
10   she says to me, 'and how your eyes were wet,
and how, compelled by time, I left you then?

'I had no power nor wish to speak of it;
now I can say as something tried and true:
hope not to see me on this earth again.'

P267: *Oimè il bel viso, oimè il soave sguardo*

Alas, the lovely face, the sweet regard,
alas, the gait where pride and grace combined;
alas, the speech by which the rebel mind
was humbled and the coward given heart!

and O, alas, the smile that sent the dart
which now makes death the only hope I find:
most royal soul, worthy to rule mankind,
if you had not descended here so late!

Still must I breathe in you, still burn again,
10   since I was yours; and, robbed of you, the less
can any other sorrow grieve the mind.

With hope you filled me and desire when
I parted from the highest living bliss:
but all your words were taken by the wind.

P272: *La vita fugge e non s'arresta un'ora*

Life flees before, not stopping on the way,
and death with daylong marches follows fast,
and all things present join with all things past
and with the future to make war on me;

forethought and memory bring such dismay,
now one and now the other, that at last,
but for self-pity that still holds me fast,
I would already from these thoughts be free.

If any joy has lightened this sad heart,
10   it now returns to mind; then all around
I see the winds against my sailing bent:

I see a storm in port, and, tired out,
my pilot there, the mast and rigging down,
and the bright stars I contemplated spent.

P279: *Se lamentar augelli, o verdi fronde*

If the lament of birds, or the green leaves
in summer breezes softly quivering,
or the hoarse murmur of translucent waves
are heard on some fresh bank where flowers spring,

there, where I sit and write the thought love brings,
one shown by heaven, hidden by the grave,
I see and hear, and know that ever-living
she answers from afar the heart that grieves.

'Ah why untimely wear away the years?'
she says with pitying voice, 'why shed
from sorrowing eyes this bitter flood of tears?

'Weep not for me, know that my days were made
in death eternal; when I closed my eyes,
towards the inner light they opened wide.'

P293: *S'io avesse pensato che sì care*

If I had ever reckoned that so dear
would be the sighs that in these rhymes resound,
from the first sigh I would have made them sound
in greater numbers and in style more rare.

Since she is dead who made me speak of her
and who alone amid my thoughts stood crowned,
I cannot hope, the file no more is found,
to make the rough dark verses smooth and clear.

Indeed, my only study at that time
10 was all to give the sorrowing heart relief
in some poor fashion; fame was not the spur.

My grief sought tears, not honour for my grief:
now would I wish to please; but she, sublime,
beckons me, mute and weary, after her.

P302: *Levommi il mio penser in parte ov'era*

My thoughts had lifted me to where she stood
whom I still seek, and find on earth no more:
among the souls that the third circle bore,
she came with greater beauty and less pride.

She took my hand and said: 'If hope can guide,
you will again be with me in this sphere:
for I am she who gave you so much war
and closed my day before the eventide.

'No human mind can understand my bliss:
10 you I await and what you loved so much,
the veil I left below where now it lies.'

Why did she loose my hand? Why did she cease?
for at such pitying and unsullied speech
I almost could have stayed in Paradise.

P346: *Li angeli eletti e l'anime beate*

On my dear lady's passing, that first day,
the chosen angels and the spirits blest,
the citizens of heaven, came and pressed
with reverence and wonder round her way.

'What light and what new loveliness?', they say,
'for never has a form so finely dressed
mounted from errant earth to this high rest
while all the present age has passed away.'

And she, contented to have changed her state,
10   among the perfect ones stands no less rare,
and often, turning back, she seems to wait

to see if I am following her there:
so that to heaven I raise all hope and thought,
hearing her bid me hasten in her prayer.

P362: *Volo con l'ali de' pensieri al cielo*

I fly on wings of thought to paradise
so often that I almost seem to enter
the company that there keeps all its treasure,
leaving on earth the veil that shattered lies.

At times a trembling and sweet chill will rise
within my heart as she who drains my colour
says: 'Now, my friend, I give you love and honour,
for you have changed your fur and changed your ways.'

She leads me to her Lord, and there I bow,
10   humbly praying that he will let me stay
to look on one and on the other face.

And she replies: 'Your fate is certain now,
and though some twenty, thirty years' delay
seem long to you, it is a little space.'

P363: *Morte à spento quel sol ch'abbagliar suolmi*

Death has put out the sun that dazzled me,
in darkness are those pure and constant eyes;
my cause of cold and heat, earth where she lies;
to oak and elm is turned my laurel-tree:

in this, though I still grieve, my good I see.
No-one compels my mind to fall and rise
with fear and courage as I burn and freeze,
nor fills with hope and loads with misery.

Free of the hand that healed and wounded me,
that once inflicted on me such long pain,
I find a bitter and sweet liberty;

and to the Lord, whose governing glance holds fast
the heavens, whom I adore and thank, I turn
tired of living, sated at the last.

P364: *Tennemi Amor anni ventuno ardendo*

For twenty-one long years Love made me burn,
glad in the fire, hopeful in my pain;
my lady took my heart to heaven's domain,
and so he gave me ten more years to mourn;

Now I am weary, and my life I spurn
for so much error that has almost slain
the seed of virtue, and what years remain,
high God, to you devoutly I return,

contrite and sad for every misspent year,
for time I should have put to better use
in seeking peace and shunning passions here.

Lord, having pent me in this prison close,
from everlasting torment draw me clear:
I know my fault and offer no excuse.

P365: *I'vo piangendo i miei passati tempi*

I keep lamenting over days gone by,
the time I spent loving a mortal thing,
with no attempt to soar, although my wing
might give no mean example in the sky.

You that my foul unworthy sins descry,
unseen and everlasting, heavenly King,
succour my soul, infirm and wandering,
and what is lacking let your grace supply;

so, if I lived in tempest and in war,
10   I die in port and peace; however vain
the stay, at least the parting may be fair.

Now in the little life that still remains
and at my dying may your hand be near:
in others, you well know, my hope is gone.

NICHOLAS KILMER (1941–)

Kilmer is a painter, dramatist, novelist and translator of Ronsard, Petrarch and Dante. Three poems from *Songs and Sonnets from Laura's Lifetime* (1980).

P6: *Sì traviato è'l folle mi' desio*

I've come this far. My foolhardy desire
Follows her escape. She is airborne,
Careless. I can hear the four feet under me.

The less he listens to me the more I call,
Bawling directions, cautioning towards safe highways.
Neither spurring, nor yanking the reins, makes any difference.
Love, the need of it, makes his nature restive.

His rage keeps the bit and the rein.
I am become already a dead rider,
10   Bucketing about in the saddle, out of control.

He paws, stamps at the foot of the laurel.
I take its bitter fruit in my mouth. Tasting it
Makes my wounds more desperately known.

P13: *Quando fra l'altre donne ad ora ad ora*

Now and then she stands among other ladies.
Love comes into her face, and desire
Is as alive in me, as she is more beautiful than they.

There is honor in the distance my soul has travelled
Since the place, moment – they are in my mind –
When I looked upward for the first time.

What little I know of love is her gift:
My glimpse of perfect grace, and my ability
To follow it are hers; my knowledge
10   That what men want mostly is worthless.

I am proud of what she allows me to hope,
Her beckoning me to some distance from sin:
Light, love, air – my own soul's future.

P188: *Almo sol, quella fronde ch'io sola amo*

You were this tree's first lover, sun;
Tree whom I love now; and kept her loveliness
Green always, unequalled since Adam's sin
Stood out clearly before us.

We will look at it together.
Yet you leave my prayer in the shadow of hills
Lengthening; take daylight and my vision.

The shadow falling from the low hill
Where my bright flare gleams,
10   Where the great laurel was a frail sapling,

Growing while I speak, invades my eyes,
Darkens the dwelling where her brightness was,
Takes my heart's shelter.

MARION SHORE (1952–   )

Shore is a poet and translator. Two poems from *For Love of Laura:
Poetry of Petrarch* (1987).

P2: *Per fare una leggiadra sua vendetta*

To take his sweet revenge on me at last
and right a thousand wrongs with one swift blow,
in secret Love took up his deadly bow
and lay in ambush for me as I passed.

All my old resistance was amassed
about my heart to guard against the foe,
when the mortal arrow chanced to go
where every dart was blunted in the past;
    thus shattered in the first attack, my will
10 had neither time nor vigor to remain
and arm itself against the coming darts,
    nor strength to climb the steep and lofty hill
wherein it might escape the grievous pain
from which it would, but cannot shield my heart.

P20: *Vergognando talor ch'ancor si taccia*

Ashamed sometimes, my lady, that I still
cannot express your beauty in my rhyme,
I wander to that sweet and distant time
when you alone gained power of my will.
    But even there I find no guiding skill,
no strength to scale a height I cannot climb,
for such a task demands a force sublime,
at whose attempt I fall back, mute and still.
    How often do I move my lips to speak,
10 and find my voice lies buried in my breast –
but then, what sound could ever rise so high?
    How often in my verses do I seek
to find the words my tongue cannot express,
but pen and hand are vanquished with each try.

CODA: PARODIES AND REPLAYS

We are reminded by Katherine M. Wilson that 'Taken seriously sonnet talk would be blasphemous',[1] and she, of course, is right. Blasphemy is quite simply parody of the deity, and from the invention of the sonnet by Giacomo da Lentino (thirteenth century), long before Petrarch saw the light of day, the love-talk of the sonnet played with other, conflicting meanings of love that gave a space to the outcries of human desire within a larger intellectual world, epitomized by Barnabe Barnes's 'My god, my god, how much I love my goddess'. St Augustine, very early on in the Christian tradition, had outlined in *De doctrina cristiana* the human confusion of *caritas* and *cupiditas*. The opposition is not our modern opposition between love and lust. *Caritas* is first of all the love of God and second the love of his created things because he created them ('Thou shalt love the Lord with thy whole soul, thy whole mind, and thy whole heart – and thy neighbour as thyself'). *Cupiditas* is the love of any created thing for itself alone. The confusion between the two is evident in one of Giacomo's earliest sonnets, which I quote in Dante Gabriel Rossetti's charming translation:[2]

> I have it in my heart to serve God so
> That into Paradise I shall repair,
> The holy place through the which everywhere
> I have heard say that joy and solace flow.
> Without my lady I were loath to go, –
> She who has the bright face and the bright hair;
> Because if she were absent, I being there,
> My pleasure would be less than nought, I know.
> Look you, I say not this to such intent
> As that I there would deal in any sin:

> I only would behold her gracious mien,
> And beautiful soft eyes, and lovely face,
> That so it should be my complete content
> To see my lady joyful in her place.

So much for the beatific vision! The absurdity of the poet–lover's decency and decorum turns the poem into a parody of itself. Neither Dante nor Petrarch resorts to such naked blasphemy, but the threat of blasphemy and parody inheres in their works, especially when they have conveniently killed off their Ladies, and therefore it is important for us as readers to be careful about what we call 'Petrarchan parody'.

The most famous example of putative Petrarchan parody is Shakespeare's sonnet 130, which, in spite of Helen Vendler's most skilful efforts to domesticate it as a nice poem, is nonetheless in the mainline of Petrarchan imitation because it still idolizes the lady, although its choice of laudable physical desiderata is lower than anything that Petrarch would have chosen:

> My Mistress eyes are nothing like the Sunne;
> Currall is farre more red, then her lips red,
> If snow be white, why then her brests are dun;
> If hairs be wiers, black wiers grow on her head.
> I haue seene Roses damaskt, red and white,
> But no such Roses see I in her cheeks,
> And in some perfumes is there more delight
> Then in the breath that from my Mistres reekes.
> I loue to heare her speake; yet well I know,
> That Musicke hath a farre more pleasing sound:
> I graunt I neuer saw a goddesse goe,
> My Mistres, when shee walkes, treads on the ground.
> And yet, by heauen, I thinke my loue as rare
> As any she beli'd with false compare.[3]

After the initial denial of her eyes as the sun, a definite Petrarchan metaphor, we learn that her lips are not particularly red, that her breasts are not white, that her hairs are kinky, that her cheeks are not rosy, that she has halitosis and that her voice is not pleasant. It is enough to turn one off, except for the poet-lover's assertion that she is 'as *rare* / As any she beli'd with false compare'. She is rarified only by the poet's desire, and this places the Dark Lady as much in the Petrarchan tradition as any she who is belied by any other form of idolatry.

Shakespeare's poem was preceded in the English tradition by a more complicated version of the same idolatry in Sir Philip Sidney's sonnet to Mopsa in the *Arcadia*. In this example, Sidney adopts Dante's trick of using a 'screen lady' to praise his real beloved, in this case, the ugly servant girl Mopsa to stand in for the prince's real love, Philoclea, who is listening to the whole recital of the prince's poem to Mopsa:

> What length of verse can serve brave Mopsa's good to show,
>   Whose vertues strange, and beuties such, as no man them may know?
> Thus shrewdly burden'd then, how can my Muse escape?
> The gods must help, and pretious things must serve to shew her shape:
>   Like great God Saturn fair, and like faire Venus chaste:
> As smooth as Pan, as Juno milde, like goddesse Iris faste.
> With Cupid she fore-sees, and goes god Vulcan's pace:
> And for a tast of all these gifts, she borowes Momus' grace.
>   Her forhead jacinth like, her cheekes of opall hue,
> Her twinkling eies bedeckt with pearle, her lips as Saphir blew:
> Her hair pure Crapal-stone; her mouth O heavenly wide;
> Her skin like burnisht gold, her hands like silver ure untryde.
>   As for those parts unknowne, which hidden sure are best:
> Happy be they which well beleeve, and never seeke the rest.[4]

Never has sonnet lady been so grounded as Mopsa, but one also has to wonder about Philoclea's response to this pseudo-praise of woman. What could she expect? But Sidney gives us the up-beat side of this praise in the river Ladon episode of the *Arcadia* when the prince, disguised as an Amazon, accompanies the ladies for a skinny-dip and sings his praise of Philoclea, in which the midpoint of the lush poem is a description of her navel (indicated by [★])!

> What tongue can her perfections tell
> In whose each part all pens may dwell?
> Her hair fine threads of finest gold,
> In curled knots man's thought to hold;

But that her forehead says, 'in me
A whiter beauty you may see.'
Whiter indeed, more white than snow,
Which on cold winter's face doth grow.

   That doth present those even brows
Whose equal line their angles bows,
Like to the moon when after change
Her horned head abroad doth range;
And arches be to heav'nly lids,
Whose wink each bold attempt forbids.

   For the black stars those spheres contain,
The matchless pair, ev'n praise doth stain.
No lamp whose light by art is got,
No sun which shines, and seeth not,
Can liken them without all peer,
Save one as much as other clear;
Which only thus unhappy be
Because themselves they cannot see.

   Her cheeks with kindly claret spread,
Aurora-like new out of bed,
Or like the fresh queen-apple's side,
Blushing at sight of Phoebus' pride.
Her nose, her chin pure ivory wears:
No purer than the pretty ears.
So that therein appears some blood,
Like wine and milk that mingled stood.
In whose incirclets if ye gaze,
Your eyes may tread a lover's maze,
But with such turns the voice to stray,
No talk untaught can find the way.
The tip no jewel needs to wear;
The tip is jewel of the ear.

   But who those ruddy lips can miss,
Which blessed still themselves do kiss?
Rubies, cherries, and roses new,
In worth, in taste, in perfit hue,

Which never part, but that they show
Of precious pearl the double row,
The second sweetly-fenced ward
Her heavenly-dewed tongue to guard,
Whence never word in vain did flow.

   Fair under these doth stately grow
The handle of this precious work,
The neck in which strange graces lurk.
Such be, I think, the sumptuous towers
Which skill doth make in princes' bowers.

   So good a say invites the eye
A little downward to espy
The lovely clusters of her breasts,
Of Venus' babe the wanton nests,
Like pommels round of marble clear,
Where azur'd veins well mix'd appear,
With dearest tops of porphyry.

   Betwixt these two a way doth lie,
A way more worthy beauty's fame
Than that which bears the milken name.
This leads unto the joyous field,
Which only still doth lilies yield;
But lilies such whose native smell
The Indian odours doth excel.
Waist it is called, for it doth waste
Men's lives, until it be imbraced.

   There may one see, and yet not see
Her ribs in white all armed be,
More white than Neptune's foamy face
When struggling rocks he would embrace.

   In these delights the wand'ring thought
Might of each side astray be brought,
But that her navel doth unite,[*]
In curious circle busy sight,
A dainty seal of virgin-wax,
Where nothing but impression lacks.

Her belly there glad sight doth fill,
Justly entitled Cupid's hill;
A hill most fit for such a master,
A spotless mine of alabaster,
Like alabaster fair and sleek,
But soft and supple, satin-like.
In that sweet seat the boy doth sport.
Loath, I must leave his chief resort;
For such an use the world hath gotten,
The best things still must be forgotten.

Yet never shall my song omit
Those thighs (for Ovid's song more fit)
Which flanked with two sugared flanks,
Lift up their stately swelling banks
That Albion cliffs in whiteness pass;
With haunches smooth as looking glass.

But bow all knees, now of her knees
My tongue doth tell what fancy sees
The knots of joy, the gems of love,
Whose motion makes all graces move;
Whose bought incaved doth yield such sight
Like cunning painter shadowing white.
The gartring place with childlike sign
Shows easy print in metal fine.
But there again the flesh doth rise
In her brave calves, like crystal skies,
Whose Atlas is a smallest small,
More white than whitest bone of whale.

There oft steals out that round clean foot,
This noble cedar's precious root;
In show and scent pale violets,
Whose step on earth all beauty sets.

But back unto her back, my muse,
Where Leda's swan his feathers mews,
Along whose ridge such bones are met,
Like comfits round in marchpane set.

Her shoulders be like two white doves,
Perching within square royal rooves,
Which leaded are with silver skin,
Passing the hate-spot ermelin.

And thence those arms derived are;
The phoenix' wings be not so rare
For faultless length, and stainless hue.

Ah, woe is me, my woes renew.
Now course doth lead me to her hand,
Of my first love the fatal band,
Where whiteness doth for ever sit:
Nature herself enamell'd it.
For there with strange compact doth lie
Warm snow, moist pearl, soft ivory.
There fall those sapphire-coloured brooks,
Which conduit-like with curious crooks,
Sweet islands make in that sweet land.
As for the fingers of the hand,
The bloody shafts of Cupid's war,
With amethysts they headed are.

Thus hath each part his beauty's part;
But how the Graces do impart
To all her limbs a special grace,
Becoming every time and place,
Which doth even beauty beautify,
And most bewitch the wretched eye!
How all this is but a fair inn
Of fairer guests, which dwells within.
Of whose high praise, and praiseful bliss,
Goodness the pen, heav'n paper is,
The ink immortal fame doth lend.
As I began, so must I end.

No tongue can her perfections tell,
In whose each part all pens may dwell.[5]

These three poems are examples of the *blason*, a kind of poem that Petrarch himself never wrote. He wrote in praise of eyes and other parts of the beloved's body, but he never gathered them all together in a compendium as in these three poems. Nancy Vickers has written a well-received essay on Petrarch's anatomizing of Laura as a re-membering of the dis-memberment of the woman, forgetting, alas, that a poetic portrait must proceed one element after another, by virtue of the nature of language.[6] Her article has given new life to the erroneous suggestion that Petrarch originated this laundry-list of femi-nine traits. He did not. In the Petrarchan tradition the *blason* was inevitable, but it is a realignment of separate elements in his poetry.

The earliest and possibly the most famous *blason* is the 'Crin d'oro crispo e d'ambra tersa e pura' of Pietro Bembo (1470–1547), which was almost immediately parodied by Francesco Berni (1497/8–1535) in his 'Chiome d'argento fine, irte ed attorte'. Thus was established in Italy both the laudatory and the parodic. In spite of this contemporary but earlier outbreak of the *blason* in Italy, it is commonly assumed that the *blason* was a French invention, if not Petrarchan. Clément Marot (c. 1496–1544) is so credited for his *Blason du beau tétin*, and he may have been responsible for a poetic contest that resulted in the anthology *Blasons anatomiques du corps feminin* (1536), but from this point on catalogues of feminine items were in. One might look at Joachim du Bellay (1523–60), 'Contre les Petrarchistes', or at least the first of its 52 stanzas:

> J'ai oublié l'art de pétrarquiser
> Je veux d'amour franchement deviser
> Sans vous flatter, et sans me déguiser
>   Ceux qui font tant de plaints.

More insidious and hilarious is the internalized *blason* of Barnabe Barnes in his *Parthenophil and Parthenophe* (1593), of which the title alone is sufficient proof of the commodification of the mistress (to use a current critical velleity). The poet-lover's easy accommodation to his desires is really nothing more than intercourse inside-out.

Ioue for Europaes loue tooke shape of Bull,
    And for Calisto playde Dianaes parte
    And in a golden shower, he filled full
    The lappe of Danae with coelestiall arte,
Would I were chang'd but to my mistresse gloues,
    That those white louely fingers I might hide,
    That I might kisse those hands, which mine hart loues
    Or else that cheane of pearle, her neckes vaine pride,
Made proude with her neckes vaines, that I might folde
    About that louely necke, and her pappes tickle,
    Or her to compasse like a belt of golde,
Or that sweet wine, which downe her throate doth trickle,
    To kisse her lippes, and lye next at her hart,
    Runne through her vaynes, and passe by pleasures part.[7]

More decorous examples occur in this anthology under Thomas Lodge and an anonymous poem from *The Phoenix Nest*, all of which were derived from Ronsard's *Amours*, I.12 (1552):[8]

Je vouldroy bien richement iaunissant
En pluye d'or goute à goute descendre
Dans le beau sein de ma belle Cassandre
Lors qu'en ses yeulx le somne va glissant.
Je vouldroy en toreau blandissant
Me transformer pour finement la prendre,
Quand elle vapar l'herbe la plus tendre
Seule à l'ecart mille fleurs rauissant.
Je vouldroy bien afin d'aiser ma peine
Estre un Narcisse & elle une fontaine,
Pour m'y plonger une nuict à sejour
Durast tousjours sans que jamais l'Aurore
D'un front nouueau nous r'allumast le jour.

The parody need not cleave to the physical. It can also appropriate the spiritual as in Daniel's *Complaint of Rosamond* (1592), a complaint poem appended to Daniel's sonnet sequence, *Delia*, in which the soul of Rosamond Clifford appeals to the poet to tell her story so that she may get across the river Styx, with the added inducement to the poet that Delia, hearing her story, would add her sighs to waft poor Rosamond over; to which one can only suppose that, having heard Rosamond's story, Delia would be a stupid ninny not to recognize the perils of Rosamond's submission to the king. Barnes does this irony one better in an ode that invokes the aid of the Blessed Virgin Mary to assist him in his conquest of Parthenophe, for the simple reason that she too is a virgin.

> Vpon an holy Saintes eue
> (As I tooke my pilgrimadge)
> Wandring through the forrest warye
>   (Blest be that holy sainte)
> I mette the louely Virgine *Marye*
>   And kneeled with long trauell fainte
>   Performing my dew homage,
> My teares fore told mine hart did greeue
> Yet *Mary* would not me releeue.
>
>
>   Her I did promise euery yeare,
> The firstling foemale of my flocke
> That in my loue she would me furder:
>   I curst the dayes of my first loue,
> My comfortes spoiles, my pleasures murther:
>
>   She, she alas did me reproue,
>   My suites (as to a stonie rocke)
> Were made, for she would not giue eare.
>   Ah loue, deare loue, loue bought to deare!
>
>
>   *Mary*, my sainte chast, and milde
> Pittie, ah pittie my suite;
> Thou art a virgine, pittie mee:
>   Shine eyes, though pittie wanting
> That she by them my greefe may see
>   And looke on mine hart panting:

> But her deafe eares, and tonge mute
> Shewes her hard hart vnreconcil'de,
>   Hard hart, from all remorse exil'de.[9]

This kind of blasphemous Renaissance play is forgotten in the Romantic period, most notably by Byron, who in the third canto of *Don Juan* utters his famous invocation of the Muse and does a descant on the subject of romance and marriage with specific reference to Petrarch.

1

HAIL, Muse! et cetera – We left Juan sleeping,
  Pillowed upon a fair and happy breast,
And watched by eyes that never yet knew weeping,
  And loved by a young heart, too deeply blest
To feel the poison through her spirit creeping,
  Or know who rested there, a foe to rest,
Had soiled the current of her sinless years,
And turned her pure heart's purest blood to tears!

2

Oh, Love! what is it in this world of ours
  Which makes it fatal to be loved? Ah why
With cypress branches hast thou wreathed thy bowers,
  And made thy best interpreter a sigh?
As those who dote on odours pluck the flowers,
  And place them on their breast – but place to die –
Thus the frail beings we would fondly cherish
Are laid within our bosoms but to perish.

3

In her first passion Woman loves her lover,
  In all the others all she loves is Love,
Which grows a habit she can ne'er get over,
  And fits her loosely – like an easy glove,

As you may find, whene'er you like to prove her:
One man alone at first her heart can move;
She then prefers him in the plural number,
Not finding that the additions much encumber.

4

I know not if the fault be men's or theirs;
But one thing's pretty sure; a woman planted
(Unless at once she plunge for life in prayers) –
After a decent time must be gallanted;
Although, no doubt, her first of love affairs
Is that to which her heart is wholly granted;
Yet there are some, they say, who have had none,
But those who have ne'er end with only one.

5

'T is melancholy, and a fearful sign
Of human frailty, folly, also crime,
That Love and Marriage rarely can combine,
Although they both are born in the same clime;
Marriage from Love, like vinegar from wine –
A sad, sour, sober beverage – by Time
Is sharpened from its high celestial flavour
Down to a very homely household savour.

6

There's something of antipathy, as 't were,
Between their present and their future state;
A kind of flattery that's hardly fair
Is used until the truth arrives too late –
Yet what can people do, except despair?
The same things change their names at such a rate;
For instance – Passion in a lover's glorious,
But in a husband is pronounced uxorious.

7

Men grow ashamed of being so very fond;
They sometimes also get a little tired
(But that, of course, is rare), and then despond:
The same things cannot always be admired,
Yet 't is 'so nominated in the bond,'
That both are tied till one shall have expired.
Sad thought! to lose the spouse that was adorning
Our days, and put one's servants into mourning.

8

There's doubtless something in domestic doings
Which forms, in fact, true Love's antithesis;
Romances paint at full length people's wooings,
But only give a bust of marriages;
For no one cares for matrimonial cooings,
There's nothing wrong in a connubial kiss:
Think you, if Laura had been Petrarch's wife,
He would have written sonnets all his life?

With this delightful couplet Byron comes to his real subject, the
relationship of love and poetry, and his example is, needless to say,
Petrarch and Laura, which leads him on to those two other epic
venturers who both had marital difficulties, Dante and Milton.

9

All tragedies are finished by a death,
All comedies are ended by a marriage;
The future states of both are left to faith,
For authors fear description might disparage
The worlds to come of both, or fall beneath,
And then both worlds would punish their miscarriage;
So leaving each their priest and prayer-book ready,
They say no more of Death or of the Lady.

10

The only two that in my recollection,
Have sung of Heaven and Hell, or marriage, are
Dante and Milton, and of both the affection
Was hapless in their nuptials, for some bar
Of fault or temper ruined the connection
(Such things, in fact, it don't ask much to mar);
But Dante's Beatrice and Milton's Eve
Were not drawn from their spouses, you conceive.

11

Some persons say that Dante meant Theology
By Beatrice, and not a mistress — I,
Although my opinion may require apology,
Deem this a commentator's phantasy,
Unless indeed it was from his own knowledge he
Decided thus, and showed good reason why;
I think that Dante's more abstruse ecstatics
Meant to personify the Mathematics.

Here the singing of the poet is not the sign of his laureation but the
sign that he knows it is all a game. Byron is the nineteenth-century
Sidney, with an added twist, that he throws away in the first stanza of
the fifth canto of the poem.

When amatory poets sing their loves
In liquid lines mellifluously bland,
And pair their rhymes as Venus yokes her doves,
They little think what mischief is in hand:
The greater their success the worse it proves,
As Ovid's verse may give to understand;
Even Petrarch's self, if judged with due severity,
Is the Platonic pimp of all posterity.

Petrarch has been taken as far as he can go from his original intentions;
he has become the Early Modern poet that serves so many of our
interests today. Gone is the false spirituality of the fourteenth century;

gone is the connection between the poet's linguistic brilliance and his putative love. He becomes the 'Platonic pimp' of all mankind, and that is a very long journey for any poet. Petrarch's initial proposition that he loved a woman and suffered much for this unrequited love in his life and in his poetry gets undone in the nineteenth century in two ways. Either it is spiritualized, as in many of the nineteenth-century poems in this volume, which flicker around the altar of Wagner's *Tristan und Isolde*, or it becomes secularized as in this early poem, 'Silet', by Ezra Pound:[10]

> When I behold how black, immortal ink
> Drips from my deathless pen – ah, wellaway!
> Why should we stop at all for what I think?
> There is enough in what I chance to say.
>
> It is enough that we once came together;
> What is the use of setting it to rime?
> When it is autumn do we get spring weather,
> Or gather may of harsh northwindish time?
>
> It is enough that we once came together;
> What if the wind have turned against the rain?
> It is enough that we once came together;
> Time has seen this, and will not turn again;
>
> And who are we, who know that last intent,
> To plague to-morrow with a testament!

Desire satisfied does not need poetry, should not use poetry as a 'testament', but Pound nonetheless did write a poem, and it could not have been written without a Petrarch, somewhere at the bottom of the heap. Poetry has been thrown out of the realm of love, which has become just 'coming together'. No need to satirize marriage, or wives or husbands; it is no longer a major concern. This is twentieth-century *laissez-faire*. Where do we go from here?

It has been my good fortune to have been sent two poems by women who learned from Christopher Ricks that I was compiling this volume. I include them because they continue the monologue begun by Petrarch, as we used to say, from the distaff side.

Sonnet after Wyatt after Petrarch

The poets swear their love in little cubes
with tidy borders: stressed, unstressed and rhyme.
As if by slicing our lives up in lines
the regiments of words would follow rules
in life like in those sonnets: it's not true
This 'in the field with him to live or die'
looks good on paper, no? But it's a lie.
At least I know I couldn't see it through.
Not for this guy I sleep with every night.
If our love dies it's dying on its own.
Words like these could bring on domestic strife;
maybe he'll leave. I'll cry after the fight.
But if he finds some other girl to bone
I do recall I liked living alone.

Jill McDonough

The Lover Resorts to Commerce

To ——

Not, Oh not by me shall you get fame.
I will not line, O love, this box with you.
My lips are brazen, dustless, Delphic, warm,
While yours sprout veins of cobalt blue, and cold
Your eyes to match your stones. A crusted sac
Your heart, your head, your hair unwired is.
If I a rosebud, lush plush red red, am,
You, a fusty muffled ointment-daubed worm, are.
Your fingers, though they're ten, can't sum love's knot.
I'll carry not, O love, to fame your name.
I'll praise a tomcat (though unstoned), swiss cheese
(Though partial), Bromsgrove poems (although no though).
    Yet if you spend with me the course of sluttish time,
        And love me night by night, Oh, then what I will write!

Marcia Karp

When all is said and done, are we not back to the original premise of Petrarch? Man loves woman; woman loves not man. Neither the reason for not loving, nor the gender of who is writing matters, but write we will. Where do we go from here?

I think the answer lies in a recent volume called *The Triumph of Love* by Geoffrey Hill, who has obviously been influenced by Petrarch but who takes as his starting point the final poem of the *Canzoniere*, the very beautiful hymn to the Blessed Virgin, 'Vergine bella, che di sol vestita', a poem, the elaborate stanzaic form of which has not been imitated in English except by Milton in his 'On the Circumcision', the most minor of Milton's minor poetry (see above). The exactitude of Milton's duplication of the stanzaic form cannot be questioned, once George Watson's *Bibliography* pointed it out. Circumcision is not a subject congenial to lyric poetry, and perhaps Watson is correct in suggesting that a hymn to the Virgin was equally uncongenial to a Protestant poet, but I think that Milton did not chuckle while writing his poem. The circumcision of Jesus was the first blood-letting of the infant God-man and anticipated his dying on the Cross. I think it more likely that Milton was taking from the Mater Dolorosa to give proper praise to the Son. At any rate Milton is giving praise to Petrarch's poem in appropriating its verse form. Hill, by using the *Vergine bella* as a leitmotif in his poem, is calling our attention back to a voice in Petrarch that has not been listened to in five centuries. His poem is a fitting finale to this volume.

> *Vergine bella* – it is here that I require
> a canzone of some substance. There are sound
> precedents for this, of a plain eloquence
> which would be perfect. But –
> ought one to say, I am required; or, it is
> required of me; or, it is requisite that I should
> make such an offering, bring in such a tribute?
> And is this real obligation or actual
> pressure of expectancy? One cannot purchase
> the goodwill of your arduously simple faith
> as one would acquire a tobacconist's cum paper shop

or a small convenience store
established by aloof, hardworking Muslims.
Nor is language, now, what it once was
even in – wait a tick – nineteen hundred and forty-
five of the common era, when your blast-scarred face
appeared staring, seemingly in disbelief,
shocked beyond recognition, unable to recognize
the mighty and the tender salutations
that slowly, with innumerable false starts, the ages
had put together for your glory
in words and in the harmonies of stone.
But you have known and endured all things
since you first suffered the Incarnation:
endless the extortions, endless the dragging
in of your name. *Vergine bella*, as you
are well aware, I here follow
Petrarch, who was your follower,
a sinner devoted to your service.
I ask that you acknowledge the work
as being contributive to your high praise,
even if no one else shall be reconciled
to a final understanding of it in that light.[11]

Notes

1. Katherine M. Wilson, *Shakespeare's Sugared Sonnets* (1974), p. 34.
2. Dante Gabriel Rossetti, *The Early Italian Poets* (1861).
3. Helen Vendler, *The Art of Shakespeare's Sonnets* (1997), pp. 556–8. The text is from the first edition (1609).
4. *The Countess of Pembroke's Arcadia* (*The Old Arcadia*), ed. Jean Robertson (1974), pp. 30–31.
5. Ibid., pp. 238–42.
6. Nancy J. Vickers, 'The Body Re-membered: Petrarchan Lyric and the Strategies of Description', in *Mimesis: From Mirror to Method, Augustine to Descartes*, ed. John D. Lyons and Stephen G. Nichols, Jr. (1982).

7.   Barnabe Barnes, Sonnet 43, *Parthenophil and Parthenophe*, ed. Victor A. Doyno (1971).

8.   Pierre de Ronsard, *Les Amours*, eds. Henri and Catherine Weber (1963).

9.   Barnes, Ode 3, *Parthenophil and Parthenophe*.

10.   *The Ripostes of Ezra Pound* (1912).

11.   Geoffrey Hill, *The Triumph of Love* (1998).

PETRARCHAN ORDER OF THE
SELECTED TRANSLATIONS

All the Petrarchan numbers are to sonnets unless followed by a letter: b = *ballata*; c = *canzone*; m = *madrigale*; s = *sestina*. *TM* is *Tottel's Miscellany*; *Bohn* is *Bohn's Illustrated Library*

51   *Bohn*: Anon.

52m Musa

53c Musa

54m Bishop

57   *TM* 94: Wyatt

61   *Phoenix Nest*; Wrangham

62   Hough

70c Musa

71c Musa

72c Musa

73c Musa

77   Penn

82   *TM* 38: Wyatt

84   Constable

90   C. Smith; *Bohn*: Anon. Ox. 1795

99   Kennet

102   *TM* 45: Wyatt; *Paradise of Dainty Devices*: Earl of Oxford

106m Ayres

108   *Bohn*: Anonymous 1777

112   Drummond; *Bohn*: Anonymous 1777

119c Cayley

121m *TM* 69: Wyatt; Ayres

122   Wrangham

123   Wrangham

124   *TM* 95: Wyatt

126c Jones; Hunt

128c Dacre

129c Dacre

132   Chaucer; Watson, *Hekatompathia*; Ayres

134   *TM* 49: Wyatt; Watson, *Hekatompathia*; Lodge, *Phillis*; Ayres

138   Symonds

140   *TM* 6: Surrey; *TM* 37: Wyatt

145   *TM* 12: Surrey; *Phoenix Nest*; Drummond; Habington; Ayres

148   Drummond

153   *TM* 77: Wyatt; Carew; Cartwright

156   Nott

159   Campbell; *Bohn*: Anon.

163   Wrangham

164   *TM* 10: Surrey; Drummond

169   *TM* 41: Wyatt

ACKNOWLEDGEMENTS

I would like to thank first of all Professor Christopher Ricks who felt that I could do this task and secondly Professor George Watson, without whose *Bibliography* the task would have been impossible. Also my two 'Lauras', Laura Barber, my kind and patient editor at Penguin Books, and Laura McPherson, who submitted Petrarch to the rigors of the computer, as well as those Princeton students, who came to my rescue at moments of technological despair: Cynthia Snyder, Genelle Gertz-Robinson, Todd Barry, Kate Mackenzie and Nick Merritt. And lastly, my eternal gratitude to Monica Schmoller, who 'tweaked' the whole mess into shape with patience, goodwill and a relentless eye. I would also have liked to thank, but must only acknowledge, my indebtedness to Professor Thomas Bergin who first taught me Petrarch in translation when I was a Yale undergraduate now more than fifty years ago. Finally, my profound gratitude to all those teachers of Italian who have tried to make me competent in that language: Guelfo Frulla at Yale, Frank Soda of Princeton High School and Luisa Rapaccini of the Istituto Britannico in Florence.

Thanks are due to the following copyright holders for permission to reprint material used in this anthology:

The Anvil Press Poetry for Nicholas Kilmer's translation from *Songs and Sonnets from Laura's Lifetime* (1980), by permission of the author; Appleton-Century-Crofts for Thomas Bergin's translations from *Petrarch: Selected Sonnets, Odes, Letters* (1966); Gerald Duckworth & Co. for Graham Hough's translation from *Legends and Pastorals* (1961); Faber for Ezra Pound's 'Silet' from *Collected Shorter Poems* (1952); Heinemann for Agnes Tobin's translations from *On the Death of Madonna Laura by Francesco Petrarca, Rendered into English* (1906); Indiana University Press for Morris Bishop's translations from *Petrarch and His World* (1963) and Mark Musa's translations from *Petrarch: The Canzoniere, or, Rerum vulgarium fragmenta* (1996); Longman, Green and Co. for Joseph Auslander's translations from *The Sonnets of Petrarch* (1931); New York State University at Binghamton Press for James Wyatt Cook's translations from *Petrarch's Songbook Rerum Vulgarium Fragmenta: A Verse Translation* (1995); Ohio State University Press for Ruth Hughey's edition of *The Arundel Harington Manuscript of Tudor Poetry* (1960), by permission of Professor Hughey's estate; Penguin Books Ltd for Geoffrey Hill's translation from *The Triumph of Love* (1999) and Anthony Mortimer's translation of *Petrarch's Canzoniere: Selected Poems* (2002) by permission of the translators; University of Arkansas Press for Marion Shore's translations from *For Love of Laura: Poetry of Petrarch* (1987), by permission of the author; and L. Raley for Helen Lee Peabody's translations from *Madrigals and Odes from Petrarch* (1940).

Marcia Karp's sonnet 'The Lover Resorts to Commerce' and Jill McDonough's 'Sonnet after Wyatt after Petrarch' are published here for the first time by permission of the authors.

Every effort has been made to trace or contact all copyright holders. The publishers will be glad to make good any omissions brought to their attention.

Princeton, 19 July 2004

INDEX OF TITLES AND FIRST LINES

INDEX OF AUTHORS/
TRANSLATORS